Applied Innovation and Knowledge Management in Organizations

Innovatives Wissensmanagement
Innovative Knowledge Management

Herausgeber
Editor

Tit. Univ.-Prof. Dr. Dr. Dr. habil. Bernhard F. Seyr
Europäische Gesellschaft für Wissensökonomie
European Association for Knowledge Economy – EURECO

Band 3

Zur Qualitätssicherung und Peer Review der vorliegenden Publikation

Die Qualität der in dieser Reihe erscheinenden Arbeiten wird vor der Publikation durch externe, von der Herausgeberschaft benannte Gutachter geprüft.

Notes on the quality assurance and peer review of this publication

Prior to publication, the quality of the work published in this series is reviewed by external referees appointed by the editorship.

Bernhard F. Seyr (ed.)

Applied Innovation and Knowledge Management in Organizations

Angewandtes Innovations- und Wissensmanagement in Organisationen

PETER LANG

Bibliographic Information published by the Deutsche Nationalbibliothek

The Deutsche Nationalbibliothek lists this publication in the Deutsche Nationalbibliografie; detailed bibliographic data is available online at http://dnb.d-nb.de.

Library of Congress Cataloging-in-Publication Data

A CIP catalog record for this book has been applied for at the Library of Congress.

ISSN 2699-6324
ISBN 978-3-631-87414-1 (Print)
E-ISBN 978-3-631-87436-3 (E-PDF)
E-ISBN 978-3-631-87437-0 (EPUB)
DOI 10.3726/b19483

Peter Lang – Berlin · Bern · Bruxelles · New York · Oxford · Warszawa · Wien

This publication has been peer reviewed.

www.peterlang.com

Contents

List of authors

in alphabetical order of the surnames

Noor ul Ain
PhD Scholar, School of Business and Economics, University of Management & Technology, Lahore (PK).
E-Mail: noorulain_13@yahoo.com

Caspar von der Crone, PhD
CEO der CD Consulting gUG, IG Bio-Initiative e. V. (DE).
E-Mail: info@ig-bio.de

Prof. Dr. Mariska van der Giessen
Professor of International Entrepreneurship at NHL Stenden University of Applied Sciences, Academy of Commerce & International Business, Leeuwarden (NL).
E-Mail: mariska.van.der.giessen@nhlstenden.com

Dr. Volker C. Horsthemke
Organizational Development, HR Development, Knowledge and Ideas Management, currently Head of HR in the private sector (DE).
E-Mail: volker.horsthemke@outlook.de

Neha Jain
PhD Candidate, International Joint Cross-Border PhD Programme in International Economic Relations and Management, University of Applied Sciences Burgenland (AT) – University of Economics in Bratislava (SK).
E-Mail: nehajain.knp@gmail.com

Prof. Dr. Horst Lang
Universität Sopron, Alexandre Lamfalussy Fakultät für Wirtschaftswissenschaften (HU).
E-Mail: horst.lang@uni-sopron.hu

Ing. Daan Linnartz, MBA
Alumnus MBA Programme – Fontys International Business School, Venlo (NL).
E-Mail: daanlinnartz@hotmail.com

Prof. Dr. Markus Mau
Dekan der Fakultät für Ökonomie der E.H.E. Europa Hochschule EurAKA (CH).
E-Mail: markus.mau@euraka.ch

Ing. Dr. Martin A. Moser, MSc, MA
Head of Quality Management Pharma Division, Constantia Flexibles International GmbH (AT).
E-Mail: martin.a.moser@icloud.com

Prof. Dr. Vincent Pijnenburg
Research Chair Cross-Border Business Development – Fontys International Business School, Venlo (NL).
E-Mail: v.pijnenburg@fontys.nl

Tit. Univ.-Prof. Dr. Dr. Dr. habil. Bernhard F. Seyr
Generaldirektor der Europäischen Gesellschaft für Wissensökonomie – European Association for Knowledge Economy – EURECO; Tit. Prof. der Universität Sopron, Alexandre Lamfalussy Fakultät für Wirtschaftswissenschaften (HU); Sachverständiger beim Landesgericht Salzburg (AT), Personal- und Unternehmensberater.
E-Mail: seyr@seyr.at

Ali Akbar Sohail
PhD Candidate, International Joint Cross-Border PhD Programme in International Economic Relations and Management, University of Applied Sciences Burgenland (AT).
E-Mail: aliakbarsohail@gmail.com

Dr. Patrick Szillat
Research Chair Cross-Border Business Development – Fontys International Business School, Venlo (NL).
E-Mail: p.szillat@fontys.nl

Editorial

Band 3 der Schriftenreihe *Innovatives Wissensmanagement* beinhaltet aufgrund seiner internationalen Ausrichtung vorwiegend Beiträge in englischer Sprache.

Der erste Beitrag stellt den aktuellen Forschungsbericht des internationalen Forschungsprojekts der Europäischen Gesellschaft für Wissensökonomie (EURECO) zu Auswirkungen innovativer Innenarchitektur in öffentlichen Gebäuden dar.

Der zweite Artikel beschäftigt sich mit der Ausgestaltung und Akzeptanz von Systemen des Customer Relationship Managements (CRM) im Hinblick auf ihre Rolle als Instrument des Wissensmanagements.

Daran anschließend wird im folgenden Kapitel untersucht, inwiefern die COVID-19-Pandemie zu einem rascheren Wissensaustausch geführt hat.

Der nächste Beitrag stellt den Wissenstransfer im Change Management und Wissensmanagement in den Vordergrund.

Kapitel 5 befasst sich hingegen mit dem Problem der Leistungsmessung im Bildungssystem der Niederlande.

Die Umsetzung von offenen Innovationen durch die Fähigkeit einer Organisation zur Zusammenarbeit wird in Kapitel 6 als neues Werkzeug zur Erreichung von Wettbewerbsvorteilen betrachtet.

Das abschließende Kapitel ist dem Thema Tierschutz gewidmet und beleuchtet innovative Möglichkeiten, wie das Verbot des Kükentötens in Deutschland auch ökonomisch sinnvoll in der Lebensmittelindustrie umgesetzt werden kann.

Wie aus diesen Beiträgen deutlich wird, bietet auch Band 3, wie bereits die beiden vorangehenden Bände der Schriftenreihe, dem interessierten Publikum ein breites Spektrum an theoretischen und praxisorientierten Ansätzen des Innovations- und Wissensmanagements aus verschiedenen Blickwinkeln.

Salzburg, im Jänner 2022

Tit. Univ.-Prof. Dr. Dr. Dr. habil. Bernhard F. Seyr
Herausgeber

1. Innovative forms of interior office design and its effects on the well-being and absenteeism of employees in non-profit organizations: An international study of the European Association of Knowledge Economy (EURECO) in the Netherlands, Germany, Austria and Hungary

Mariska van der Giessen, Vincent Pijnenburg & Bernhard F. Seyr

Abstract: This paper investigates the effects of modern interior office design on employees, especially with regard to their well-being and absenteeism. In this context, modern *open-plan* offices in public buildings and universities in the Netherlands, Germany, Austria and Hungary are evaluated by qualitative in-depth interviews and a quantitative survey. The results reveal that modern *open-plan* offices often increase the well-being of employees. Such modern office designs are able to improve communication, cooperation, flexibility, knowledge sharing and productivity as well as the physical movement within the offices. An important success factor for the implementation of new office plans is the early integration of the employees in pilot projects. In general, there is no evidence that the interior office design has significant effects on absenteeism of employees.

1.1 Field of research, research questions and research design

1.1.1 Field of research

1.1.1.1 Introduction

After a general introduction in this first section, this chapter introduces innovative office designs and its effects, and consequently, a short literature review on office design and well-being. After that, the research questions of this research project are formulated and the research design is explained.

According to DeJoy & Wilson (2003, p. 34), employee well-being represents the physical, psychological and emotional aspects of employee health. Research on employee well-being is well documented in organizational studies. However, comprehensive understanding, conceptual clarification and the definition of employee well-being remain largely unclear and unresolved. The term "well-being" can be defined as a state of being comfortable, healthy, and happy. In this regard, employee well-being implies the physical, psychological and emotional health, comfort and happiness of employees (Pradhan & Hati, 2019, p. 3). Further research on employee well-being states that the term consists of six aspects including a manageable workload, personal control, support by colleagues and supervisors, positive job relationships, a clear role and certain control of involvement in organizational change (Jain, Giga & Cooper, 2009, p. 258). Pradhan and Hati (2019) define "well-being" from the human side in comparison to the aspects and prerequisites that are related to the employee well-being. The latter can lead to a human well-being as a consequence in Jain, Giga and Cooper's (2009) study. It can be said that both definitions are linked to each other and both studies recognize that employee well-being influences organizational outcome such as job satisfaction, organizational commitment, and turnover. For example, Samad (2015) conducted a study among 193 employees at an Australian university and found a significant relationship between well-being and job satisfaction. Moreover the study found that there is a negative relation between well-being and turnover as well (Samad, 2015, p. 44).

Keyes, Shmotkin and Ryff (2002) present a different stream of analysis on the term well-being. Their research organizes the field of well-being into two broad traditions: one dealing with happiness, and one dealing with human potential.

According to research by Bakker and Demerouti (2018), employees reported about their job demands, resources and well-being in which a relation with individual performance was found. The study states that employees can react sensitive and undermine themselves by creating more job demands. On the other hand, employees can be proactive and optimize their own job demands and resources. It seems that this bottom-up perspective complements the existing top-down approaches. In addition to this, keeping in mind the active role of the relevant stakeholders, i. e. employer and staff, the question rises how various stakeholders interact. Therefore, it is crucial that researchers identify the different factors that influence employee well-being (Bakker & Demerouti, 2018, pp. 5–15).

Job resources have been found to influence commitment and well-being, especially the contribution of individual and team-level resources in the motivational processes. Beyond the supply of job-level resources, organizational- and team-level resources are key motivational developments. These developments support an explanation of how levels of commitment and well-being can be increased. Additional resources, such as job involvement, and organizational and team factors, such as vision clarity and psychological safety, can be assessed for either a direct or indirect impact on job resources and engagement (Albrecht, 2012, p. 853).

Simultaneously, these aspects affect individuals by complex means. There is not a general consensus on the best aspects of employee well-being. Yet, many types of employee well-being affect the organization, either positively or negatively. Many theories and research focus on physical health, mental health, job satisfaction, motive, morale, stress, organization commitment, and climate (Grawitch, Gottschalk & Munz, 2006, p. 134).

Seligman's theory describes five characteristics of well-being (Seligman, 2012). *Positive emotions* include feelings such as happiness, pleasure, and comfort. Within this characteristic, positive emotions serve as a marker for personal well-being. Frederickson (1998) proposes that positive emotions produce personal prosperity and are worth to manage. According to her Broaden-and-build theory, positive emotions like happiness can enhance awareness and lead to new ideas and actions (Fredrickson, 1998). The factor *engagement* refers to being interested and engaged in a particular activity, organization, or purpose. Additionally, Kahn (1990) defines that engagement is the willingness of employees to invest in their work roles (Kahn, 1990), physically and emotionally. The element of *relationships* includes feelings of being integrated in society or a community. Moreover, feelings of being cared by loved ones and being satisfied with one's social network belong to this category/aspect. Many experiences of individuals revolve around other individuals. Therefore, support from social relationships has been connected to a decrease in depression, increase of physical health, and lower mortality rates. Research has proven that there is evidence that social relationships are beneficial for health, absenteeism, and self-management (Tay, Tan, Diener & Gonzalez, 2012). *The characteristic of meaning* is to have sense of purpose and direction in life and feeling connected to something larger than the individual. Individuals who claim to be happy and satisfied with their live often state that their lives are more meaningful. Nevertheless, a meaningful life is not naturally a happy life (Baumeister et al., 2013). *Accomplishment as the fifth element* indicates making progress to the individuals' goals or objectives. By achieving these goals or objectives, one can gain external recognition and an internal sense of accomplishment. The term accomplishment can be understood in a subjective way, in this sense it can be affected by individual ambition, drive, and personal characteristics. For example, an individual who raises a child might consider life as successful, while the other defines success as earning a promotion to become a manager (Seligman, 2012).

1.1.1.2 Innovative office designs

The *activity-based flexible office* (A-FO) is realized at many non-profit organizations on global scale. The concept of A-FO has the goal to improve usage of office space, increase performance, and decreases costs of facilities. The concept aims to provide various workspaces that fit work activities and environmental preferences of employees. In addition to this, the A-FO might offer several benefits. The concept aims to stimulate interaction, to increase employee productivity and satisfaction, to attract and to bind staff, to reduce the environmental footprint, and to obtain a positive image among internal stakeholders and often also to reduce employers costs. The A-FO concept is also named as new offices, flexible offices, *flex* offices or non-territorial offices (Babapour & Rolfö, 2019, p. 18).

There exist also radically innovative and creative forms of working: For example, Rudokas et al. (2020) propose the *forest-office administrative movement* (FO-AM) that allows staff to move from sitting to walking while working in created or adapted forest areas. This futuristic approach is based on the idea of a heritage that aims to connect between the past and future. Not only the connection between the past and future is important, merging together nature and culture, biology and technology as well. Furthermore, the FO-AM concept aims to ensure quality of life and employee well-being for all ages, promotes sustainable organizational growth, employment, and favourable work conditions (Rudokas et al., 2020, p. 45). Sustainability is seen here as a concept that allows to exploit material resources in order to satisfy the needs of the present generation without reducing the chances of future generations to do so.

Oseland, Catchlove and Miller (2013) proposed the concept of *living offices* where ergonomics plays an important role. Their concept includes a shift in tools, management and places that improves creativity, productivity, connectivity, and ergonomics in the workplace. For example, employees who want to chat might seek a semi-private area that enables them to do so. Whilst other individuals want to show and tell contents, they might look for a meeting space in which tables, seats, and technology support employees with the ability to share digital content (Catchlove & Miller, 2013, p. 201).

1.1.1.3 Effects of office designs

In previous research many valuable conclusions are drawn with regards to the effects of interior office design. However, minimal attention is paid to the difference between successful and unsuccessful cases. According to Brunia, de Been and van der Voordt (2016), organizations that consider implementing new ways of working in *activity-based work* (ABW) settings can benefit from other organizational experiences that already carried out activity-based work. On the other hand, the unsuccessful offices are mainly characterized by failure factors from ABWs. Therefore, it is expected that once pre- and post-evaluations are taken into account by the heads of departments, an increase of employee well-being will be the result. ABWs and A-FO are expected to be successful due to certain design or process characteristics (Brunia, de Been & van der Voordt, 2016, p. 33).

Ching and Binggeli (2018) state that there should be a fit of the form of sustainable of interior space and the own body dimensions. For example, this can be a static form in which one sits in a chair or in a dynamic form. The dynamic form contributes to human movement in terms of walking up a stairway, move through the rooms and halls of a building. It appears that space which encourages or discourages movements has a positive influence on employee well-being. Another advantage, besides the positive influence on well-being, is that physical activity has been shown to stimulate psychological activity. Furthermore the design of sustainable workspaces for different functions has both a positive physical and psychological impact on employees (Ching & Binggeli, 2018, pp. 45–55).

Summing up, *open-plan* offices (A-FO) and activity-based offices (ABW) have become more popular in the recent years. The reasons behind the implementation of these new office concepts are not only employee-oriented but they also serve the goal of decreasing costs, saving space and increasing flexibility in office use (Rolfö, Eklund & Jahncke, 2017, p. 645).

1.1.1.4 Office design and well-being

As basis for the regarding research project the following points can be distilled out of the academic literature:

Research on employee well-being in organizations is extensively documented. Nevertheless, studies focussing non-profit organizations remain limited. Previous research of Pradhan and Hati (2019) formulated that the term "well-being" is a state of comfort, healthiness, happiness, meaning that employee well-being implies the physical, psychological, and emotional health that determines the comfort and happiness of employees. This humanistic approach is questioned by Jain, Giga and Cooper's (2009) research in which employee well-being is presented in six aspects: workload, personal control, colleague and supervisor support, work relationships, organizational roles, and organizational involvement. Based on these findings, it can be stated that Jain, Giga and Cooper's (2009) work consists of an organizational approach in comparison to the humanistic approach chosen by Pradhan and Hati (2009). Thus, DeJoy and Wilson (2003) represented the physical, psychological, and emotional aspects that affect the employees' health. These findings present an interpretation of how different aspects determine employee well-being. These aspects affect employees by complex means and can be best identified by Seligman's theory (2012). Seligman's theory (2012) postulates that each aspect of well-being must have three characteristics: (1) It needs to contribute to well-being, (2) individuals need to pursue goals for their own benefit, and (3) well-being is defined and measured separately of the other aspects. These five aspects – as described above – are: positive emotions, engagement, relationships, meaning, and accomplishment. In this case each aspect of employee well-being consists of a humanistic and an organizational approach, meaning that it determines the physical, psychological, and emotional health effects on employee well-being.

1.1.2 Research questions and research design

Based on the research interest of the European Association of Knowledge Economy (EURECO) that initiated the study, the following research questions are defined with regard to non-profit organizations:

1. Which effects do modern forms of interior offices designs have on employees, especially concerning their well-being?
2. Is there an effect of such modern office designs on absenteeism?

The research has an international focus and includes the Netherlands, Germany, Austria and Hungary and refers to buildings of public authorities and universities (of applied science).

As a first part, the researchers conducted a qualitative study with in-depth interviews with seven higher ranked officials of public institutions like town halls or public administrations. Additionally, eight experts of universities were interviewed in the first half of the year 2021. The choice of the interview partners was selective following the special expertise that was needed to answer the questions profoundly. It has to be stated clearly that the qualitative interviews reflect the opinions of managers and office planners, and not of the staff. In contrast to this, the view of the employees has been investigated by the quantitative part of this research project.

As a second part, also in the first half of 2021 a quantitative study was executed with 150 participants in the Netherlands and Germany. The questionnaire was distributed to the employees by the universities that also participated in the qualitative study as an internet link. Unfortunately, the number of participants in Austria and Hungary was too small in order to obtain valid results. Thus the interpretation of the quantitative results only reflects the data of the Netherlands and Germany, and the quantitative data of Austria and Hungary was not taken into account.

It has to be clearly stated that the results of this study have an explorative and hermeneutic character, and that the study does not aim to gather representative data.

There also has to be mentioned a significant limitation of this research project: All interviews were conducted by different researchers from different nationalities due to the language skills. All interviews were based on guidelines instead of strict questionnaires and with that, the structure and the focus of the interviews differ as well as the chosen terms.

1.2 Aspects of interior office design

This chapter will identify interior office design in terms of functionality, aesthetics, ergonomics and quality of life as well as sustainability.

Ching and Binggeli (2018) describe interior office design as the planning, layout, and design of interior office spaces within buildings. The researchers state that these physical settings satisfy a basic need for protection and shelter. Furthermore, such settings create the standards for the shape of individual activities, they nurture aspirations, express ideas, and affect our mood and personality. Therefore, the purpose of interior office design is to improve functionality and ergonomics, enhance aesthetics, and the quality of life.

Educational institutions are often using the term interior architecture when focusing on creative design processes. The creative design processes focus on the needs of the people who are using the buildings, rather than just the buildings as objects (Ching & Binggeli, 2018, p. 35).

1.2.1 Improvement of functionality

Meel (2000) mentioned that in order to understand interior office design it is important to look at the function that the building fulfils. Office buildings are regarded as factors of production, like human resources, technology, finance, and information. The main purpose of these buildings is to facilitate and support the main processes of the organization using the office. Therefore, the interior design of offices needs to be based on the analysis of organizational functionality and business processes. An important aspect is that one must know what kind of purpose the building fulfils before decisions can be taken. Thus, one must consider the organizational aspect as well. These aspects include variables such as the size, structure, and activities performed by the organization (Meel, 2000, p. 40).

According to Fan and Jin (2020), Google's office furniture design is usually based on the employee's needs, that focuses on creation of own workspaces. The reason is that Google, as an organization, believes that employees need more free space and stimulation of new things to improve creative inspiration.

This cultural characteristic of the organization especially focuses on employees who are engaged in creative and design work, and where work efficiency and functionality has to be increased by aesthetics in interior office design (Fan & Jin, 2020, p. 2).

After the analysis of organizational functionalities and business processes the actual interior space needs to be designed. In many cases interior space consists of individual workstations or desks and their environment. Thus, it may occur that interior space includes the entire inner space of the office building, excluding the architectural outer shell and technical installations. Interior office space design includes the use of spatial elements, lighting, surface finishing, furniture, and accessories to realize the required functional and desired visual quality. Elements of interior space design are more frequently and more easily changed than technical installations and the building construction. Therefore, the elements provide quicker wins to adjust the work environment (Colenberg, Jylha & Arkesteijn, 2020, p. 3).

1.2.2 Aesthetics

Today's rapid development of economy and internet technology is a trigger for the production of office furniture to be manufactured more intelligent and humanized. Additionally, the design of office furniture is often adapted to the needs of organizational image and culture. Innovative and personalized office design is an important representation of an organization's identity, culture, and core values. Aesthetics in interior office design is a crucial condition for creating a personalized workspace or office space. Not only the personalized aspect is important, it also acts as one of the main visual communication media to express organizational culture (Colenberg, Jylha & Arkesteijn, 2020).

Many previous research projects have focused on aesthetics in interior office design and interior architecture. The majority of these research projects deal with topics that are related to the concepts of aesthetics and the social aspects. Furthermore, topics related to the demand for aesthetic office furniture and their materials are important issues. These aesthetic aspects include the use of colours, availability of daylight and personalization.

Overall it is difficult to consider factors of "aesthetics" separately to the factors functionality, sustainability and ergonomics. For example noise reduction has to be taken into account when planning offices and also the question how to use and produce the required materials of these elements (Rashdan & Ashour, 2017, p. 255). The way how solutions for practical questions as the reduction of noise can be found is often also a question of aesthetics. Alfuraty (2020) suggests in his research that aesthetic aspects should be more included in the manufacturing process of components of the interior environment. Moreover, the producers should respect environmental strategies that would reduce energy consumption by the use of natural light (Alfuraty, 2020, p. 37). In addition to that, three years earlier Rashdan and Ashour's (2017) research presented a suggestion of having a set of functional and effective standards to ensure aesthetical interior design solutions. These criteria focused on mechanisms for selecting furniture, patterns and colours to enhance employee functionality and productivity in the office (Rashdan & Ashour, 2017, p. 314). These criteria are supported by Hayles (2015) when he recognizes that these materials became of importance in interior office design. He also emphasizes the role light and colours play (Hayles, 2015, p. 66).

1.2.3 Sustainability and quality of life

In 2015, Hayles studied the current supply and demand for green, sustainable products and the improvement of the quality of life by interior office design. Within his study, Hayles (2015) made use of different materials separated in five categories: window treatments, fabrics, flooring, surface material, and walls and ceilings. Hayles' (2015, p. 102) research concluded that employees demand better sustainable solutions to improve their quality of life.

Employees seek sustainable solutions to improve quality of life in the organization as well as for the improvement of psychological and physical health at the workplace. Designers find it challenging to include these sustainable materials in the switch from environmental irresponsibility to an environmentally responsible interior design (Hayles, 2015, p. 104). However, the centre of all efforts is the human character. In the recent years there can be detected an increasing willingness to contribute to an environment that does not have a negative effect on quality of life and health. The interior and the internal space of the building provide a positive impression and feeling, and motivating work conditions. Sustainable interior components such as floors, walls, ceilings, furniture, and equipment guarantee the implementation of the functional processes for which quality of life in interior office is designed. These components also increase the quality of life in the workplaces and enhance comfort and well-being of employees (Lee, Allen & Kim, 2013 p. 15).

The demand for green and sustainable products that improve the quality of life leads to the rise of concepts such as eco-style and ecological interior. According to Zymina (2020), eco-style includes interiors where natural elements are visually present. This concept uses natural components of interior as well as graphic natural forms and objects, such as trees, rocks and sea. In essence, any office interior can be ecological if sustainable materials are used. These sustainable materials can be either natural or artificial such as wood, clay, natural stone, brick, glass, and textiles. Even synthetic or artificial materials can be sustainable if they do not harm the nature or individual health. Due to the use of these materials the interior can be considered as ecological (Zymina, 2020, p. 4).

In this context, Zymina (2020) perceives the human being as the centre of efforts and thoughts. The study recognizes that the interior office environment should not have a harmful effect on health, and it should provide an aesthetic impression and positive working conditions (Zymina, 2020, p. 4). Another advantage of sustainable interior office design is that sustainable design seeks to produce workspaces that use energy and natural resources efficiently and effectively. Moreover, the sustainable design process aims to find solutions that protect both the natural environment and multiple forms of quality of life. The main characteristics of sustainable interior office design are the reduction, reuse and recycling of materials. Additionally, a thorough evaluation on factors that influence quality of life at the workplace such as health impacts, and access to natural light and fresh air are included (Ching & Binggeli, 2018, p. 48).

One of the most essential benefits of these interior office designs is that these are designed as places for human movement, activity and leisure. Ching and Binggeli (2018) stated that form of office design contributes to the physical movement of employees in terms of walking up a stairway, moving through the rooms and halls of a building. Whether office space encourages or discourages movements has a positive influence on employee well-being. Another advantage, besides the positive influence on well-being, is that physical activity stimulates mental activity. More so, the design of sustainable workspaces for different functions has both a positive physical and psychological impact on employees (Ching & Binggeli, 2018, pp. 45–55).

While sustainable interior office design is generally a positive goal, the literature shows that there are also disadvantages to sustainable interior office design as well. The sustainability of production materials is not the single question because moreover, the practicability, manufacturing processes and their energy consumption as well as the ways of transport have to be considered. For example, bamboo is often considered to be a sustainable product in comparison to hardwood. Bamboo regenerates more quickly than wood, however, the material must be shipped to Europe from China, while several species of wood are available from sustainable managed forests in Europe itself. Therefore, interior office designers should consider which products are recyclable, how far the materials must travel, and evaluate the environmental and social responsibility of the manufacturers (Templeton, 2011, p. 48).

1.2.4 Ergonomics in interior office design

Ergonomics in interior office design is defined as the consideration of physical human characteristics for the design of workplaces. Nowadays, many offices are based on the concept of *open-plan* offices, *or flex* workspaces, in which a given desk, office or workplace is intended to be used by different employees at different times. When changing to these forms of office design, the focus must be set on the employees' needs, wants and behaviour (Chandra et al., 2009, p. 913). Moreover, ergonomics in interior office design is an aspect that is focused on closing the gap between employees and the environment in which employees work. Interior office design should be user-friendly in order to result in an increase of functionality for the organization. Besides that, previous research recognizes an increase in employee productivity in which a safer, healthier, and efficient environment can be realized (Olabode, Adesanya & Bąkare, 2017, pp. 817–820).

As mentioned above, ergonomics in interior office design has increasingly developed in recent years. Rebuilding traditional cellular office environments to *open-plan* offices or *flex* offices has stimulated an open area for group work, meetings, and common facilities (Vos & van der Voordt, 2001, p. 50). Due to the introduction of these different forms of workplaces three interesting developments have been recognized as advantages. First, research has shown that work becomes more personalized and customized, as a result workplaces become more diverse and integrated. Therefore, interior office design will need to provide personalized, professional, and customized options (Fan & Jin, 2020, p. 2). Second, to improve the effective utilization of office space it is important to track office space usage.

Moreover, collecting data, sharing space and proportioning furniture, can be seen as other advantages of innovative interior design in office spaces. Simultaneously, the collected data is used to observe the ergonomics that effect employee well-being. Previous psychological research has shown that the employees' ergonomics and well-being have a considerable influence on employee efficiency and motivation (Rolfö, Eklund & Jahncke, 2017, p. 642). At last, social changes have increased living standards and the individuals' demand for individuality as well. These various developments of society resulted in a shift of the office character from a single form to a diversified form. As a beneficial effect, technological innovation promotes the development of the design of office furniture. Therefore, user experience might play an important role in the design of office interior. These current and future technological innovations can be useful for employees in terms of interaction, efficiency and self-development on the workplace (Fan & Jin, 2020, p. 3).

Vos and Van der Voordt (2001) address two major issues that are related to office layout. Research results state that if there is an increase in shared areas and a decrease in fixed workplaces, concentration and effective hours worked decrease. Furthermore, it appears that office noise and inappropriate office use increase (Vos & van der Voordt, 2001, p. 60). Rolfö, Eklund and Jahncke (2017), are aware of these disadvantages in their research and they have found out that a high "people to workstation ratio" in connection with unsuitable arrangements of workstations and the absence of rules are problematic. Moreover, the study acknowledges that the changing occupation of workplaces leads to the separation of teams (Rolfö, Eklund & Jahncke, 2017, p. 655). Finding the right balance of private and shared areas requires a detailed assessment of individual needs as well as the needs of teams. Once the office space is built, there will be an additional demand to continually evaluate and manage the office space. This highlights a need for active workplace management to ensure that the office environment constantly remains supportive for organizational and individual needs (Haynes, 2008, p. 191).

1.2.5 Summary

In order to understand the connection of interior office design on employee well-being and absenteeism it is important to identify different influencing factors. As shown above, these factors include the functionality, aesthetics, sustainability, quality of life, and ergonomics in interior office design. At first, in order to understand interior office design, it is important to look at the function of the building. Employees at organizations use their buildings for different purposes such as information, production, and service. Moreover, literature explains that the interior office includes the use of spatial elements, lighting, surface finishing, furnish, and accessories to realize the required functional and desired visual quality (Colenberg, Jylha & Arkesteijn, 2020). Thus, the study of Rashdan and Ashour (2017) states that personalized work spaces can be considered as main visual communication channels to express organizational culture. Besides the importance of improving the functionality in interior office design, aesthetics are crucial. The creation of a personalized workspace or office space is of importance. Aesthetics in interior office design are influenced by factors such as the use of colours, availability to daylight, and personalization of the workplace.

It can be stated that quality of life in interior office design has become more important in recent years. Hayles (2015) indicates there are five physical categories within the design: window treatments, fabrics, flooring, surface material, and walls and ceilings. The literature states that the use of materials that contribute to quality of life is related to the functional processes organizations and leads to the rise of new office concepts. As mentioned before, these new interior office concepts can be seen as eco-style and ecological interior concepts. According to a study of Ching and Binggeli (2018) these new concepts stimulate dynamic forms of human movement. It appears that space encourages or discourages movements, and it can have a positive or negative influence on employee well-being. Thus, not only do these concepts improve employee well-being based on physical health, but also in terms of emotional health.

Lastly, many offices are based on the concept of *open-plan* offices, or *flex* offices, in which a given desk, office or workplace is intended to be used by different employees at different times. Furthermore, ergonomics in interior office design attempts to close the gap between employees and the office environment. Thus, Olabode (2017) stated that ergonomics results in an increase in functionality, employee productivity, and efficiency. Furthermore, ergonomics contributes to a safer and healthier environment as well. However, one cannot assume that once the interior office space is designed it can be interpreted as final. Ergonomics needs to be constantly evaluated and improved based on individual needs and organizational functionality.

1.3 Qualitative study

The qualitative expert interviews have been conducted with managers and experts responsible for new built office areas of an organization, such as executives, HR managers, housing managers, and facility managers and advisors. The interviews identify the expert insights on thoughts and opinions of employees at universities and town halls as well as selected other non-profit organizations within the interview guidelines. The information described in these cases provides a practical point of view that includes real-life examples. The interviews focus on the effect of interior office design on employee well-being and absenteeism at non-profit organizations, such as town halls, public buildings and universities in the Netherlands, Germany, Austria, and Hungary.

In the interviews the researchers investigate potential effects of interior office design on employee well-being and how the organizations act or do not act regarding matters of employee well-being. Furthermore, the goal of this study is to get insights into potential effects of office design on absenteeism and how it is related to employee well-being.

1.3.1 Town halls and public buildings

This part includes seven expert interviews with representatives of:

- three town halls in the Netherlands (Leeuwarden, Groningen, Zwolle)
- two town halls in Germany (Oldenburg and Osnabrück).
- one ministry in Austria (Vienna)
- one regional administration office in Hungary (Murakeresztúr)

The functions that these experts carry out are facility managers (interviewee I1 and I2), a HR manager (interviewee I3), housing managers (interviewee I4 and I5), a higher ranked civil servant in the HR development in a ministry (I6), and an executive of a regional administration (I7).

1.3.1.1 The Netherlands

In the Netherlands, the different forms of interior office design at town halls vary from traditional structures to *open-plan* offices. In the town hall of Leeuwarden, the organization created *open-plan* offices in all departments, in which employees can go to another room to make a phone call. According to I1, the reason for these types of interior office spaces was due to the fact that the organization found it necessary to move on with new innovative ways to improve the workspaces for employees. The office is furnished based on the housing concept a*ctivity-based working* (AGW). I1 stated that it is important to the organization that employees feel at home. As employees feel comfortable, they start to be more productive in which ultimately absenteeism will decrease.

A similar concept has been used by the town hall of Groningen as well. According to I2, the starting point for the renovation has been to create a more open structure. However, the organization still holds on to traditional structures in some departments. Although the town hall of Groningen hoped for positive effects of interior office design on well-being and absenteeism, individuals tend to not fully utilize available *open-plan* office spaces. In addition to this, internal research recognized that employees tend to be happier with a fixed location in the traditional office structure. This internal research indicated that especially older employees, between 55 and 60 years of age, prefer a fixed location in which the designated location feels like a safe haven. Therefore, the changes in interior office design to *open-plan* offices had a negative influence on employee well-being.

The town hall of Zwolle introduced another concept than the *open-plan* office compared to the town hall of Leeuwarden and Groningen. In the concept of Zwolle, the organization introduced *flex* concepts and co-working offices combined with concentration spaces which can be utilized by one or two individuals for extensive work. All three organizations offer quiet spaces for three to four people where employees can cooperate for municipal projects. According to I3, this trend has mainly emerged in profit organizations, and it showed that it stimulates employees to be more productive. The motivation to introduce these interior office designs at the town hall of Zwolle was to encourage employees to work in teams and to consult more often with others. However, the organization had to keep in mind that the workspace was not too noisy.

At the town hall of Leeuwarden, I1 expressed that *open-plan* offices have a positive effect on employee well-being. The employees of the town hall seem to be very satisfied with these working conditions. Nevertheless, it took some time to accommodate to the new forms of office design, because employees no longer had a fixed workplace. Of course, employees still have their own department, but it is organized in such a way that the employees can determine what is necessary and needed for their daily activities in the office space. For example, when an employee finds it necessary to utilize a quiet room, the employee can reserve a time slot online. According to I1, employees find this satisfactory in terms of flexibility and comfort. The organization also currently investigates a partnership with a catering company to support healthy food consumption by employees in the organization.

The *open-plan* office at the town hall of Groningen has not led to the expected effect and had negative effects on well-being. It can be stated that this correlation might be influenced by more practical issues, as I2 described that due to cold air drafts in the winter, the organization had to cope with health issues that immediately caused problems regarding employee productivity and organizational performance. Within that period the absenteeism ratio increased from 4 % to 5 %. Regarding physical and psychological health, I2 thinks that much more can be controlled with healthy catering. Significant financial resources are invested in innovation and sustainability in terms of the creation of a more healthy environment for employees. The situation presented by I2 is in contrast to the effect on employee well-being and absenteeism at the town hall of Leeuwarden although some employees still find it difficult to adapt to the new work environment. I1 stated that this problem to adapt is recognized among elderly employees. Nevertheless, the organization did not identify a substantial decrease in absenteeism. As mentioned earlier, the town hall of Leeuwarden is constantly looking for improvement in workspaces and its acoustics. The organization identified a slight decrease (from 3 % to 2 %) in absenteeism when the new interior office design was introduced. Moreover, the organization is constantly working to increase the employees' experience, comfort, positivity, and productivity. Based on these factors, I1 thinks that the organization improved in comparison to previous interior office design.

According to the interviewee I3, the *flex* concepts and co-working office introduced by the town hall of Zwolle have led to a positive effect of the interior office design on employee well-being and absenteeism. The organization has noted that the absenteeism rates have decreased slightly. In addition to this, I3 expresses that these forms of interior office design have had a positive effect on employee well-being if it is used properly in the organization. Within the organization it worked out reasonably well: the noise distraction decreased, and an internal benchmark found that employees are very satisfied with the new office design. Simultaneously, the organization recognized a slight decrease in absenteeism when the new interior office design was introduced. The town hall of Zwolle already has evaluated the situation after the reconstruction among the employees, and the outcomes show that absenteeism has slightly decreased from 7 % to 6 % since the introduction. Besides that, the workspaces left a positive impression among employees according to the internal benchmark.

1.3.1.2 Germany

In Germany, the town hall of Oldenburg consists of various forms of interior office design, such as flexible workspaces, *open-plan* offices and informal communication areas. I4 stated that the employees at the town hall of Oldenburg still lack the motivation to use these new opportunities. Moreover, the organization wanted to make use of space more efficiently in terms of storage and archiving. When the new interior office design was introduced, the reuse of sustainable materials was very important in order to increase the quality of life, according to I4.

Similar to the introduced *flex* concepts at the town hall of Oldenburg, there are the new built office spaces at the town hall of Osnabrück. The reason for these types of interior office spaces was due to the fact that the organization needed renovation, but it was cheaper to create a new building. Furthermore, the organization found that collaboration between the departments was not optimal, so the organization aimed for more crossovers. The building is designed to be more open in order to simplify meetings. Additionally, the flexible working spaces made it possible to plan a smaller building. The most important factor for the future to increase functionality and productivity is the variety of types of working places. In terms of employee well-being, the town hall of Osnabrück measured an increase in well-being. The organization conducted an internal survey that indicated that at least 50 % of the people who moved, consider themselves satisfied to have moved. 90 % of participants of the surveys are happy that they are in this building, and they would not like to move back. Furthermore, the internal survey results have shown that headaches and skin diseases among employees have decreased. Employees perceive a great air quality and thermal quality, and that exceeds their expectations. Furthermore, the organization makes use of a restaurant that offers healthy and local meals. Besides that, elevators are almost hidden so that people would be incentivized to take the stairs, and programs and workshops are offered to educate people to quit smoking or to create awareness of the sources of foods and drinks.

Based on these *flex* concepts, the town hall of Oldenburg recognizes an increase in productivity, which is probably positively related to well-being. Nevertheless, I4 argues that this factor was not measureable due to unreliable data of other studies in which they participated. A positive effect arises when employees have the feeling to have more freedom of movement. In this organization, the new interior office design obviously increases physical health. The employees tend to stay in their daily routine on the workplace and no further noises are heard. The effect of interior office design on absenteeism has not been recognized at the town hall of Oldenburg. In this sense, I4 states that the management and head of departments did not recognize a decrease in absenteeism due to these changes. According to I4, this is due to the fact that employees tend to be more satisfied when they can finish a task on one desk. I5 recognizes that the interior office designs have an influence on the absenteeism rates at the town hall of Osnabrück. However, she also states that the hierarchy is a lot stronger with more physical distance. Nonetheless, I5 recognizes a slight decrease in absenteeism when the new interior office design was introduced. The organization conducted a benchmarking project after the reconstruction among employees, and the outcomes show that absenteeism slightly decreased from 10 % to 8 % since the introduction. Besides that, the new workspaces left a positive impression among employees according to the internal benchmark.

1.3.1.3 Austria

I6 explained that the reasons behind the new built office areas in the ministry – which are *open-plan* offices, co-working spaces and flexible workspaces – were the wish for a change in the business culture, to foster entrepreneurial spirit, to increase the number of innovations, as well as the goal to improve the flow of communication, breaking up "silo-thinking", and to foster networks within the organization. This goes hand in hand with the modernization of the working environment and the improvement of the "employer brand", and, last but not least, the customer orientation as well as the improvement of the customer service.

According to interviewee I6, the ministry uses *open-plan* offices, co-working spaces, flexible workspaces for "loud work" and for "silent work" for four to five persons within one workspace. It is applied to all departments, except the top management who use personal offices. The latest technical equipment is used for all employees (laptops, mobile phones, collaboration tools).

The innovative office design should serve as example of best practice and should increase the image of the organization. An employee survey and the needs of the staff were the foundation of the project. The employees' representatives played an important role in the project. The aim was a modernization of the working environment and the working style. This process can be seen as a work in progress.

Process innovations should be stimulated by open communication spaces.

Regarding communication (intensity, team work), there is a positive effect, according to the interviewee(s): a different style of personnel communication can be observed. All employees are more open for direct communication, and they are friendlier towards all customers of a certain process.

Concerning innovation and knowledge generation, unfortunately there is no effect observed. Ideas for innovations are still predominantly generated and established top-down.

Knowledge sharing has obviously increased. Employees have more general knowledge and knowledge about the work of their colleagues.

IP6 states that his ministry paid attention to aspects of sustainability as well as to the legal requirements.

In combination with mobile working or home office there are no disadvantages of this new office design which has been used for approx. 5 years now, according to the interviewee.

The new interior office design has a positive effect on the employees regarding the following points: reduction of absenteeism, more freedom regarding the working hours and self-management of the employees, also in combination with mobile working. However, the effects on well-being depend on the personality of the employees (introverted and extroverted). According to the opinion of the interviewee, there is a positive effect on employee well-being. An important aim for the introduction of the innovative office design was to increase freedom regarding working time and working spaces, and to create modern workspaces based on best practices from other countries (e. g. the Netherlands).

Another effect is the different behaviour of the employees, they are more open for communication, also for informal communication, and they started to dress in a more modern way.

Plants, the use of light and the ability of free movement have positive effects on employee well-being. The better the working conditions, the more comfortable employees feel.

I6 explained that they had implemented two home office days per week with the new office concept. Furthermore, I6 thinks people also work from home on these two days when they feel a little sick. Thus absenteeism is reduced.

1.3.1.4 Hungary

I7 is mayor and head of the municipal office Murakeresztúr, and as a patron institution it is responsible for four villages. I7 explained that a new building for the joint municipal office was constructed due to the fact that the old building was about 40 years old, built in the socialist era. A renovation would have been necessary because the building has not been touched in the last 30 years. New facilities are: the meeting room, a co-working office for more flexibility, a new kitchen area that is big enough for all the employees to have their lunch, tea or snack together. Therefore, it strengthens the human relations among the employees. There is also a new archive. A meeting room was needed for staff meetings and representative meetings. If a lawyer or the deputy mayor comes and wants to work here for a few hours, there used to be no place for them. Now, such guests can use the co-working office. To make use of the new office form, collaborative programs and team-building trainings are planned to strengthen relationships. Since the renovation, there has been a staff meeting every Monday. Employees in the finance department need to share knowledge often, so they are working in one separate room now.

Aspects of sustainability have been taken into account for the building renovation, e. g. solar panels, external insulation, modern windows and doors for a better insulation, modern heating and electrical network. For social sustainability, there are new places (kitchen, meeting room) which support communication and exchange now.

The reasons to introduce the new office design were to invest in the most important asset, the employees, and to improve communication and co-working.

The renovation of the building started in October 2020 with participation of local companies and was finished in April 2021.

The authority will see how the workplaces suit everyone, and if there are any further requirements, they will be met in the next office furniture investment. At the moment, the experience is absolutely positive, and customer feedback is very positive as well.

The goal of I7 is to offer workplaces that are motivating for the employees. New amenities were created, e. g. new lights, air conditioning for more comfort, modified tables as temporary solutions (to be replaced in future). Some people have their own flowers on the desk.

There is no direct evidence for a reduction of absenteeism due to the new office design, but in many cases the holidays from last year have not been taken, and there have been no COVID cases in the office.

1.3.2 Universities

This chapter includes eight expert interviews with universities of applied science in Leeuwarden, Groningen, Zwolle, Oldenburg, and Osnabrück. The functions that these experts carry out are facility manager (I8.1 and I9), HR manager (I10), housing managers and advisors (I11, I12, I8.2). Furthermore, two interviews were conducted in Austria at the two Universities of Applied Sciences in Vienna with two heads of departments: FH Wien (I13) and FH Technikum Wien (I14).

1.3.2.1 The Netherlands

Universities of Applied Sciences in the Netherlands use various forms of interior office design. These forms include *open-plan* offices, *flex* offices, and co-working spaces. Nevertheless, the traditional office structure is still present at the Hanze Hogeschool in Groningen. The NHL Stenden University of Applied Sciences in Leeuwarden converted to an integrated workplace development program, meaning that there are areas in which individuals do not have their own workplace but where employees choose a workplace based on their daily activities. This can be either an *open-plan* office or a *flex* office. Moreover, the organization made these changes based on new educational and research concepts: *design-based education* (DBE) and *design-based research* (DBR). Within this educational- and research-concepts, workshops, open spaces and contact areas between employees, students, researchers and lecturers are necessary.

This means that the amount of traditional closed office structures had to be reduced. From 2017 onwards, NHL Stenden in Leeuwarden started using the majority of new built areas in the organization, such as additional buildings, conference rooms and auditoria that fit the criteria.[1] Interviewee I8.1 of Hanze Hogeschool Groningen presents a similar *open-plan* office structure in which the organization aimed to stimulate synergy and collaboration among employees. Besides that, Hanze Hogeschool still utilizes a traditional office, the cellular office, in which employees are satisfied, according to the interviewee. Nonetheless, it occurred that some departments wanted to move from a traditional structure to an *open-plan* office. According to I8.2, housing advisor at Hanze Hogeschool, the project group *Vitale Hanze* had to determine what the needs and wants of that specific department where and how they could stimulate vitality by plants, comfortable furniture, and factors that stimulate creativity, such as colours and shapes. A similar concept appears at Windesheim Hogeschool in Zwolle in which the organization utilizes *open-plan* offices, *flex* work spaces, and traditional offices as well. However, the organization has added concentration space for one or two individuals. I9 stated that within these new concepts the organization wants to stimulate employees in their vitality and promote sustainable living. Besides that, they want to promote creativity at every department through plants and colours.

In the Dutch universities of this study, the above-mentioned forms of interior office design had a positive effect on employee well-being. According to I11, the social and professional connection between employees at NHL Stenden has increased. As a result, employees found it more comfortable, colourful, and functional to work in a chosen space. The organization has been able to realize areas in which employees can meet or interact with each other. Besides the social connection, the positive effect of the *open-plan* offices is that employees can learn faster, increase productivity and efficiency. Due to the shorter lines of communication employees are more able and willing to share ideas and knowledge. Similarly, the case of the Hanze Hogeschool supports the findings at NHL Stenden. According to I8.2, the organization does not only look at the needs and wants of the team or individuals, but also at the physical activities. When deciding about the office spaces, the needs of the departments are taken into consideration as well as the use of sustainable materials. In this process, different factors are considered, such as employee movement and green zones, e. g. a department might want to decide to move away from the coffee corner to

---

1 The two former Universities of Applied Science Stenden and NHL merged in January 2018. In preparation of the official merge, new concepts of education and research were elaborated. That developments needed also new planning of office and the facilities of the UAS buildings and their usage.

stimulate physical activity of employees. The motivation and purpose at Hanze Hogeschool were to stimulate physical activity among employees and a healthy office environment. Moreover, the organization offers several workshops to stimulate different desk positions, e. g. sitting to standing, importance of movement, and interaction with colleagues. The need for physical activity and health is also acknowledged by Windesheim Zwolle. I9 stated that organization recognized a need to develop and contribute to the sustainable issues we face as a society. Therefore, the organization sought a balance between sustainable and modern furniture. The organization utilizes desks where you can stand and cycle. This contributes to the ergonomics and quality of life for employees in the long term. According to I9, the HR reports showed a slight decrease in absenteeism from 3 % to 2 % since the introduction.

1.3.2.2 Germany

In Germany, the Osnabrück University of Applied Sciences introduced *flex* concepts and *open-plan* offices within their office environment. In this new built office environment different facilities, such as meeting rooms, conference rooms and healthy catering were implemented. This decision was driven by studies that consider open workspaces and *flex* offices to stimulate employees in their productivity and efficiency. Additionally, the organization aimed to improve interaction between teaching, staff, research, and the science areas for a successful development of the university. The case of Osnabrück differs from the office environment of Jade University of Applied Sciences in Oldenburg. Their office environment still consists of a traditional office structure. Traditional in this context means the cellular office space that can be identified as small functional offices. These office spaces can be occupied by a maximum of 6 people. The original building has not been renovated recently. Many years ago, the University of Applied Sciences in Oldenburg upgraded the organization with two new buildings behind the main building, but the traditional office structure remained. According to I10, HR manager at Jade University, the organization is relatively small, and their budget to make improvements is limited. Nevertheless, the organization uses plants, different colours, and paintings to give the building some more character. In addition to this, the parallel traditional office structure brings some advantages to employees in terms of privacy, concentration, and less noise distraction.

I12, housing manager at the Osnabrück University, mentioned that the organization has conducted research that was vital in the decision-making process of the interior office design. The outcomes of the research revealed that more light, more open spaces, healthy food consumption and movement, e. g. stairways, contribute to employee well-being. Besides that there is also an effect of interior office design on employee well-being at Osnabrück University of Applied Sciences. The influence of interior office designs on absenteeism has been recognized as well. As stated by I12, the organization conducted a benchmark after the reconstruction among employees, and the outcomes showed that absenteeism slightly decreased from 6 % to 5 % since the introduction of the new office design. Although the Jade University in Oldenburg did not change their office environment, the organization continuously looks for improvements based on functional and ergonomic aspects that can have effect on employee well-being. This is implemented by means of ergonomic chairs and adjustable desks. Additionally, the organization has taken measures to increase the oxygen levels by using plants and changing the air ventilation. Taking the above mentioned points into account, I10 mentioned that the organization did not recognize a change in absenteeism compared to the traditional workplaces. It appears that employees find the workplace enjoyable, and they are satisfied with the air purification, daylight and ergonomic solutions that support their productivity.

1.3.2.3 Austria

According to I13 at the FH Wien, one main reason behind the newly built office areas was the need for space. A large proportion of employees at the university who spend a lot of time in the lecture hall still have their own desk. Other reasons were facilitating collaboration and modern working, and workplace efficiency (making better use of the empty workstations).

At the moment there are the following forms of innovative office design and organization:

- "home bases": eight workstations at the university, for office work
- "think tanks": maximum of two workstations, for concentrated work, for correction of exams or preparation, preparation and follow-up for teaching
- meeting spaces
- kitchen areas
- twice a week, working from home is allowed

In the following departments a classical office design is in use: administration, human resources, finance, and management. In teaching and research the new system ("smart working" as described above) is applied.

Employees in teaching and research spend a lot of time in the lecture hall, not at the workplace, but still have their own desk. This situation needed to be optimized. Each employee is allowed to choose his or her own workstation every day, depending on the work they have to execute on that day. This enables a cross-divisional exchange. This system will not be changed in the near future, but the focus will be set more on digitalization and virtual conferences.

The new office system promotes communication: it makes it easier to exchange ideas, you hear more from other colleagues and other areas, and it promotes team work. The new office design makes innovation, knowledge generation and sharing easier and information is spread more quickly.

FH Wien dedicated a lot of time to the topic "office design" in order to find the right solution for the long-term future. The pilot project was run in 2016, and in 2017 it was rolled out to the whole teaching and research. Several innovative variants were tested in the selection process. The employees' needs were taken into account by surveys. Colours and plants play an important role in the office concept. Sustainability is seen as strategically very important at the FH Wien. For example, the Nespresso capsule coffee system was converted to coffee machines in order to protect the environment and to save resources.

The new system leads to a higher flexibility, better interaction, and the possibility to a rapid reformulation of groups, project teams. Creativity is also supported. The new office design keeps the people flexible in a mental sense and of course in the sense of mobility. New employees can be integrated faster.

A lack of privacy is one of the disadvantages, as well as the restricted willingness of the employees to look for free desks over several floors. Moreover, the personalization of the workplace is not possible. Teachers work a lot with books. Books are heavy, and they need a lot of space. The university is not yet as digitalized as they would like to be.

Regarding absenteeism and well-being, effective data do not exist. In the regarding department sick leaves and absences do not seem to have changed in any way as a result of the new office design. There is very positive feedback from the employees, which might have an influence on their well-being.

At the *FH Technikum Wien* the change of the interior office design was a top-down decision. The new design should strengthen the image of a progressive university. According to the I14, the FH Technikum Wien was the first university that converted to a "new work" concept. As a first step, the pilot project has been launched, afterwards it will be rolled out floor by floor. Mistakes are corrected based on the feedback and the learning outcomes from the pilot project.

The reasons for choosing new interior office forms were more freedom for employees and the need for innovative solutions. A workplace is increasingly becoming a place where people can meet and work together creatively. In addition, there are more home office solutions now.

There is a think tank area for concentrated work with four to six seats inside. The home base for normal routine work is designed for 14 seats. A lodge area is used for informal meetings.

I14 explains his ideas for the future: With height-adjustable tables desk bikes can be put under the table. There could also be fitness area with table tennis and showers, gymnastics classes, and a storage room. The future offices could be comparable with Google which is an ecosystem of its own. Space at a university should not be limited to the offices, but certainly also to the lecture halls and to the laboratories. I14 posed the question why the students actually have to sit, and why there are no standing possibilities. Interactive, action-oriented didactics should support the spatial change. The following ideas should be discussed: mobile tables for group work, instead of flip-charts writing on the walls, boxes with materials for prototype construction, and design thinking tools.

Due to the new office design, there was a lot more communication across departments. Because of the change process, two institutes that were clearly divided before now form a kind of community of fate, and the people have grown together. Many more ideas came up to do things together, the change supported the cross-departmental collaboration and cooperation.

The new office design supports inter-departmental communication and collaboration, and it is a trigger for digital work skills to improve.

Home office can be an attraction for young people and new employees. It is economically beneficial, because space can be used more efficiently.

The interviewee, however, also notes the following disadvantages:

- Meetings have to be scheduled.
- Employees feel they lose a lot of privacy and their individual office desk with their plants and personal things.
- All the books pile up and they have to be put away every day.
- Employees lose their freedom in terms of work organization.

Furthermore, interviewee I14 explains the following issues:

The losses of the old office structures can cause a lot of negative emotions among employees, and so employers have to give people something that makes this new work concept a win, in order that people can see that it is positive. Such positive gains can be opportunities for physical movement and visually attractive work environments. In order to make such losses more bearable, the employer has to communicate these advantages to the employees repeatedly. Employees do not have to do everything right away, but there are possibilities and offers. The FH Technikum Wien gives their employees the best possible support in their efforts to achieve the highest possible productivity.

The employees were asked about their working habits, about their percentage of work that is done very concentrated on their own, and the percentage of routine work. The pilot project allows everybody to test the new solutions, and everybody can evaluate the furniture. During the change process, there was a lot of negative energy because some information was not passed on immediately. The whole change unsettles people and when people are unsettled, then of course they deal primarily with themselves and their fate and less with their work. If people feel threatened there, then they start to think and gossip. But after a year, people seem to be settled again and satisfied.

Regarding sustainability, interviewee I14 states: Sustainability is an issue in the furniture selection, sourcing the furniture from local suppliers. Sustainability is also promoted by the more efficient use of the existing resources (also regarding office space). This implies lower electricity costs and lower cleaning costs. Sustainability can be seen from the ecological, environmental and social dimensions, but also from the social dimension, i.e. when the employer does something that is attractive for the employees (like exercise programs, height-adjustable desks etc.).

Sustainability becomes an issue for employees later. First, people deal with themselves, with their own destiny, and then comes the sustainability when people are completely free of fear and have no other problems.

In the opinion of I14, there is no effect on absenteeism, neither in the short term nor in the long term.

1.3.3 Summary

In this chapter the results are summed up and categorized regarding well-being and absenteeism of employees due to innovative interior design which means especially modern *open-plan* offices without fixed workplaces. The following table visualizes the outcomes of the 16 interviews regarding the main categories.

Main Categories Interview Partner (City, State)	**Effects on employees**	**Absenteeism related to changes in office design**
	Public Administration Buildings	
I1 (Leeuwarden, NL)	Well-being was improved, satisfaction of employees increased	Slight decrease of absenteeism
I2 (Groningen, NL)	Well-being decreased, employees are averse from *open-plan* offices, they prefer fixed desks	Absenteeism slightly increased due to air draft
I3 (Zwolle, NL)	Positive effects on well-being, high satisfaction of the employees, productivity increased	Slight decrease of absenteeism
I4 (Oldenburg, D)	Employees are sceptical against the new office design, no substantial evidence for an increase of productivity	No decrease of absenteeism
I5 (Osnabrück, D)	Employees have a positive impression of the new office design	Slight decrease of absenteeism
I6 (Vienna, A)	Predominantly positive effects, e. g. more flexibility for the employees, better communication and knowledge sharing	Decrease of absenteeism
I7 (Murakeresztúr, HU)	Better communication, motivating for the employees	No direct effect on absenteeism
	Universities	
I8.1, I8.2 (Groningen, NL)	*Open-plan* offices in combination with fixed (cellular) offices, stimulating creativity, synergies and cooperation, stimulating physical activity in the offices, new system is interesting for groups of employees in order to switch from the cellular offices to *open-plan* offices	No data

Main Categories Interview Partner (City, State)	Effects on employees	Absenteeism related to changes in office design
I9 (Zwolle, NL)	Stimulating employees in their vitality and promoting sustainable living and creativity, parallel structure with traditional cellular offices for certain departments	Slight decrease of absenteeism
I10 (Oldenburg, D)	Employees find the workplace enjoyable, parallel structure with traditional cellular offices for certain departments	no decrease of absenteeism
I11 (Leeuwarden, NL)	Social and professional connection between employees increased, employees find it more comfortable, colourful, and functional to work in a chosen space, they learn faster, increase of productivity and efficiency, sharing ideas and knowledge is facilitated.	No data
I12 (Osnabrück, D)	Positive effects on well-being, more light, more open spaces and physical movement in the offices contribute to employee well-being	Slight decrease of absenteeism
I13 (Vienna, A)	More flexibility and creativity, better communication, possibility to a rapid reformulation of groups and project teams, but several disadvantages still exist	No effect on absenteeism
I14 (Vienna, A)	Generally positive effects on well-being, more communication, but several disadvantages and start-up difficulties	No effect on absenteeism

Note: Bright shading: positive effects; dark shading: no effects or negative effects.

Summing up the outcomes of the qualitative expert interviews, it can be stated that there is some evidence that modern *open-plan* offices can promote the well-being of employees, and they promote communication, creativity, productivity and flexibility as well as the physical movement within the offices. An important success factor for the implementation of new forms of office design is the early integration of the employees in pilot projects and therefore to implement it bottom-up instead of top-down.

Overall, the expert interviews show that in the Netherlands the argumentation for a change in office designs, the effects of the changes and the evaluation or observations after a change was made are "human-centred". All Dutch respondents answered by taking the perspectives of the staff in first place and not the organization as a whole. Remarkably, in the Dutch interviews aspects as "stimulating employees vitality" or "promote sustainable living" were mentioned and can be appointed as "human-centred" aspects. While the German, Austrian and Hungarian respondents almost always gave reasons for the change of office designs as "functionality", "enhancing efficiency and/or productivity" which can be seen in first place as benefits for the organizations as a whole.

In some universities, *open-plan* offices are seen sceptically because of the need of some scientists for a fixed and silent workplace. The drive to new flexible office designs is often influenced by the requirement to use limited office space more efficiently. Regarding the employees' absenteeism there is no or no clear evidence that modern interior office design in terms of *open-plan* offices lead to a decrease of absenteeism.

These are the outcomes of the interviews with experts and responsible persons for the introduction of *open-plan* offices but it is important to compare them to the employees' opinions that are evaluated in the quantitative study.

1.4 Quantitative study

This part describes information of the executed quantitative survey. The survey questions are developed around the topics interior office design, well-being, and absenteeism. Each question within the survey carries the aim to get insights in the effect of interior office design on well-being and absenteeism of employees. The topics that were covered within this survey are spatial comfort, visual comfort, acoustic comfort, wellbeing and absenteeism.

The total amount of responses at the time of withdrawal was 150 responses in the Netherlands and Germany. Although the surveys were completed anonymously the participants were asked to fill in their country of origin, gender, age, type of organization, type of interior office design and if the participants fulfil a part-time or full-time job position. The pie chart below illustrates the participant's country of origin (Fig. 1).

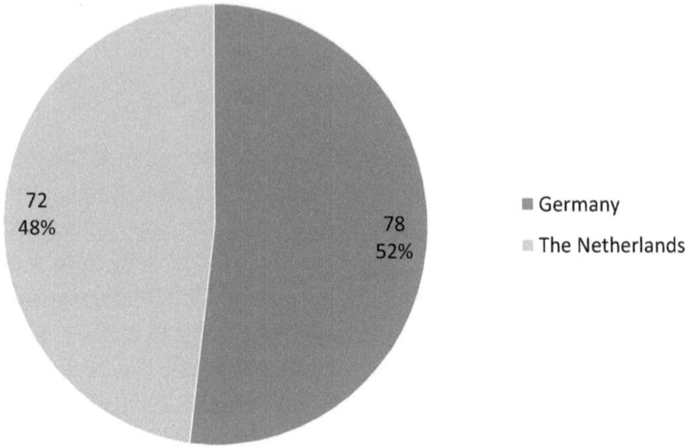

Fig. 1: Participant's country of origin

Fig. 2 illustrates in what type of interior office design the participants operate in. This contributes to get insight in the effect of these office designs in terms of well-being and absenteeism. It can be seen that 23 % of the participants work in an *open-plan* office with their own space. In addition to this, 20 % of the total participants work in an *open-plan* office without own space (both with separation by physical barriers). Moreover, the percentage that represents the participants that work in an *open-plan* office without separation, such as physical barriers, is 9 %. The participants that work in a private office at their organization are represented by 15 %. At last, 33 % of the participants work in a private which they share with others.

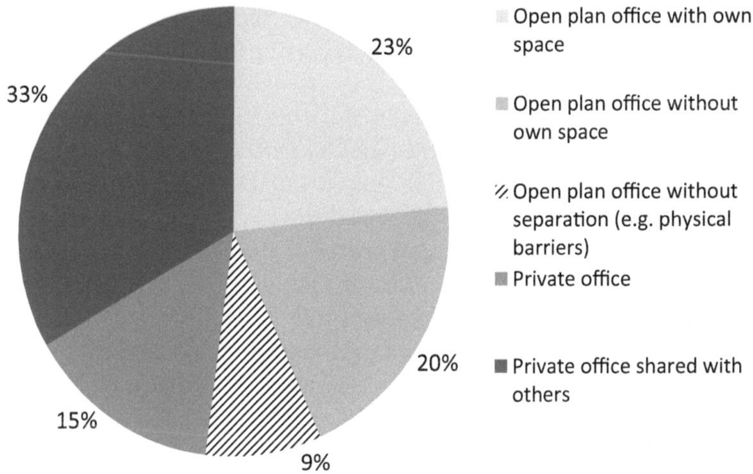

Fig. 2: Type of interior office design

1.4.1 Results

This paragraph aims to provide insight on thoughts and opinions of employees that could not be identified through interviews. This paragraph is supporting the factors that are described in the literature on interior office design that includes functionality, aesthetics, ergonomics, and quality of life. In addition to this, the paragraph examines the effect on well-being and absenteeism in the Netherlands and Germany. Simultaneously, the difference and similarities between these two countries are described.

1.4.1.1 Functionality

The participants were asked several questions based on the spatial comfort at their offices space in which they are interviewed about the functionality within this space. 25 % of the participants in the Netherlands agree that the building offers enough space for breaks and relaxation. On the contrary, 6 % does not agree and 6 % has a neutral feeling towards this. In Germany, 19 % of the participants agree and 17 % disagree. In addition to this, the percentage of a disagreement is higher in Germany (17 %) in comparison to the Netherlands (6 %).

Furthermore, the results from participants in the Netherlands have shown that the workspaces offer enough room fit to the employee function. The survey results illustrate that 21 % agree and 10 % disagree. On the contrary, 23 % of the

German participants agree and 12 % disagree. Yet, the German 2 % participants tend to strongly agree in comparison to 3 % participants in the Netherlands on this matter.

Besides that, the workspace within the Dutch non-profit organizations showed a mix of results based on the room for personal storage of documents, folders and reports. This means that the majority of the Dutch participants either agrees (23 % of 150) or strongly agrees that there is enough space for storage (4 % of 150). Yet, 9 % of 150 strongly disagree on this matter. In comparison to German participants, it can be seen that the percentage of agreement is lower (21 %) and the percentage that strongly agrees (9 %) is higher.

In the Netherlands, the ability to work under unwanted interruptions by other individuals is perceived as satisfactory by 34 % of the employees (34 % of 150). On the contrary, 19 % expressed dissatisfaction based on distractions and unwanted interruptions. Besides that, approximately 33 % have a neutral feeling towards this matter. German participants are slightly less satisfied (33 %), yet 11 % are very satisfied on the ability to work under unwanted interruptions. Moreover, 22 % of the German participants are dissatisfied or share a neutral feeling.

In general, the German participants seem to be more satisfied with the ability to work based on distractions, such as sound and movement. 38 % of the German participants are satisfied with the ability to do their work and 16 % is dissatisfied. Yet, 34 % still shares a neutral opinion on this matter. In comparison to the Netherlands, the percentage of dissatisfaction is much higher (22 %). Moreover, the Dutch participants that are very dissatisfied are 11 % in comparison to 5 % of the German participants. Nevertheless, the majority of the participants in the Netherlands seem be satisfied (37 %) with the ability to work based on distractions.

It can be seen in Fig. 3 that 33 % of the Dutch participants found that the workplace had a positive effect on their productivity. Moreover, 36 % of German participants were positively affected. In addition to this, German and Dutch participants share an almost similar negative effect on productivity; 21 % (Germany) and 22 % (the Netherlands). Yet, the neutral feeling of both countries is relatively high; Germany (31 %) and the Netherlands (28 %).

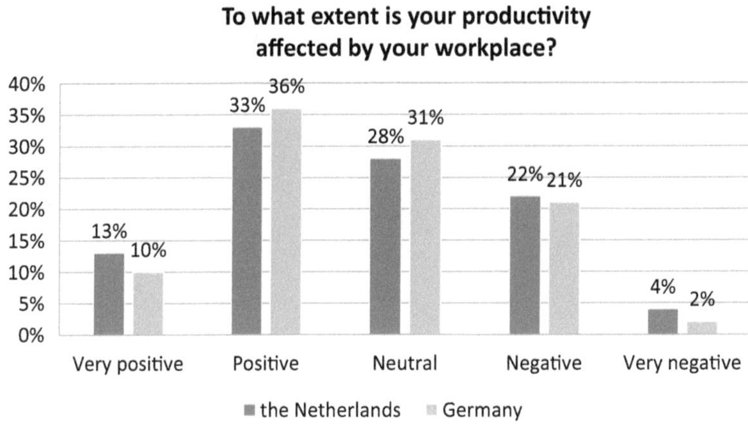

Fig. 3: Employee productivity by the workplace in the Netherlands and Germany

1.4.1.2 Aesthetics

When taken a look at the factor of aesthetics, that also includes movement, use of daylight, and temperature in this research, the survey results that in the Netherlands 35 % of the participants are satisfied about the air quality in the workspace. Nevertheless, 17 % are still dissatisfied about the air quality and 35 % share a neutral opinion. Additionally, the data shows that German participants seem to be more satisfied (40 %) with the air quality in the workspace compared to the Netherlands with 35 %. In comparison to the Netherlands, this is supported by a slight decrease is dissatisfaction of 3 %. Nevertheless, as Fig. 4 shows, 7 % of the German participants appear to be very dissatisfied about the air quality. Contrarily, in the Netherland the percentage of strong dissatisfaction is 0 %.

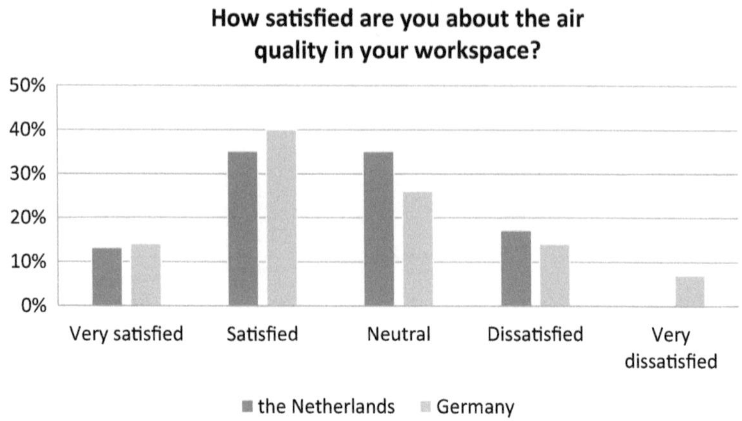

Fig. 4: Air quality at the workplace in the Netherlands and Germany

Moreover, with their visual comfort in terms of daylight 52 % of the Dutch participants are either satisfied or very satisfied about the light comfort in their workspace (e. g. blinding, reflections, contrast). Only a few Dutch participants (13 %) are dissatisfied about the light comfort. On the other hand, it can be seen that German participants are less satisfied; this is represented by a satisfaction rate of only 36 % vs. 52 % in the Netherlands.

The amount of daylight that is available at their workspace is also found satisfactory (54 %) or even very satisfactory (22 %) by participants in the Netherlands. Contrarily, only 7 % is dissatisfied about the available amount of daylight at their workspace. In Germany, 41 % of the participants are very satisfied about the amount of daylight available in their workspace. However, the percentage of dissatisfaction among German participants is higher (12 %) in comparison to the Netherlands (7 %).

1.4.1.3 Ergonomics

As can be seen in Fig. 5, Dutch participants find the comfort of furniture (e. g. desk, chair, office material) at their workspace important (39 %) or very important (43 %). The data also illustrates that 2 % of the participants find it somewhat important and 15 % fairly important. In Germany, 55 % the participants find the comfort of furniture in their workspace very important. Moreover, this difference is presented by a difference of 12 percentage points in comparison to the Netherlands. Besides that, 9 % of the German participants find the furniture somewhat important, which results a difference of 7 percentage points in comparison to Dutch participants.

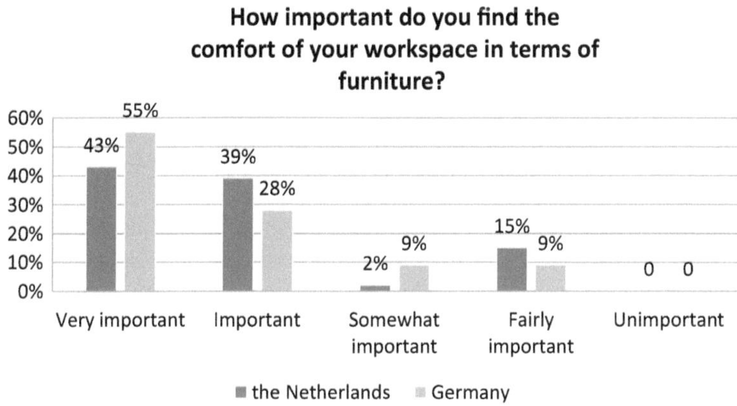

Fig. 5: Comfort of the workplace in terms of furniture in the Netherlands and Germany

The survey results show also that in the Netherlands the importance of ergonomics at the workspace is found very important (53 %) by participants. Yet, it appears that German participants find ergonomics even more important (62 %) in comparison to Dutch participants. It can be stated that the research recognized a difference of 9 percentage points between the Netherlands and Germany.

Besides these findings, the research recognizes that the general sound and distractions in the workspace are found satisfactory by 43 % of participants in the Netherlands. Furthermore, 28 % of the Dutch participants are dissatisfied about the general sound and distractions. Simultaneously, the German participants share an almost similar opinion on this matter. 21 % of the German participants are dissatisfied. However, approximately 26 % of the German participants share a neutral feeling. In comparison to the Netherlands, this illustrates a difference of 17 percentage points, since only 9 % of the Dutch share a neutral feeling.

1.4.1.4 Quality of life

The outcome of the survey demonstrates that in the Netherlands 46 % of the participants agree that their workspace can be adjusted to their needs and wants. Moreover, 11 % of the Dutch participants strongly agree. Additionally, 22 % of the participants disagree and 11 % have a neutral feeling towards this question. In Germany, only 36 % of the participants agree and 17 % strongly agree. Yet, German participants seem to disagree more as well. A slight difference of 2 percentage points has been identified in terms of disagreement. Yet, German participants appear to less strongly disagree (5 %) in comparison to Dutch participants (11 %).

Furthermore, participants were asked if the building offers enough formal and informal workspaces for teamwork. More than a half of the Dutch participants (54 %) agree that the buildings offer these types of workspaces for teamwork. Contrarily, the results demonstrate that on the German side only 34 % agree that the buildings offer these types of workspaces. Furthermore, 20 % of the Dutch participants strongly agree and 9 % strongly disagree. An interesting fact is that 22 % of the participants in Germany share a neutral opinion towards this matter. When taken a look at the results from the Netherlands this percentage is represent by 0 %.

Furthermore, in the Netherlands the participants find (social) interaction with colleagues of major importance; very important (37 %) and important (46 %). On the other hand, a minority of 7 % finds it fairly important and 2 % even unimportant. As the results show, German participants find social interaction with colleagues even more important (59 % see it as very important and 0 % as unimportant).

Dutch and German participants were asked to what extent their well-being is affected by their workplace. As can be seen in the graph below, 52 % of the Dutch participants recognize either a positive influence (41 %) or a very positive (11 %) on well-being by their workplace. Yet, 30 % express a negative (26 %) or very negative (4 %) influence based on this question. Moreover, 17 % express a neutral feeling regarding their well-being. As can be seen in the graph below, the neutral feeling of the German participants shows a difference of 17 percentage points compared to the Dutch. The negative effect differs by 14 percentage points. But in general, most of the German participants find that their well-being is positively affected by their workplace.

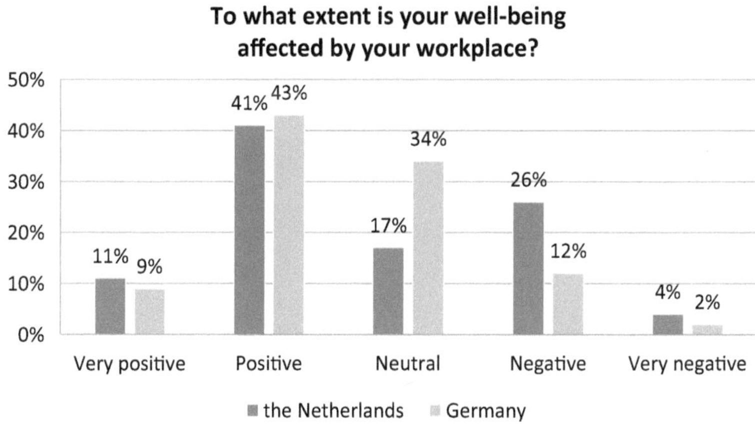

Fig. 6: Well-being affected by the workplace in the Netherlands and Germany

Lastly, 33 % of the Dutch participants express that their absenteeism is affected positively by their workplace, meaning that their absenteeism decreases due to their actual workplace (Fig. 6). Contrarily, the research identifies a negative effect of 9 % in which the absenteeism increases. Additionally, a majority of 46 % has a neutral feeling towards the effect of the workspace on their absenteeism. In Germany, the neutral feeling towards this effect is perceived higher (+ 4 percentage points) in comparison to the Netherlands. Additionally, the negative effect among the German participants results in an outcome of 19 %, as is shown in Fig. 7, meaning that 19 % of the German participants find that their absenteeism increases due to their actual workplace.

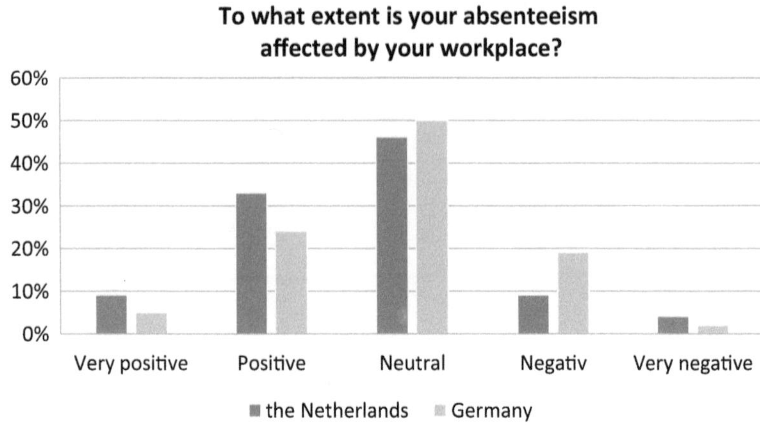

Fig. 7: Absenteeism affected by the workplace in the Netherlands and Germany

1.4.2 Summary

Based on the survey outcomes, it can be concluded that most employees of non-profit organizations in the Netherlands (41 %) and Germany (40 %) are satisfied about the interior office design. Nevertheless, it can be concluded that German employees seem to be more dissatisfied than Dutch employees as there are 7 percentage points difference regarding the satisfaction between Germany and the Netherlands. Moreover, it can be stated that employee well-being is positively affected by the interior office design for Dutch and German employees.

Considering all data in average in both countries, there are no extreme positive or negative answers. In sum, the differences in opinions and experiences of the Dutch and German participants can be valued as not significant.

1.5 Conclusions

After extensive qualitative and quantitative research it can be concluded that different forms of interior office design, such as *open-plan* offices, or *flex* offices, influence employee well-being at town halls and universities.

Additionally, this research concludes that in the Netherlands the influence of interior office design on employee-wellbeing and absenteeism can be interpreted as positive based on the results. This can mainly be related to the fact that Dutch non-profit organizations do include the needs and wants of employees before creating an office space. Moreover, the conclusion can be drawn that the office design at Dutch non-profit organizations has a positive effect on employees. In the Netherlands, the absenteeism ratio decreased at many universities and town halls since the introduction of *open-plan* offices and *flex* offices.

It can be concluded that interior office design aims to meet the purpose to improve functionality, ergonomics, enhance aesthetics, and improve quality of life in the workspace at non-profit organizations. Moreover, this research finds that interior office design has a close connection to employee well-being at non-profit organizations. Additionally, that employee well-being is affected by physical, psychological and emotional health. Besides that, the relation between absenteeism and employee well-being is a process that includes perception of meaningfulness of work, productivity, and engagement. Additionally, it can be concluded that the effect of interior design on employee well-being and absenteeism at town halls and universities in the Netherlands slightly differs in the specific form of office design.

Furthermore, employee perception of these different forms of interior office design shows different results as well. Some town halls in the Netherlands still hold on to the traditional office which has been positively received by elderly employees. On the other hand, universities in the Netherlands adopt the new office environments to a larger extent than the other types of institutions in this research project. Generally, a clear effect of the office design on absenteeism cannot not be recognized. Besides that, town halls and universities alike are constantly looking for improvement in workspace based on employee functionality, employee productivity, vitality, physical and psychological health.

In Germany and Austria, it can be concluded that the effect of interior office design on employee well-being and absenteeism at public institutions and universities is based on prior research executed by the organizations. Dutch non-profit organizations rely on feedback based on the employees' needs and wants. Based on these findings it can be concluded that the German and Austrian non-profit institutions tend to operate from a top-down communication structure in which management makes decision based on research, whereas in the Netherlands the employees' perspective and their well-being is taken more in consideration. Nevertheless, this research recognizes some positive developments that occur in German town halls and universities, i. e. in German non-profit organizations the need for improvement based on movement, daylight, and healthy food consumption is taken into account. An internal benchmark of Osnabrück University of Applied Sciences resulted in a decrease of 1 % in absenteeism since the new built office environment has been introduced which is not significant.

Additionally, this research concludes that the perceived satisfaction with *open-plan* offices depends on the employees' habits and routines that must be adapted during time.

Furthermore, thorough research on employee well-being and absenteeism found that employee well-being is affected by physical, psychological, and emotional health. Besides that, the relation between absenteeism and employee well-being is a factor that includes perception of meaningfulness of work, productivity, and engagement. And in line with that, office design can only be considered as one of the factors that influences well-being of employers.

With that, many factors influence the employees' well-being and absenteeism: The above mentioned perception of meaningfulness of work, productivity and engagement is represented in the physical, psychological, and emotional health in which the research is focussed on. This is supported by literature provided by Fedrickson (2003) which describes that psychological and emotional health is determined by employee engagement and organizational performance by means of finding meaningfulness for employees. In addition to this, it can be stated that when employees find more meaningfulness in their work the absenteeism ratio will decrease. The office design itself has no significant influence on absenteeism.

In order to understand the effect of interior office design on employee well-being it is important to identify the different factors that might of influence. This research shows that these factors include the functionality, aesthetics, quality of life, and ergonomics in interior office design. Moreover, it can be concluded that to understand interior office design it is important to look at the functions of the buildings such as information, production, and service.

Based on the *survey outcomes* it can be concluded that most employees of non-profit organizations in the Netherlands (41 %) and Germany (40 %) are satisfied about the interior office design. Nevertheless, it can be concluded that German employees seem to be more dissatisfied than Dutch employees (with a difference of 7 percentage points between both countries). Moreover, it can be stated that employee well-being is positively affected by the interior office design by Dutch and German employees.

The research concluded that the office environments and buildings offer plenty of room to fit employee functionality in the Netherlands and Germany alike. Additionally, similar results have been presented that the office space offers enough room for personal storage of documents and folders in both countries. Moreover, the effects of new office designs on employee productivity can be positive or negative in the participating countries. Therefore, these countries have been considered to be similar. Lastly, it can be concluded that employees in the

Netherlands and Germany share a similar opinion about the general sound and distraction in the office environment in which approximately 40 % of the employees of both countries find it satisfactory.

Although town halls and universities in the Netherlands and Germany share some similarities, differences between these two countries do exist. Therefore, the research concludes that the decision-making process is based on research carried out by the management, and that needs and wants are not always implemented in Germany. It can be surely stated that the hierarchical approach in Germany and Austria still overrules employees. Thus, in the Netherlands a bottom-up approach is preferred to support employees in terms of ergonomics, aesthetics, functionality, and vitality. The results show that Dutch employees at town halls and universities are more satisfied about space for breaks and relaxation, temperature during winter and summer, daylight, comfort and availability, ability to work under unwanted interruptions, and available formal/informal workspaces for teamwork.

On the contrary, it can be concluded that German employees are more satisfied about the ability to work despite distractions. Additionally, it can be surely stated that factors such as air quality, comfort of furniture, interior office ergonomics, (social) interaction are more important among German employees.

1.6 Summary, limitations and future outlook

Within this international research collaboration, a comparison is made between new office designs in public authorities and universities (of applied sciences) in the Netherlands, Germany, Austria and Hungary. Whereas the qualitative research part focuses on the perspectives of the planners and managers of public organizations, the qualitative part focusses on the opinion and experiences of the staff itself in all the participating countries.

This research gives a detailed insight on several aspects of (new) office designs in relation to well-being of the staff in public organizations in the several participating countries. However, this research has several limitations in its approach as described in Section 1.1.5. In future research some of these limitations must be eliminated beforehand.

To result in more representative outcomes, the future research on office design and well-being needs more respondents in all participating countries. Due to the limitations of this research, the outcomes and results of this research collaboration can only be considered as indications and a first glance at an interesting international comparison.

Without repeating all detailed findings of this project (as summarized above), we will summarize the key findings below:

- While in the German speaking countries and Hungary, argumentation, reasons and the effects of changing office designs can be described as organizational oriented – by using terms as "functionality" and "efficiency" – in the Netherlands there can be seen a more "human centred" perspective by using terms as "employer vitality" and "sustainable living".
- Both perspectives (human-centred and organizational-oriented) can be closely connected to the implementation process of new office designs in public organizations which can be described as bottom-up-procedures in the Netherlands, and contrarily in Germany, Hungary and Austria as top-down procedures.
- Changing office designs lead in all countries of this study to side-effects. It can be stated that most of the respondents show a growing awareness of healthcare for the staff. Offering healthy food, sport facilities etc. to the staff lead in this direction.

References

Albrecht, S. L. (2012). The influence of job, team and organizational level resources on employee well-being, engagement, commitment and extra-role performance. *International Journal of Manpower*, *33*(7), 840–853. https://doi.org/10.1108/01437721211268357

Alfuraty, A. B. (2020). Sustainable environment in interior design: Design by choosing sustainable materials. *IOP Conference Series: Materials Science and Engineering*, *881*, 012035. https://doi.org/10.1088/1757-899x/881/1/012035

Babapour Chafi, M. & Rolfö, L. (2019). Policies in Activity-based Flexible Offices – "I am sloppy with clean-desking. We don't really know the rules." *Ergonomics*, *62*(1), 1–20. https://doi.org/10.1080/00140139.2018.1516805

Bakker, A. B. & Demerouti, E. (2018). Multiple levels in job demands-resources theory: Implications for employee well-being and performance. *Handbook of Well-Being*, 1–13. https://nobascholar.com

Baumeister, R. F., Vohs, K. D., Aaker, J. L. & Garbinsky, E. N. (2013). Some key differences between a happy life and a meaningful life. *The Journal of Positive Psychology*, *8*(6), 505–516. https://doi.org/10.1080/17439760.2013.830764

Brunia, S., De Been, I. & van der Voordt, T. J. M. (2016). Accommodating new ways of working: lessons from best practices and worst cases. *Journal of Corporate Real Estate*, *18*(1), 30–47. https://doi.org/10.1108/jcre-10-2015-0028

Chandra, A., Chandra, P., Deswal, S. & Kundar, R. (2009). Ergonomics in the office environment: A review. *International Conference on Energy and Environment*, Chandigarh, India. https://www.researchgate.net/publication/270888471_Ergonomics_in_the_Office_Environment_A_Review

Ching, F. D. K. & Binggeli, C. (2018). *Interior Design Illustrated* (4th ed.). Wiley.

Colenberg, S., Jylhä, T. & Arkesteijn, M. (2020). The relationship between interior office space and employee health and well-being – a literature review. *Building Research & Information*, 1–15. https://doi.org/10.1080/09613218.2019.1710098

DeJoy, D. M. & Wilson, M. G. (2003). Organizational health promotion: Broadening the horizon of workplace health promotion. *American Journal of Health Promotion*, *17*(5), 337–341. https://doi.org/10.4278/0890-1171-17.5.337

Fan, Y. & Jin, Y. (2020). research on the development and future trend of office furniture design. *E3S Web of Conferences*, *179*, 02075. https://doi.org/10.1051/e3sconf/202017902075

Fredrickson, B. L. (1998). What good are positive emotions? *Review of General Psychology*, *2*(3), 300–319. https://doi.org/10.1037/1089-2680.2.3.300

Grawitch, M. J., Gottschalk, M. & Munz, D. C. (2006). The path to a healthy workplace: A critical review linking healthy workplace practices, employee well-being, and organizational improvements. *Consulting Psychology Journal: Practice and Research*, *58*(3), 129–147. https://doi.org/10.1037/1065-9293.58.3.129

Grove, J. (2017). *Interior Design: A Professional Guide* (1st ed.). RIBA Publishing.

Hayles, C. S. (2015). Environmentally sustainable interior design: A snapshot of current supply of and demand for green, sustainable or Fair Trade products for interior design practice. *International Journal of Sustainable Built Environment*, *4*(1), 100–108. https://doi.org/10.1016/j.ijsbe.2015.03.006

Haynes, B. P. (2008). The impact of office layout on productivity. *Journal of Facilities Management*, *6*(3), 189–201. https://doi.org/10.1108/14725960810885961

Jain, A. K., Giga, S. I. & Cooper, C. L. (2009). Employee well-being, control and organizational commitment. *Leadership & Organization Development Journal*, *30*(3), 256–273. https://doi.org/10.1108/01437730910949535

Kahn, W. A. (1990). Psychological conditions of personal engagement and disengagement at work. *Academy of Management Journal*, *33*(4), 692–724. https://doi.org/10.2307/256287

Keyes, C. L. M., Shmotkin, D. & Ryff, C. D. (2002). Optimizing well-being: The empirical encounter of two traditions. *Journal of Personality and Social Psychology*, *82*(6), 1007–1022. https://doi.org/10.1037/0022-3514.82.6.1007

Lee, E., Allen, A. & Kim, B. K. (2013). Interior design practitioner motivations for specifying sustainable materials: Applying the theory of planned behavior to residential design. *Journal of Interior Design*, *38*(4), 1–16. https://doi.org/10.1111/joid.12017

Meel, J. (2000). *The European Office*. 010 Publishers.

Olabode, S. O., Adesanya, A. R. & Bakare, A. A. (2017). Ergonomics awareness and employee performance: An exploratory study. *Economic and Environmental Studies*, *17*(44), 813–829. https://doi.org/10.25167/ees.2017.44.11

Oseland, N., Catchlove, M. & Miller, H. (2013). Personality and Preferences for Interaction. *workplace unlimited.*

https://www.workplaceunlimited.com/Personality%20and%20Interaction%20v1.1.pdf

Pradhan, R. K. & Hati, L. (2019). The measurement of employee well-being: Development and validation of a scale. *Global Business Review*, 097215091985910. https://doi.org/10.1177/0972150919859101

Rashdan, W. & Ashour, A. F. (2017). Criteria for sustainable interior design solutions. *The Sustainable City XII*, 311–322. https://doi.org/10.2495/sc170271

Rolfö, L., Eklund, J. & Jahncke, H. (2017). Perceptions of performance and satisfaction after relocation to an activity-based office. *Ergonomics*, *61*(5), 644–657. https://doi.org/10.1080/00140139.2017.1398844

Rudokas, K., Armagan Dogan, H., Viliūnienė, O., Vitkuvienė, J. & Gražulevičiūtė-Vileniškė, I. (2020). Office-nature integration trends and forest-office concept FO-AM. *Architecture and Urban Planning*, *16*(1), 41–47. https://doi.org/10.2478/aup-2020-0007

Samad, A. (2015). Towards an understanding of the effect of leadership on employee well-being and organizational outcomes in Australian universities. *The Journal of Developing Areas*, *49*(6), 441–448. https://doi.org/10.1353/jda.2015.0121

Seligman, M. E. P. (2012). *Flourish (A Visionary New Understanding of Happiness and Well-Being)* (1st ed.). Atria Books.

Singh, T., Chetty, N. & Karodia, A. M. (2016). An investigation into the impact of absenteeism on the organizational performance of a private security company in Durban, Kwazulu-Natal. *Singaporean Journal of Business Economics and Management Studies*, *4*(11), 105–159. https://doi.org/10.12816/0027227

Tay, L., Tan, K., Diener, E. & Gonzalez, E. (2012). Social relations, health behaviors, and health outcomes: A survey and synthesis. *Applied Psychology: Health and Well-Being, 5*(1), 28–78. https://doi.org/10.1111/aphw.12000

Templeton, A. (2011, July). *Perceptions of Practicing Interior Designers: Motivations that Encourage their Sustainable Design Practices* (No. 1). http://hdl.handle.net/10217/48140

Vos, P. & van der Voordt, T. (2001). Tomorrow's offices through today's eyes: Effects of innovation in the working environment. *Journal of Corporate Real Estate, 4*(1), 48–65. https://doi.org/10.1108/14630010210811778

Zymina, S. (2020). Types of ecological relationships in the system "nature, artificial environment, humans". Peculiarities of modern eco interior development. *IOP Conference Series: Materials Science and Engineering, 907*, 012010. https://doi.org/10.1088/1757-899x/907/1/012010

2. Prerequisites, design and acceptance of Customer Relationship Management (CRM) systems as components of corporate knowledge management

Martin A. Moser & Bernhard F. Seyr

Abstract: In highly competitive markets, companies must secure their existence by building and assuring long-term competitive advantages by the use of Customer Relationship Management (CRM) systems. The design of CRM systems has a direct influence on the future development and the profit of corporations, and it should be seen as a success factor of corporate knowledge management. The overall goal of this scientific article is the identification of design features and prerequisites for CRM systems which contribute to an increase in sales, the development of corporate knowledge base, as well as organizational development. The empirical study was executed 2019 in the Austrian packaging industry (Moser, 2021). As a result, particular attention has to be paid to the identification of requirements of a CRM system that lead to an increase in acceptance by the users. The identified design criteria can be used for the implementation of future CRM projects in order to ensure a proper usage and approval, and furthermore for the design of a holistic CRM approach that integrates corporate knowledge management.

2.1 Introduction

The importance of consumers plays a decisive role in buyer markets. In the industrial age, corporations developed control systems that supported the effective handling of material and financial funds (Chandler, 1977, p. 21). In order to be competitive and to meet the customer needs in the digital age, an organization must be optimally supported and controlled (Binckebanck & Elste, 2016, p. 48).

The highest potential to generate unique competitive advantages lies within the qualitative arrangement of the customer interfaces (Helmke, Uebel & Dangelmaier, 2017, p. 5). The operation of professional CRM systems offers an opportunity to differentiate from the competitors (Swift, 2001, p. 14). A possibility to achieve the fulfilment of strategically important activities more effectively is through the use of CRM systems, which tries to win and establish valuable and long-term relationships via the assistance of IT-solutions (CRM systems). It can help to increase profit through cost reductions and sales increases (Stokburger

& Pufahl, 2002, pp. 16–17). It is not a temporary limited project or a single IT-solution, but a holistic approach and customer-oriented strategy, which needs to be implemented within a continuous organizational learning process (Hippner & Wilde, 2004, p. 15).

The acceptance by employees is a decisive and mandatory factor for the success of a CRM system, because it is only as good as the employees who implement and use it (Schüller, 2007, p. 11). Without acceptance, the success of the implementation of a CRM system is doubtful (Hildebrand, 2015, p. 13). It is significant to analyse influence factors on the daily use and acceptance of a CRM system in a sales department (Homburg, Wieseke & Kuehnl, 2009, pp. 159–168). The most common reasons for employee resistance are insecurity and the fear of being overwhelmed by innovations (Helmke, Uebel & Dangelmaier, 2017, pp. 280–281).

There is a close connection to various important economic disciplines, like e. g. knowledge management, organizational development, and change management. Systematic handling of knowledge is called knowledge management (Kohl, Mertins & Seidel, 2016, p. 1). Successful knowledge management leads to competitive advantages in fast-changing business environments. Newly adapted mechanisms are investigated with respect to their sufficiency for the strategic evaluation and development of knowledge bases in organizations (Seyr & Hoffer, 2020, p. 1).

Organizational development is also a relevant issue for most companies. They are constantly faced with the question of a suitable or improved organization. Change management generally deals with the optimal control of corporate change (Lauer, 2019, p. 6). CRM helps to strengthen the sales functions, the bundling of all sales activities in one overall responsibility, the strengthening of product management, and the review of management margins (Schifferer & von Reitzenstein, 2018, p. 20). On the way to Industry 4.0, the creation and exchange of data between machines will continue to increase ("Big Data"). Added value is only created, if it is possible to generate new knowledge from data and information. The employees and organizational knowledge bases still belong to the most important success factors and productivity reserves.

2.2 Objectives, research gap and research questions

Anticipating changing customer needs, identifying market opportunities and differentiation potentials, as well as exploiting new markets and target groups are factors that will strongly decide about the optimization of value creation (Stokburger & Pufahl, 2002, pp. 16–17).

The overall aim of this article is the identification of design features and prerequisites for a CRM system as an important part of knowledge management in order to contribute to an increase in sales and the overall development of corporations. It is important to illuminate the corresponding management concepts that show the individual phases of the customer relationship and thus enable profitable and customer-oriented processing. The objective is to generate decisive competitive advantages through knowledge about the design features and prerequisites for a CRM system which have a positive impact on development and sales, and ensure lasting and profitable customer relationships. As a result of which, long-term competitive advantages and the existence of the company can be guaranteed (Stokburger & Pufahl, 2002, pp. 16–17).

This article is furthermore dealing with the identification of requirements of a CRM system that increase the acceptance by the users including the employees of corporations. The identified acceptance criteria can be used for further implementations of CRM systems to ensure a proper usage and approval, and furthermore the achievement and assurance of the intended purpose of a holistic CRM approach. The factors influencing the acceptance of CRM systems by its users will be identified and the goal is to derive a requirement profile, which will be accepted by the employees and applied accordingly. Likewise, their motivation to use the system should increase accordingly.

Within the scope of this article, measures are developed based on a representative case study that help corporations with the introduction of a CRM system in sales. The focus is on finding out dimensions and factors of acceptance and assessing the influence of sales employees when introducing CRM systems. It is also important to analyse, in which phase of the introduction of CRM systems which dimensions of acceptance can be assigned.

The potentials of a CRM system with regards to an increase in sales can be achieved when CRM is considered as an integrated approach which focuses on customer orientation and not solely on product orientation. Besides the customer-related orientation of the organization, the implementation of a CRM system also requires the reorientation of different organizational and technological processes. The important and useful functionalities of a CRM system will be identified within a requirement analysis. It is necessary to select those which reveal the highest possible application benefit for the company (Holland, 2004, pp. 25–26).

The primary goal of CRM is an increase of the corporate value via higher customer satisfaction and customer retention. The lack of empirical studies measuring the success of CRM implementations are in contrast with the great interest in practical CRM concepts. Thus, there is scientific interest to close this gap.

Empirical studies, dealing with methods for the determination of financial CRM success, have been carried out to answer the question to what extent the promise of an increase in value could be redeemed. However, these studies have not been executed industry-specifically and over a broad range of company sizes. The methodological challenges which have been examined in detail regarding this matter were only partially solved (Selchert, 2004, p. 27). Varajão and Cruz-Cunha (2016) describe the main motivations for the introduction of CRM systems in a study that was carried out in Portuguese companies, but they do not examine the reasons for a possible impact on sales (Varajão & Cruz-Cunha, 2016, p. 1269). Li and Mao (2012) place the focus of their case study on internal sales management using CRM and the resulting advantages for companies. They also do not describe possible sales-affecting design features of CRM systems (Li & Mao, 2012, p. 269).

To fill these research gaps the following **research questions** are derived:

1. Which design features of CRM systems (as part of the corporate knowledge management) have an impact on the turnover of corporations and which general requirements need to be fulfilled?
2. Which are the necessary criteria and recommendations in order to increase the user acceptance and furthermore the success of CRM systems to contribute to the overall goal of an increased profitability and development of corporations?

2.3 Research methodology

The case study has been chosen as the overall research design. It is characterized by the concentration on a representative single social element as the object of investigation. In the respective case, an internationally leading corporation of the packaging industry was investigated in 2019. Based on scientific literature and on the conclusions from the qualitative study, hypotheses were formed and tested by the quantitative survey in a second step.

The acquisition of qualitative data was carried out via problem-centred and guided interviews. The interview guidelines consist of an opening and a central section. In the central section, questions were asked about possible design features of a CRM system with a view on increasing sales and the overall development of corporations. The quantitative survey aims to detect the elements that affect the acceptance of CRM systems by employees.

In this course, the gained qualitative data has been separated into categories and evaluated afterwards. The outcomes are debated in this article and put into relation to the corresponding literature (Mayring, 2016, pp. 115–116).

The goals of the quantitative investigation are to detect possible barriers to acceptance when introducing and using sales-supporting CRM systems, to define their importance for sales employees, and to filter out the best possible design features for the use or implementation of CRM systems in sales, so that they are able to contribute to the overall goal of having a positive influence on the development of corporations. In addition, the aim is to generate an effective, acceptance-oriented technology design so that the sales employees are motivated to deal with CRM systems and work with them without encountering resistance and rejection. The investigation has both practical and theoretical relevance. When introducing sales-supporting CRM systems, there is a very high risk of failure. In order to minimize this risk, the focus must be set on an acceptance-oriented technology design. Furthermore, the corresponding research must find out the causes of failure. Lack of correspondence between the product properties of the new CRM system and the customers' needs must therefore be minimized and the flop rate when implementing CRM systems reduced. This requires employees to be involved in the implementation process at an early stage in order to be able to measure success in the system planning and system implementation phases. Due to the high costs and risks, the investigation is of essential importance for other corporations that have planned the introduction of new systems in sales. The target persons of the quantitative survey are people in sales departments who have already worked with or who are currently implementing CRM systems. The survey is carried out by using a standardized online questionnaire. Only closed questions based on Likert-scales are used in the standardized questionnaire in order to guarantee the possibility of comparison and to filter out the importance of properties, activities, and concerns of CRM systems. Structural data, such as age and education, are also queried. A partial survey is used to carry out the quantitative study. The method of conscious selection was chosen for the survey. The quota method, a method of the conscious selection, was chosen for the quantitative research. Here the sample is constructed independently, and the respondents are selected according to relevant characteristics. In the quantitative survey of this article, the quota method is limited to a few dimensions that are known in the distribution of the population. In addition, it must be considered that dimensions are chosen that play a decisive role for the object of investigation (Berekoven, Eckert & Ellenrieder, 2009, p. 49). The quota selection is related to internal sales staff. It is therefore important to consider the characteristics of the sales staff that works with CRM systems or deal with various IT-systems.

Since the selection of sales employees as respondents is already an enormous limitation, they can still be divided according to the following characteristics: sales employee in industry, and sales employee in packaging industry. If these relevant characteristics are used for determining the quota, the distribution of these characteristics in the packaging industry must also be determined, for example from statistics, and converted numerically to the intended sample size. According to the resulting quota plan, the number of people to whom the questionnaire should be sent is calculated. If carried out correctly, a sample is created that corresponds to the composition of the population in terms of all individual quota characteristics. The quota method is inexpensive, fast, and flexible to use. The sample of the quota procedure was calculated based on statistical data, as shown in Tab. 1. The total number of all employees (white-collar and blue-collar workers) in the packaging industry in Austria, which was 14,961 in 2019, was generally used. Of these 14,961 total employees in Austria, around 4,125 are white-collar workers (WKO, 2019). The sales staff in the packaging industry in Austria is among these white-collar workers. In order to find out how many employees are in sales, a general percentage was used for the calculation. On average, 3 % are employed in sales (WKO, 2019).

Tab. 1: Quota procedure

Quota procedure
Number of total employees in the packaging industry: 14,961
Number of white-collar workers in the packaging industry: 4,125
Sales force approx. 3 % of the white-collar workers
~ 120 sales employees to be surveyed

Source: Authors' figure

The statistics program SPSS was used to organize existing data of market research, to prepare it for and to carry out the evaluation. Descriptive statistics respectively frequencies are used for the evaluation as well as cross-tables in order to test the hypotheses. The hypotheses are derived from the analysis of the qualitative research.

2.4 CRM as holistic concept

Rapidly changing market conditions require organizations to focus more on CRM. In this context, the focus is not set on the respective product, but rather on the relationship with the customer. All company activities must be systematically planned, carried out, controlled, and adjusted with a view to the profitable customer relationship. In addition to customer satisfaction and customer loyalty, considerations about systematic and individualized management of customer relationships play a decisive role (Meffert, Pohlkamp & Böckermann, 2010, pp. 5–6).

The implementation of CRM enables the identification of essential actions and dimensions. The management of knowledge across interaction and time channels in order to coordinate the continuous client relationship is methodically associated with CRM. Generally, CRM enables corporations to utilize information to advocate their perception of how to manage clients. Corporations take advantage of the data in CRM systems to be able to win new clients, keep current clients, and improve these associations via cross-selling and custom-built communications (Palmatier, Kumar & Harmeling, 2018, p. 58). CRM means the integral handling of an organization's interaction with its clients. Distribution, communication, and supply policies must be integrated in line with customer requirements. Client satisfaction is the central measure of CRM success. It is an indicator of client loyalty and ultimately for the long-lasting success of an organization (Helmke, Uebel & Dangelmaier, 2017, p. 7). CRM focuses on identifying, building up, and securing a profitable customer base and by this way it contributes to the optimization of a company's customer portfolio (Sperl, 2016, pp. 41–43). CRM is based on a new customer-oriented corporate strategy, and it requires the reorientation of business processes and responsibilities (Leußer, Hippner & Wilde, 2011, p. 18). CRM systems are part of Information Technology (IT) instruments, supporting various administrative actions from a technological viewpoint. The development clearly leads in the direction of a more holistic understanding of CRM and its various aspects (Perna & Baraldi, 2014, p. 57).

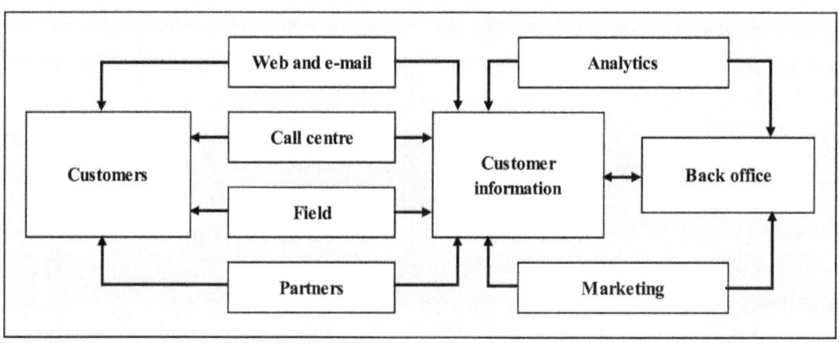

Fig. 1: Customer Relationship Management (CRM)
Source: Authors' figure

As shown in Fig. 1, customer interactions must be managed across multiple communication channels, like e. g. call centres, web applications and e-mails, dealers or partners, and field sales. The coordination and linkage of direct customer processing and the back-office is significant for success. All customer information must be collected, analysed, and used in a meaningful way. The challenge lies in making it simple for clients to do commercial activities in a manner they like to do it anytime, via any channel, and in every currency or language (Rai, 2013, p. 31).

With the usage of CRM, a perceptible advantage must arise for the customer as well as the supplier through advantages in efficiency and effectiveness. On the customer side, this could lead to a risk reduction or a general cost advantage while the supplier may have a higher intensity of customer relationship and a resulting long-term business relationship (Meffert, Pohlkamp & Böckermann, 2010, pp. 7–8). Companies with a stable and close collaboration with their clients achieve a higher profitability of relationships than other organizations. The primary causes are the positive effects of partnerships and customer relationships being induced by targeted (CRM-) measures. The literature points out that the design of supplier-buyer-relationships in B2B-environments creates special demands towards supplier companies and therefore CRM is of high importance (Schumacher, 2005, p. 28). Client-specific demands and procedures make it a challenge to classify customers in a meaningful way. Therefore, such classifications are often not correct and logical (Narayandas & Rangen, 2004, p. 63). Clients are perceived to be solitary, whereas generalizations among them are frequently seen as preposterous (Laiderman, 2005, p. 64). CRM information and data need to be structured to enable significant longitudinal or cross-sectional evaluation (Zahay, Peltier & Krishen, 2012, p. 5).

CRM helps to gather important information about customers and should enhance confidence as well as quality of customer care, it should develop the organization's sensitiveness for customer support and service requirements, decrease the loss of customers, and reduce promotional and other associated expenditures (Stein, Smith & Lancioni, 2013, p. 855). All information related to CRM and market intelligence should be available for policymakers in the company (Rigby & Ledingham, 2004, p. 118). In most companies, only few executives are aware of the accessibility of CRM data and do not know about its utilization. This problem is directly related to the knowledge management that should also enable the distribution and the use of customer related knowledge within the whole company. Once the executives are aware of to the advantages and practical use of CRM data, it evolves into a precious advantage for the corporation's decision-making procedures. Consequently, the starting point needs to be the training of those who produce the information (sales staff) and who will be utilizing the resulting data for their decision-making process (executives). The entire profitability of CRM is unfolded by the persistence of information gathering and the adaptability in decision-making (Stein, Smith & Lancioni, 2013, p. 856).

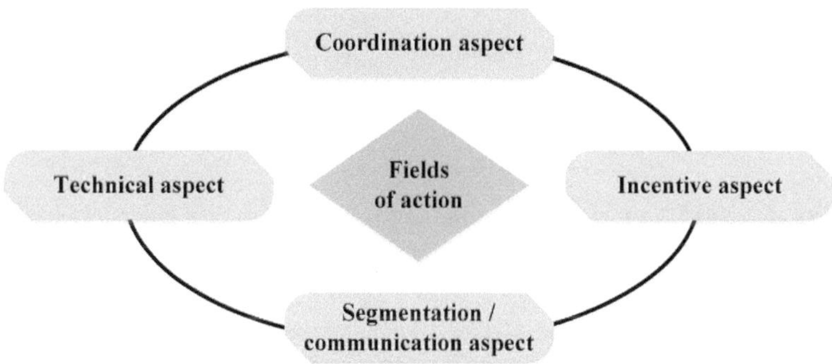

Fig. 2: Requirements for CRM
Source: Meffert, Pohlkamp & Böckermann (2010, p. 23)

There are four central prerequisites for the success of CRM and the achievement of multi-dimensional competitive advantages as shown in Fig. 2. The coordination aspect includes the management of internal and external processes, and the creation of the organizational prerequisites. Business units must be coordinated in a way that an overall view of all customers can be generated and used. The incentive aspect is a success-determining feature, which focuses on the attractiveness of customer and supplier perspective. Through an early and on-going integration of customer knowledge, new market entry barriers for competitors can be generated and the creation of unique selling propositions can be achieved. The knowledge about customers can stimulate innovations and can help to fulfill the customers' needs even better. It also helps to build change barriers and emotional bonds. This aspect is characterized by using the preferred communication media of the customer. The last prerequisite is the technical aspect, which includes IT- and system-requirements along with the usage of new technologies (Meffert, Pohlkamp & Böckermann, 2010, pp. 23–24).

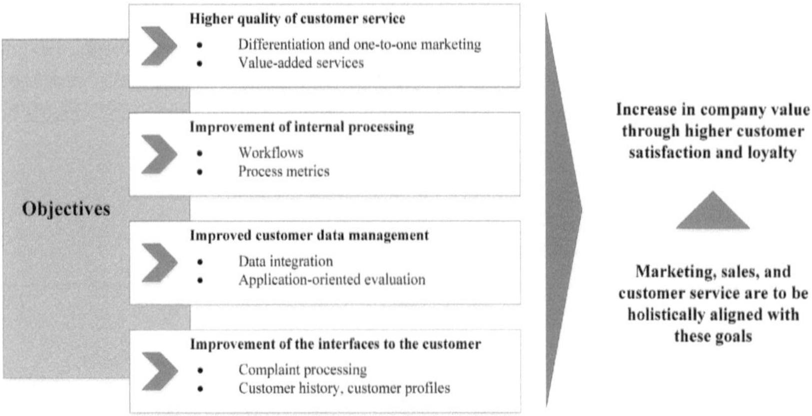

Fig. 3: Goals of the CRM approach
Source: Helmke, Uebel & Dangelmaier (2017, p. 7)

CRM is frequently diminished to its technological components or understood as a pure software project with the only tasks of acquisition, storage, and evaluation of customer data (Stauss & Seidel, 2002, p. 11). However, this single-track perspective carries the risk that the necessary framework conditions in the company are neglected. The result is that the technological possibilities are created, but the supporting processes are not geared towards the customer (Hippner, 2005, p. 116). The aim of CRM is to take customer processing to a new level of quality through a holistic focus on customer needs. The holistic concept claims the orientation on the improvement of data processing regarding customer service, internal data processing, customer data management, and the customer interfaces that should lead to an increase of the company value, a higher customer satisfaction, and customer loyalty. This should be reached by the alignment of marketing, sales and customer service in order to reach these goals. The objectives of this CRM approach are illustrated in detail in Fig. 3 (Dangelmaier, Uebel & Helmke, 2004, p. 5).

Higher client satisfaction results in a more powerful client retention, which has a beneficial impact on company profit (Helmke, Uebel & Dangelmaier, 2017, pp. 7–9). The aim of the holistic CRM approach is to distribute the information about customers more efficiently within the organization in order to use it more effectively in the context of processing customer relationships (Dangelmaier, Uebel & Helmke, 2004, pp. 5–8). First and foremost, the quality of customer processing must be increased, which can be achieved through a consistent focus on customer-oriented goals (Helmke, Uebel & Dangelmaier, 2017, pp. 7–10). Customer satisfaction, motivated by corporate practice, is a central construct in management research (Bednarek, 2014, p. 15).

Industry 4.0 and digitization are continuously changing markets. It is not a product that matters, but the value that can be offered to the customer. This is where digitization and its use in customer-oriented services offer various options that turn products into problem solutions for customers and thus significantly increase their value by individualization, better support, or sophisticated additional services (Robra-Bissantz & Lattemann, 2019, p. 3). Social media is considered as the next level of the internet progression. Out of the perspective of CRM, it stands for a significant improvement, as interactions are getting increasingly straightforward. Social media also nearly instinctively provokes worries about the confidentiality and the utilization of information and data. A significant associated incident occurred in 2018, revealing the fraudulent use of Facebook data by the data analytics corporation Cambridge Analytica (Isaak & Hanna, 2018). The latter analysed high amounts of information about users without their approval and generated comprehensive profiles about them. This occurrence induced severe discussions regarding regulations and restrictions of social media. In the end, suppliers have initiated the restriction of commercial actions and started to pay higher attention to confidentiality topics (Alt & Reinhold, 2020, p. V). Recent possibilities that support and increase the consideration of CRM include the digitization and interrelationship of service achievement, negotiation, and administrative procedures with corresponding distinction of information accessibility (Kleinaltenkamp, Plinke & Geiger, 2015, p. 290).

CRM as a holistic approach should also apply the theories of knowledge management in order that it is able to serve the whole organization as an integrated part of the company's information system. Therefore CRM must not be an isolated solution. In this context, North (2021, pp. 33–69) presents his "Knowledge Staircase". From this model it can be derived that CRM must not be reduced to the data processing (first degree of maturity) and specific single solutions (second degree of maturity), but it should be developed to an integrated component of a professional knowledge organization (third degree of maturity) and furthermore to an important resource of knowledge-oriented business management (fourth degree of maturity). In order to reach this goal, knowledge must be inter-linked and applied to achieve the third degree of maturity. For the fourth degree of maturity, also the employees' *motivation to act* accordingly, and the competence (the ability to act *correctly*) are prerequisites in order to become (or remain) a competitive and unique market participant. In short, this means that

CRM should not be a simple collection of data, but it should be a vivid basis for entrepreneurial decisions and actions, embedded in a holistic concept of knowledge management for the entire organization. The close interrelation between the success of knowledge management, CRM and innovation capabilities ought to be taken into account in this context (Migdadi, 2020).

As empirical studies reveal, a large number of organizations neglect the fact that successful knowledge management (and also CRM as a part of it) must include the following three perspectives: human, organization, and technology (Seyr, 2015, pp. 3–27). Typically the understanding of knowledge management is restricted to technology, whilst the motivation and abilities of the staff as well as the organizational implementation are widely missing. Knowledge management should not mainly be the task of the IT department, but it ought to be understood as one of the main concerns of top management in order to unfold its huge potential as productivity reserve and driver of innovation and competitiveness.

2.5 CRM systems as IT solutions

The idea connected to handling client data to comprehend who they are, how they work, their benefit as a client, and the deepness of the interaction did not start as a well-reasoned procedure or concept with the name "CRM system". They find their origins in the primary requirement to handle client data within several diversified corporations. In order to fulfil the requirement of gaining and preserving contacts and clients for all primary functions, predecessors and inceptive CRM solutions were evolved (Mathena, Yetter & Hostetler, 2009, p. 4).

Information and communication technologies are playing an essential role regarding the implementation and realization of CRM. A significant prerequisite is the technological aspect. This includes IT- and system-requirements, as well as the usage of new technologies. CRM systems are a possibility for the specific management of customer relationships (Meffert, Pohlkamp & Böckermann, 2010, pp. 23–24).

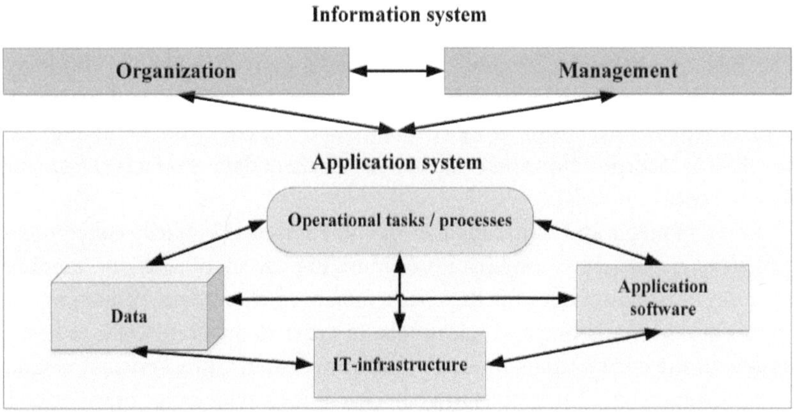

Fig. 4: Correlation between information and application system
Source: Laudon, Laudon & Schoder (2010, p. 18)

CRM systems are information and communication systems that significantly assist a CRM strategy. They are often seen as sheer application systems to collect information about customers and analyse this data collection accordingly. The aim of CRM systems is the automatization of customer-oriented processes. This IT-orientation implies the risk to forget the necessary framework conditions of corporations nowadays, which are relevant and important for a comprehensive information system (Leußer, Hippner & Wilde, 2011, pp. 17–18). Figure 4 shows the correlation between the information system with its interrelationships between organization and management, and the application system with its operational tasks and processes, data, software, and IT-infrastructure.

CRM systems are used to track and analyse the company's interactions with its customers to optimize revenue, profitability, and customer satisfaction. They simplify and support the implementation of a holistic CRM approach (Laudon, Laudon & Schoder, 2010, pp. 533–534). With their help, customer-specific data can be collected, stored, maintained, and made accessible to the entire corporation at any time and in a standardized manner.Business relevant objectives, such as maximizing customer service and customer profitability, can be identified and reconciled using a CRM system. The automation of manual work steps simplifies and shortens the company's internal processes, which means that respective savings can be achieved (Neumann, 2014, pp. 115–116). It should be noted that by improving the organizational information management system, increased customer orientation and improved competitive advantages are made possible (Torggler, 2007, p. 7). In the literature, the superior objectives and tasks of a CRM system are the coordination and integration of individual communication channels between customers and companies, the support and synchronization of the essential customer touch-points (service, sales, and marketing), and the uniform incorporation and evaluation of all client data and facts (Neumann, 2014, p. 116).

The components and functionalities of CRM systems primarily concern four main strategic targets: commercial procedure improvement in client handling, invention of novel services for the client, enhanced client data evaluation, and support of new marketing and sales-tools. In order to integrate CRM as best as possible in the corporation's internal IT-infrastructure, CRM systems integrate various components. This results in a correspondingly wide range of variation in functionalities (Helmke, Uebel & Dangelmaier, 2017, p. 10). Three CRM application areas are existing (Communicative, Operative, and Analytical CRM). In the literature, Communicative CRM is often referred to as Collaborative or Cooperative CRM. Communicative CRM is understood to mean all activities connected with the control, coordination, and support of the different communication channels between corporations and customers. Nowadays, customers mostly decide when and by which channel they are contacting a company. The customer expects that all data and information from previous interactions can be provided up-to-date, consistently, and through all available channels. Corporations must strive for a comprehensive and uniform customer experience. Additionally, clients anticipate complete and current knowledge about the corporation. For this reason, it is essential to receive a single face-to-face relationship with the customer and a uniform view of the customer in relation to the company (Neumann, 2014, pp. 116–117).

Operative CRM combines all the activities aimed at supporting, improving, and optimizing the customer contacts. The dialogue between customer and company and the related business processes need to be supported. Operative CRM includes all hardware and software that is used to assist the employees in direct contact with the customers. It includes solutions for marketing, sales, and service automation (Neumann, 2014, p. 117), as well as the necessary business processes (Hippner, Rentzmann & Wilde, 2006, p. 54). Operative CRM accommodates representatives of sales, customer service, and marketing with significant client and business data. Those staff members have constant admission to the gathered information in order to have an overview regarding the client support. Additionally, they complete the client profile, and as a result, they can take a broad picture of the client through each contact. Data regarding transmission time, inventory, etc. assist in making dependable assessments about clients. Operative CRM aspires the improvement of client support (Wilde, 2011, pp. 46–47).

Analytical CRM collects all customer-relevant data and information from customer conversations, records them systematically, and evaluates them. The overall goal is the on-going optimization of customer-related business processes. It forms the central basis for Communicative and Operative CRM (Neumann, 2014, p. 119). The essential components of an Analytical CRM system are the collection, system integration and digital processing of customer data as well as evaluation routines, like data mining or online analytical processing (OLAP) (Walter & Schmidt, 2004, p. 47). Analytical CRM supports the front and back office area in order to generate information about customer structures and customer behaviour. Ideally, this information provides knowledge on the basis on which the operational instruments and channels are to be selected in order to meet customer needs in an optimal way. Analytical CRM aims at the continuous optimization of Operational CRM processes in the form of a "closed-loop architecture", where analysis and operational businesses work together in a "learning system" (Helmke, Uebel & Dangelmaier, 2017, p. 14). The operative system generates the customer data obtained and forwards it to the analytical system where it is recorded and subjected for processing, evaluation, and interpretation. The findings and possible improvements are passed on to the operative system. The aim is to continuously optimize the customer-specific business processes (Neumann, 2014, p. 124).

2.6 Organizational and technological prerequisites

A CRM system can only exploit its full potential, when the customer-oriented strategy is coordinated with the necessary requirements. The company must set incentives for customer stimulation and primarily pay attention to reliability and constant contact persons for the customer. A customer relationship strategy inevitably results in changes for the employees, due to the alignment of all company activities with the customer. This manifests itself in changed work processes or the behavioural requirements when contacting customers. There must be a willingness to share customer knowledge within the corporation. These changes must be accepted, internalized, and actively lived in order to create the conditions for a functioning CRM concept (Georgi & Mink, 2011, p. 83).

The process and organizational structure are responsible for creating a framework that ensures the necessary customer and relationship orientation by customer-related processes and information flows (Georgi & Mink, 2011, pp. 83–84). The entire organization must be clear about what CRM means and what content is associated with this approach (Neumann, 2014, p. 138). Further success factors for CRM are the involvement of the top management from the beginning as well as its on-going commitment to the CRM strategy. Management is responsible for creating the conditions for a successful project implementation. A delegation of responsibility to managers at middle or lower levels endangers the success of a CRM project as they do not have enough influence to implement cross-departmental changes that can be necessary in the context of a CRM-project (Neumann, 2014, pp. 147–148).

A functioning CRM system must provide comprehensible, current, and complete customer-related information. The focus lies on the collection and compilation of customer data along the customer touch points, the evaluation and provision of data, and the support of all activities derived from it, especially those that have a direct impact on the customer. All company processes have to be aligned with the needs of the customers (Georgi & Mink, 2011, p. 84). In this context, ensuring data quality, timely provision for the analysis, and operational use of this data as well as compliance with data protection regulations also play an important role (Leußer, Hippner & Wilde, 2011, p. 751).

In many cases information in organizations is distributed across different systems and databases. The difficulty in aligning the processes with the customers' needs lies in the integration of existing separate data management systems and the databases in order to allow an overview of the entire company with a uniform structure. The technical integration of a CRM system with existing systems avoids redundant data storage and enables access to data from different systems (Schulze, 2002, pp. 36–37). During an implementation of an integrated CRM system, the existing structures of marketing, sales, and service processes need to be determined by creating flow and task diagrams (Schulze, 2002, pp. 158–159).

2.7 Economic effects of CRM

In the course of value-oriented management, marketing measures are examined with regards to their positive impact on the corporation's value. The difficulty in this respect lies in the reliable quantification of the intangible assets. In addition to e. g. the tacit knowledge of the organization, also the explicit knowledge about the customers as well as the value of existing customer relationships as relational capital plays a decisive role for its goodwill. By assessing customer relationships over the entire customer lifecycle, long-lasting customer loyalty can have a sustainably positive impact on long-term company success (Krafft & Götz, 2011, pp. 216–217).

Customer proximity generally describes the degree of interaction between customers and companies (Schumacher & Meyer, 2004, p. 26). It must be ensured that all customer-related information is not lost and can be used for further development and optimization of the respective product or service (Krafft & Götz, 2011, p. 218). Customer proximity can make it easier for corporations to identify their customers' expectations and needs. Products and services can be designed to meet requirements, individual customer relationships can be established, and processes between providers and buyers can be coordinated (Schumacher & Meyer, 2004, p. 27).

Customer satisfaction is understood as a positive emotional reaction to a cognitive differentiation procedure between client expectations and the perceived performance status. If the expectations are fulfilled or exceeded, customer satisfaction occurs. In addition to objective indicators, such as sales or market share, there are primarily subjective approaches to quantifying customer satisfaction. Due to its qualitative nature, no method for operationalizing and measuring customer satisfaction has prevailed (Krafft & Götz, 2011, pp. 222–223).

Customer retention is understood as the maintenance of a business relationship that is characterized by a non-random sequence of transactions and interactions between customers and suppliers. It is concretized in past, present, and future buying or ordering behaviour. Influencing factors represent economic, psychological, and social barriers to change, and furthermore customer satisfaction, and the attractiveness of competitive offers. A high level of customer retention is positively related to the intention of buying the product again, the attitude of the customer for the supplier, and the intention to recommend the product to others. Longer customer retention goes hand in hand with increased sales, more recommendations, and shorter consultation times (Krafft & Götz, 2011, pp. 226–228).

Key indicators for assessing the economic value of customer relationships are primarily the turnover, the margin contribution, the customer's share of the deliveries, and the customer's value. A review of the literature regarding the effects of customer proximity, customer satisfaction, and customer retention on the economic value proves the achievement of higher sales by long-term customer relationships. Moreover, there is a positively significant link between higher customer retention and the buying behaviour, the re-sale, and the further recommendation by customers (Krafft & Götz, 2011, pp. 231–233).

2.8 Acceptance theory

The implementation of a CRM system is usually a complex procedure, involving all processes of a corporation in a technical and organizational way. It must be considered as a strategical project, which forms and develops the prospective design of customer processing. In the scope of an extensive CRM audit, the selection of the software itself, the alignment of CRM with the strategic company goals, the identification of needs for necessary process reorganizations, as well as the needed change management must be discussed and defined. Human beings are playing the leading role during the CRM implementation. The added value of CRM, as well as the individual benefit and usefulness must be visible for every user to ensure acceptance (Helmke, Uebel & Dangelmaier, 2017, pp. 267–270).

Acceptance is a key term used in social and sociological discussions for the description of positive and negative decisions. Several different and varying definitions exist and the search for a universal and generally valid definition is relatively low (Kollmann, 1998, p. 37). Acceptance refers to the degree of willingness of a user to deal with a specific situation or system, to identify with it, and to retrieve the provided utilization potential in a task-based manner (Manz, 1983, p. 177). The term is often used as a synonym for recognition, endorsement, approval, and affirmation. Due to its partly inflationary use, a precise definition of the term is increasingly difficult (Betz, 2003, p. 97).

Despite the different conceptions of the research areas, there is an agreement in the scientific discourse that acceptance describes the relationship between an acceptance subject (individual, group) and an acceptance object (technical system, innovation, opinion) within a subject- and object-mediated acceptance context (environment). The concept of acceptance can be displayed in its ideal type in the analytical triangle (see Fig. 5) of subject, object, and context (Lucke, 1995, pp. 88–89).

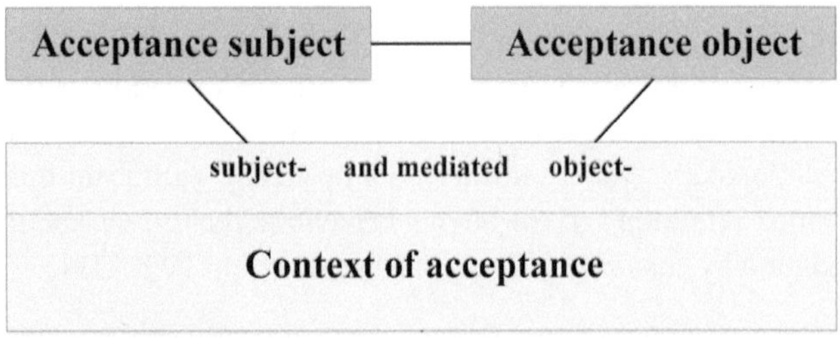

Fig. 5: Acceptance triangle
Source: Lucke (1995, p. 89)

Due to the wide range of uses, an exact definition of acceptance mostly depends on the respective objective or subject of investigation (Königstorfer, 2008, p. 10). In this scientific paper, the acceptance of CRM systems is based on recognition and willingness to use a CRM system efficiently, which is a mandatory prerequisite so that it consequently has a positive effect on the corporation's development.

Economical acceptance research differentiates between attitude and behavioural acceptance. As a result, scientific literature offers a basic framework for the different concepts and forms of use (Rengelshausen, 2000, p. 72). Attitude-oriented research is characterized by equating acceptance with attitudes. Attitudes are latent variables that are not directly measurable and must be derived from verbal and non-verbal responses (Trommsdorff, 2011, p. 159). In the academic literature, the attitude consists of three components, also called "concept of trinity" (Kollmann, 1998, pp. 51–52). The characteristic of behaviour-oriented research is the equality of acceptance and measurable behaviour or effective use. The acceptance is associated with a task-oriented use of an innovation. A prerequisite for positive behavioural acceptance is the willingness to behave. The properties of the examination object are decisive for the behaviour relevant to acceptance (Betz, 2003, p. 109).

The concept of acceptance in the viewpoint of Business Information Systems (BIS) mostly relates to the acceptance of application systems. The research concentrates primarily on the acceptance or rejection of the systems by the user and the organizational measures when introducing application systems (Amberg, Hirschmeier & Schober, 2003, p. 575). In this context, the term "technology acceptance" is used. With modern information and communication technologies, due to their interdisciplinary task, the focus is on human action regarding developments and the use of technical innovations (Dethloff, 2004, p. 18).

Based on the existing acceptance models in the literature and the definition of BIS, it can be concluded that the factors individual, task, and technology have a significant influence on the acceptance of BIS (Allerbeck & Helmreich, 1984, p. 15). In the business context, the factors organization and management are added as influencing factors of acceptance. The operational focus can be found in several acceptance models as company-related factors (Laudon, Laudon & Schoder, 2010, p. 18). It is recommended that CRM systems are implemented gradually in view of a thorough change management process. This gives users the chance to use the system as early as possible in individual sections and to get used to the system. It should also be noted that a good CRM project is never finished, but should be continuously improved. Since the marketing and sales strategy for a company changes over time, the CRM system and its functions must also be able to adapt to the circumstances (Stender, Göbel & Schulz-Klein, 2003, pp. 34–35).

The technology-related determinants represent the primary influencing factors for the formation of acceptance. They determine the properties and possible uses of information systems and influence their perception. Essential factors are the relative advantage, the compatibility, the complexity, the probability, and the communicability (Rogers, 2003, pp. 229–230). The relative advantage describes the extent to which a novelty is perceived to be better, compared to the technology used hitherto. Compatibility is the degree of perceived compatibility of technology with existing values, norms, experiences, and needs. The complexity indicates how difficult it is to perceive a technological innovation, and which application difficulties it presents to the user. The probability refers to the possibility to test the innovation before the introduction. Communicability describes how easily the features of the innovation can be communicated to future users. Apart from the complexity, there is a positive correlation between all determinants and the acceptance of an information system (Kollmann, 1998, p. 120).

Considering increasingly complex enterprise tasks and processes, management is given a central role in the adoption of BIS. For the employees, the efficient task fulfilment and automation of business processes is in the foreground, while the management requires structured and processed information. Although executives are also users of the information system, management sets the general framework for the use of the system (Laudon, Laudon & Schoder, 2010, p. 27). The planning concerns the fundamental decision regarding the goals and the conditions of the technical application. These decisions usually mean a change in the structure and process flow of the company (Kollmann, 1998, p. 127). The management has the task to organize the use of the technology for the task execution. The obligation to use the system specifies to what extent an information system must be mandatory in the corporation. A low motivation to use the system does not necessarily mean a negative acceptance of the system (Hartwick & Barki, 1994, pp. 440–443). Management can grant restrictions and freedom concerning the system usage, affecting user attitudes to the system (Hilbig, 1984, p. 322). The users of the information system must be applied according to their qualifications. The task of the management is to continuously control decisions about human resources and to redistribute them, if necessary (Picot & Reichwald, 1987, p. 170).

Organizational determinants are related to the company, as there are the application situation, the organizational environment, and the social environment within the organization in which the BIS is used. They represent the organizational framework and the basis for corporate acceptance and willingness to innovate. The higher the willingness to innovate in a company, the faster the acceptance process will proceed. The willingness to innovate depends on the organizational culture and structure (Rogers, 2003, pp. 411–413). Organizational culture reflects the individual character of an organization, expressed through values, norms, and collective patterns of order. The organizational culture is responsible for the fundamental attitude of an organization towards change (Schreyögg, 2016, p. 407).

The task-related determinants deal with the question of whether the task can even be solved with the help of a BIS. This is understood as the actual usability of the technology in the respective sphere of influence. The more difficult the task is, the higher the demands towards the system are (Reichwald, 1978, p. 33). The individual performance of the user and the associated acceptance of the system depend on the support during the task performance. Collaboration between multiple organizational units requires an integrated information system that can ensure cross-unit information sharing (Goodhue, 1995, pp. 1,828–1,833).

2.9 Empirical study

2.9.1 Qualitative data analysis and results

In order to gain access to the field and the widest possible knowledge spectrum, sales employees from all sales regions as well as different hierarchy levels (regional sales manager, key account manager, account manager) of an internationally leading manufacturer in the packaging industry were interviewed in an empirical setting in 2019 (Moser, 2021). The selection criterion for sales employees is that they must deal with CRM systems or CRM approaches in their daily work. Fourteen employees were selected for this purpose. During an experimental test of the interviews with two selected interview partners, the overall appropriateness of the interview guide was examined. In preparation of the summary content analysis according to Mayring, two category types can be generated (main and sub-categories).

In the second qualitative research, six sales employees and three external CRM experts from providers of CRM systems on the market were interviewed. The interviews of the sales staff were used to determine the needs for the acceptance of a CRM system. Interviews with the external CRM experts are the objective counterpart and are intended to bring additional specialist and industry knowledge as well as objectivity. A requirement profile for a CRM system will be derived from the results of the second qualitative research in order to increase the acceptance of the system. A criteria catalogue was created from the requirement profile in order to answer the respective research question.

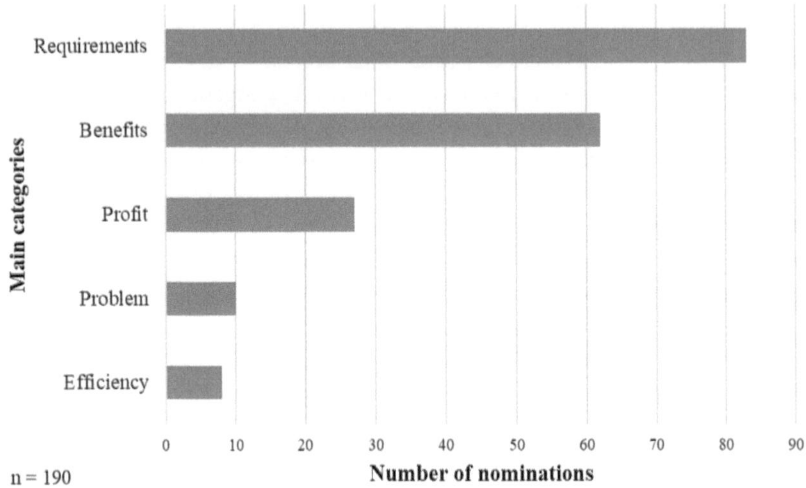

Fig. 6: Overall analysis of the main categories
Source: Authors' figure

The starting point for the presentation of the results wasan overall analysis of the main categories and the respective number of entries in the guided interviews. The sources of the statements are the conducted interviews. Figure 6 shows the overall analysis of the main categories (requirements, benefits, profit, problem, and efficiency). As a result of the summarized content analysis, 190 exploitable statements from the interviews are assigned to these categories. The main category "requirements" describes the prerequisites for the successful introduction of a CRM system with the goal that this system is appropriately used and maintained. The category "benefits" refers to the expected advantages from the usage of a CRM system. The initial research question of this article is covered by the category "profit". The main category "problem" contains possible or expected problems when working with CRM systems or CRM-approaches and the category "efficiency" refers to the prerequisites for efficient work.

When presenting the results, it must be considered that sub-categories can appear in several main categories. The respective sub-category is therefore always to be viewed and understood in relation to the concrete main category, since one and the same sub-category can influence different aspects. An example for this is the time saving that can result from working with CRM systems. According to the interviewees, this can have an impact on the profit, but is also considered as a basic prerequisite for a CRM system, an increase in efficiency, and thus a concrete benefit. The identified main category "requirements" is part of the acceptance criteria of CRM systems. As a further consequence, a subsequent detailed qualitative and quantitative analysis of this category is conducted. It provides additional in-depth knowledge and insights with regards to acceptance criteria for CRM systems, and furthermore its success contributes to the overall goal of an increased profitability and development of corporations. Based on the results of the qualitative evaluation, a profile of requirements and furthermore an overview of acceptance criteria for CRM systems is generated.

The main category "requirements" refers to the prerequisites for the successful introduction of a CRM system and the goal that the system is used and maintained appropriately by the employees. Statements on this main category can be obtained mainly from the questions about the experience when working with CRM systems and their most important characteristics. The main category "benefits" refers to the expected benefits from the use of a CRM system. In this context, the respondents already mentioned possible increases in customer satisfaction and a reduction in internal costs. The main category "profit" refers to the initial research question of this article, namely the effects of the influence of CRM systems on a company's turnover, sales, or the overall development respectively. Statements on this main category can be obtained from the specific questions regarding this influence of the interview guide. The main category "problem" refers to possible or expected problems when working with CRM systems or CRM-approaches. Statements on this main category can be gained from the questions about the users' experience with CRM systems and efficient work. The main category "efficiency" refers to the prerequisites for efficient work in general and with a CRM system. The relatively low number of nominations is based on the circumstance that statements on the main category "profit" could be incorporated more clearly in view of the initial research interest of this article.

Figure 7 shows the distribution of the main influencing factors for the acceptance of CRM systems. A certain similar distribution of the determinants (person, technology, and management) can be recognized. Task-related and organizational factors reveal the least number. This means that the acceptance of CRM systems largely depends on person-related, technology-related, and management-related factors.

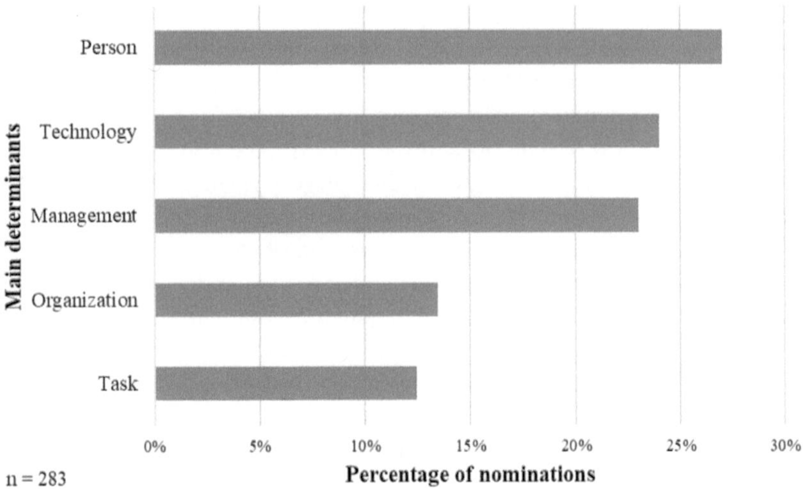

Fig. 7: Analysis of main determinants for acceptance
Source: Authors' figure

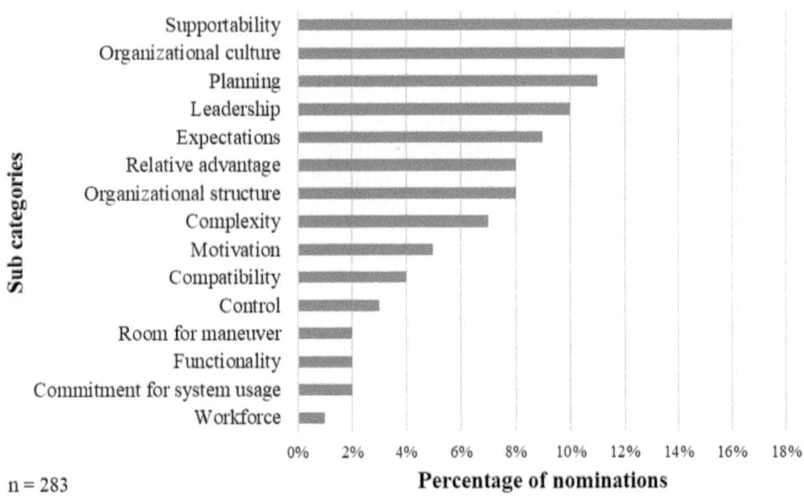

Fig. 8: Analysis of sub-categories
Source: Authors' figure

In a further step it was examined into which sub-categories the result of the distribution of the main determinants can be classified. The selection of sub-categories was based on the sub-categories of the determinants of acceptance of CRM systems, described in the theoretical part. Figure 8 indicates that the system's supportability has the biggest impact on acceptance with a level of 16 %. During the interviews, the added value has been often mentioned in this context. Only the recognition of the meaningfulness of a system and the provision of an added value for the daily work can lead to acceptance by the respective users. The employees must be convinced that the CRM system is important in terms of their daily work and their success as sales representatives. Since some people might not be open-minded enough with regards to changes, they must be convinced that the respective change brings added value to them (change management). User-friendliness plays a decisive role. The system's utilization rate will be correspondingly low, if this is not the case.

The analysis also showed the importance of an organizational culture that supports and is open for innovative technologies (12 %). The willingness to innovate should therefore be correspondingly high and knowledge must be shared. The data input must be simple and accessible from anywhere. The system should not be used as a supervision tool, but it must provide an actual benefit. Corporations should offer an introductory training during the implementation and installation phase. Furthermore, regular training is important as the CRM system is dependent on the quality of the data. The advantages of such a system need to be illustrated by clear and understandable examples. The importance must be clarified throughout the organization starting from the management level (sub-categories "planning" and "leadership"). There must be a willingness to work with the CRM system in the future. All users should be informed about the meaningfulness and importance for the corporation. The use of a CRM system may not exceed a certain amount of work and is intended to simplify work for users. CRM approaches from the past have failed due to lack of acceptance and too high complexity. Systems are regarded as controlling instruments, which are associated with additional work. As part of the generalization of the text passages and evaluation of the conducted interviews, the following criteria for the acceptance of CRM systems could have been identified: (1) added value; (2) awareness creation; (3) management, commitment, and involvement; (4) planning and implementation; (5) usability.

For the acceptance of a CRM system, the added value is crucial. Employees need to feel that the use of the system offers them additional value and advantages. The usability describes that CRM systems must be easy, fast, and mobile. The system must support the user in everyday life and should be logical and intuitive.

The awareness that the CRM system is important to the company is part of the organizational culture. The system must therefore be transparent and understood as part of the corporate strategy. As part of the planning and implementing of a CRM system, management must make fundamental decisions about goals, usage, and expectations. Employees must be involved in the process right from the start. During the empirical investigation it could be determined that certain influencing factors are responsible for acceptance. The qualitative evaluation of the interviews led to the development of a collection of criteria to promote the acceptance of CRM systems. These categories must be considered so that the system can be accepted by the employees or users.

2.9.2 Quantitative data analysis and results

Based on the interviews that were carried out and analysed, the following hypotheses were developed:

- H1 *There is a connection between the age of a sales representative and the characteristic "customizability" that a CRM system should have.*
- H2 *There is a correlation between the age of a sales representative and the "extra work" concern about a CRM system.*
- H3 *There is a connection between previous experience in dealing with CRM systems and the concern "technical overload" compared to CRM systems.*

The link to the online questionnaire was sent to 120 people. A total of 101 people took part in the survey. Thus the response rate is 84.16 %. 44 % of the salespeople surveyed were masculine and 56 % of the participants were feminine. Thirty-three of the respondents were 30 years or younger. There were 28 people each between the ages of 31 and 40 and between 41 and 50. The rest of the participants were over 51 years old. The mean age of the informants is 37.6 years. In addition, the highest level of education completed by the respondents was inquired. Four people have completed an apprenticeship. The majority of the respondents have completed a Master's/Diploma degree at a university or university of applied sciences. The holders of a bachelor's degree at a university or technical college or persons with completed secondary education are in the middle range.

The first question in the questionnaire is about a rating of the respondents' experience with CRM systems. Since the CRM system at the respective company was only recently implemented or is currently in the implementation phase, only 3 % answered that they had very good experience in dealing with CRM systems. 33 % rated their experience as good and another 39 % have mediocre experience. For the second question, "How important are the following properties that a

CRM system should have?", the most important characteristics were completeness, reliability, usefulness, and timeliness. The format was least often defined as "very important" for the respondents. The third question investigated the importance of various activities that a CRM system should have. Faster data and knowledge exchange are the most important activities of a CRM system for the people surveyed. More efficient customer service and access to customer data were named as further important activities. This was followed by the demand for support for the sales processes, and an improved opportunity and lead management. Protection against data loss, misuse, and transparency in customer care were often described as less important. Furthermore the participants were asked to which extent they were affected by specific concerns when using CRM systems. Overtime has a strong influence on over 70 % of the respondents when using it. Restrictions on freedom of work and changes in working methods are on the second and third place. Higher performance pressure and poor usability were also cited as strong concerns of the sales staff. Loss of status and excessive technical demands seem to have the least influence on the sales employees surveyed. Last but not least the frequency of use after the implementation of a CRM system in the corporation has been queried. 76 % of the persons surveyed think that they will use the CRM system every day after successful implementation and only 2 % assume that they will rarely use it.

H1 There is a connection between the age of a sales representative and the characteristic "customizability" that a CRM system should have.

Regarding H1 a correlation test between age and properties in relation to CRM systems was executed. As it can be seen in Tab. 2, p is 0.001 < 0.05 (the significance is less than alpha). Thus the study detected a connection between the age of a sales employee and the property "customizability" that a CRM system should have. Therefore, hypothesis H1 can be accepted.

Tab. 2: Correlation test between age and properties in relation to CRM systems

Related variables	Chi square, Pearson Asymptotic significance	Spearman
Age and customizability	0.001 → highly significant*	0.417 → strong correlation

* 99 % probability that there is a connection
Source: Authors' figure

H2 There is a correlation between the age of a sales representative and the "extra work" concern about a CRM system.

The correlation testing between experiences and concerns regarding CRM systems is shown in Tab. 3. $p = 0.100 > 0.05$ shows that the significance is greater than alpha. Therefore it can be said that there is no connection between the age of a sales representative and the concern about "extra work" in relation to a CRM system. Based on this study, hypothesis H2 must be rejected.

Tab. 3: Correlation test between age and concerns about extra work

Related variables	Chi square, Pearson Asymptotic significance	Spearman
Age and overtime	0.100 ➔ not significant	−0.289 ➔ no correlation

Source: Authors' figure

H3 There is a connection between previous experience in dealing with CRM systems and the concern "technical overload" compared to CRM systems.

The correlation testing between experiences and concerns about CRM systems is shown in Tab. 4. $p = 0.035 < 0.05$ shows that the significance is less than alpha. Thus it can be said that there is a connection between the experience of a sales employee in dealing with CRM systems and the concern that a CRM system is "technically overwhelmed". In this sense, hypothesis H3 can be accepted.

Tab. 4: Correlation test between experience and concerns

Related variables	Chi square, Pearson Asymptotic significance	Spearman
Experience and technical overload	0.035 ➔ 65 % significant	−0.267 ➔ no correlation

Source: Authors' figure

2.10 Conclusions

Many necessary prerequisites must be met (main category 1) in order to reach a positive effect of CRM systems on sales and the development of corporations. Furthermore, problems to be expected must be considered in advance and avoided accordingly (main category 4). After the creation of these basic requirements or framework conditions a CRM system can develop its intended and expected benefits (main category 2), have a positive effect on efficiency (main category 5) and cause increases in sales (main category 3).

Integrative CRM systems consist of organizational and technological components that are related to the interaction with customers. They are a tool for the efficient processing and design of customer processes. From the corporation's viewpoint, there is a high level of interest in employees accepting technological innovations in the company. The user must have a positive attitude towards the technology, so that there is a basic willingness to use. Five determinants were identified as influencing factors of acceptance for operational information systems: the technology-related, management-related, user-related, organization-related, and task-related determinants. In order to find out how these determinants express themselves in the acceptance of CRM systems by employees in the company, an empirical study was conducted. As a part of the qualitative evaluation of the interviews, the following criteria influencing the acceptance of CRM systems can be derived: added-value, awareness creation, management, commitment and involvement, planning and implementation, and usability. The technology-related determinants stand for the technical specifications and possible uses. The management-related determinants concentrate on the central task of management in relation to building the acceptance. The influence of personal experiences on the acceptance is the core of the user-related determinants. The organizational determinants define the organizational culture and structure in which the system is used. The task-related determinants deal with the question of whether the task can even be solved with the help of such a system.

The catalogue of criteria derived from the empirical investigation contains the criteria that must be met for employees to accept a CRM system. The added value is related to the fact that the CRM system must provide the users with additional benefits. The system must also be able to give something back to the users. Modern CRM systems offer a multitude of optimization options in order to generate this added value. A CRM system is accepted by its users when the contacts and opportunities can be entered and edited easily while on the move. For a functioning CRM system, a concrete definition of goals and expectations on both sides of management and of employees is necessary. Both sides must have the same point of view, otherwise the acceptance will be restricted. The organization must also be ready to share their knowledge with its members. Whether employees are open to innovations is not only a question of their personality, but rather a question of change management and an open organizational culture that is error-tolerant and enables the sharing of knowledge. For a successful implementation of a CRM system, the management must make fundamental decisions regarding the planning of the system use. In order to guarantee the acceptance of the system, the management should involve the employees in the planning process right from the start. The decision in favour of a CRM system is a management decision, so it is important that the management stands behind the system deployment and is continuously involved. The management has a role model function and must motivate the employees, if they are not convinced of the system at the beginning.

Nowadays a CRM system is not only used by one department. To be accepted by all users, it must be a central, fully integrated system. The derived criteria catalogue is used to answer the research question. The quantitative investigation deals with acceptance factors of sales employees in relation to the use of CRM systems. Acceptance factors regarding the acceptance subject (sales employees) and acceptance object (CRM system) were the subject of this part of research. Nevertheless, it can be stated that the results of CRM projects are in danger of not being satisfactory and that high failure rates can still occur. CRM must not be considered as only a technical problem. Rather, the employee must be seen as the central factor. The demands to pay more attention to employees during the implementation of such a system are getting louder. However, there is still a lack of detailed, holistically oriented examination of the role, i. e. the importance as well as the tasks and functions of the employee in CRM. The quantitative study refers exclusively to socio-demographic acceptance factors such as age, gender, experience, and their connection with ease of use, specifications of the CRM system, the activities to be performed, and concerns about the system.

The CRM system as an object of acceptance must have various properties in order to fundamentally facilitate sales processes and work with the system. It must be suitable for the tasks to be performed, as well as reliable and efficient. The employee, whether young or old, should by no means be overwhelmed. Aesthetic aspects, such as the visual or auditory attractiveness, are important for the design, but rather secondary in relation to other acceptance factors. The inclusion of the sales staff, who will later be users of the system, is therefore important in the implementation process. Sales employees, regardless of whether they are in the front or back office, can build up acceptance barriers against the use of CRM systems due to certain concerns. It must be considered here that there is a connection between the previous experience of a sales employee in dealing with CRM systems and concerns about the technical overload. It is important to prevent this in the implementation phase. The sales employee should fill the system with important data after it has been introduced and thereby receive support for his tasks. After all, the CRM system is meant to be used daily. Certain attitudes, (personal) norms, values and emotions can create barriers to acceptance against the use of CRM systems. Also socio-demographic elements are decisive. Therefore it was possible to establish a connection between the age of a sales employee and the characteristic "customizability" that a CRM system must have. However, no connection could be found between age and the concern "extra work". Past experiences with CRM systems also influence the quality of use. The satisfaction of the users with the CRM system stands for the success in the introduction of new systems. The involvement of the sales staff, the perceived benefits and usefulness of the system, as well as organizational support and support from management, influence the users. The employee decides, no matter whether old or young, experienced or not experienced in dealing with CRM systems, whether a CRM system is successfully implemented in the company or whether the system achieves the desired success and increase in profit and development.

It can be concluded that the current possibilities of digital support in sales are constantly increasing, which is also largely welcomed by the sales staff. However, it should be noted that sustainable successes, such as better consulting quality, sales performance, and a competitive differentiation based on this, can only be achieved, if all the seller's barriers to acceptance are taken into account in the entire conception and implementation of the CRM system. Based on the results of the empirical research, various recommendations for action can be given to the management of a corporation that is planning the introduction of a CRM system. Since the quantitative study was carried out from the operator's viewpoint, recommendations for action are given that take the sales employee into account. In addition, recommendations for action are derived, based on the factors of acceptance research. For the implementation of CRM systems, change management is an important success factor. Employees always need the opportunity to give feedback on how to improve the system and must be involved from the early start. Based on the quantitative survey, it can be stated that most sales employees would like a complete CRM system. It is therefore important that each individual sales representative knows that it is up to them to collect and process high quality data in order to ensure that the system is useful. The motivation to use the CRM system can be raised by incentive systems. The effect is the creation of better customer knowledge, better opportunity and lead management, and meaningful key figures. This leads to a win-win situation between employees (users) and management. Since more than 70 % of those surveyed in the quantitative investigation expressed the acceptance barrier of "overtime" as a very strong concern, it is important to communicate to all employees that the CRM system will not cause overtime, but that it will help to get data and information much faster. The entire corporation, from management to the sales force, must live the CRM culture. The analysis of the interviews resulted in the fact that the project team should consist of experts, who can fully concentrate on the project and do not have to do any other work. In addition, the benefits of the CRM system must be correctly communicated to the users of the CRM system and an incentive must be set so that the system is filled with high quality data. Humans are creatures of habit and a change in the way they work can only be done step by step, and it takes time. The key user concept is therefore of great value.

References

Allerbeck, M. & Helmreich, R. (1984). Akzeptanz planen: Aber wie? *Office Management, 11*, pp. 1080–1082.

Alt, R. & Reinhold, O. (2020). *Social Customer Relationship Management: Fundamental, Applications, Technologies.* Switzerland: Springer Nature. https://doi.org/10.1007/978-3-030-23343-3.

Amberg, M., Hirschmeier, M. & Schober, D. (2003). DART: Ein Ansatz zur Analyse und Evaluierung der Benutzerakzeptanz. *Wirtschaftsinformatik, 2*, pp. 573–592.

Bednarek, M. (2014). *Der Einfluss des Kundenverhaltens auf die Kundenzufriedenheit: Eine Untersuchung des Kundenkontakts aus der Anforderungen-Ressourcen Perspektive.* Wiesbaden: Springer Fachmedien. https://doi.org/10.1007/978-3-658-06579-9.

Berekoven, L., Eckert, W. & Ellenrieder, P. (2009). *Marktforschung: Methodische Grundlagen und praktische Anwendung.* Wiesbaden: Gabler Verlag. https://doi.org/10.1007/978-3-8349-8267-4.

Betz, J. (2003). *Die Akzeptanz des E-Commerce in der Automobilwirtschaft: Ausmaß, Konsequenzen und Determinanten aus Sicht von Neuwagenkäufern.* Wiesbaden: Deutscher Universitätsverlag. https://doi.org/10.1007/978-3-322-81466-1.

Binckebanck, L. & Elste, R. (2016). *Digitalisierung im Vertrieb: Strategien zum Einsatz neuer Technologien in Vertriebsorganisationen.* Wiesbaden: Springer Fachmedien. https://doi.org/10.1007/978-3-658-05054-2.

Chandler, A. D. Jr. (1977). *The Visible Hand: The Managerial Revolution in American Business.* Cambridge: Harvard University Press.

Dangelmaier, W., Uebel, M. F. & Helmke, S. (2004). *Grundrahmen des Customer Relationship Management-Ansatzes.* Wiesbaden: Springer Gabler. https://doi.org/10.1007/978-3-322-96456-4.

Dethloff, C. (2004). *Akzeptanz und Nicht-Akzeptanz von technischen Produktinnovationen.* Lengerich: Pabst Science Publishers.

Georgi, D. & Mink, M. (2011). *Konzeption von Kundenbeziehungsstrategien.* Wiesbaden: Gabler Verlag. https://doi.org/10.1007/978-3-8349-6618-6_2.

Goodhue, D. L. (1995). Understanding user evaluations of information systems. *Journal of Management Science, 41*(12), pp. 1827–1844. https://doi.org/0025-1909/95/4112/1827$01.25.

Hartwick, J. & Barki, H. (1994). Explaining the role of user participation in information system use. *Journal of Management Science, 40*(4), pp. 440–465. https://doi.org/0025-1909/94/4004/044001.25.

Helmke, S., Uebel, M. & Dangelmaier, W. (2017). *Effektives Customer Relationship Management: Instrumente - Einführungskonzepte - Organisation.* Wiesbaden: Gabler Verlag. https://doi.org/10.1007/978-3-658-06624-6.

Hilbig, W. (1984). Akzeptanzforschung neuer Bürotechnologien: Ergebnisse einer empirischen Fallstudie. *Journal of Office Management, 32*(4), pp. 320–323.

Hildebrand, A. (2015). *Vertriebsmitarbeiter und Innovationen: Empirische Studien in Business-to-Business-Märkten.* Wiesbaden: Springer Fachmedien. https://doi.org/10.1007/978-3-658-10654-6.

Hippner, H. (2005). Die (R)Evolution des customer relationship management. *Marketing ZfP, 27*(2), pp. 115–134.

Hippner, H., Rentzmann, R. & Wilde, K.-D. (2006). *Aufbau und Funktionalitäten von CRM Systemen.* Wiesbaden: Gabler. https://doi.org/10.1007/978-3-8349-9080-8_2.

Hippner, H. & Wilde, K.-D. (2004). *IT-Systeme im CRM: Aufbau und Potentiale.* Wiesbaden: Gabler Verlag. https://doi.org/10.1007/978-3-663-10414-8.

Holland, H. (2004). *CRM erfolgreich einsetzen: Warum CRM-Projekte scheitern und wie sie erfolgreich werden.* Göttingen: Business Village.

Homburg, C., Wieseke, J. & Kuehnl, C. (2009). Social influence on salespeople's adoption of sales technology: a multilevel analysis. *Journal of the Academy of Marketing Science, 38*(2010), pp. 159–168. https://doi.org/10.1007/s11747-009-0157-x.

Isaak, J. & Hanna, M. J. (2018). User data privacy: Facebook, cambridge analytica, and privacy protection. *Computer, 51*(8), pp. 56–59. https://doi.org/10.1109/MC.2018.3191268.

Kleinaltenkamp, M., Plinke, W. & Geiger, I. (2015). *Business Relationship Management and Marketing: Mastering Business Markets.* Berlin and Heidelberg: Springer-Verlag. https://doi.org/10.1007/978-3-662-43856-5.

Königstorfer, J. (2008). *Akzeptanz von technologischen Innovationen: Nutzungsentscheidungen von Konsumenten dargestellt am Beispiel von mobilen Internetdiensten.* Wiesbaden: Gabler Verlag. https://doi.org/10.1007/978-3-8349-9909-2.

Kohl, H., Mertins, K. & Seidel, H. (2016). *Wissensmanagement im Mittelstand: Grundlagen, Lösungen, Praxisbeispiele.* Berlin and Heidelberg: Springer Gabler. https://doi.org/10.1007/978-3-662-49220-8.

Kollmann, T. (1998). *Akzeptanz innovativer Nutzungsgüter und -systeme. Konsequenzen für die Einführung von Telekommunikations- und Multimediasystemen.* Wiesbaden: Gabler Verlag. https://doi.org/10.1007/978-3-663-09235-3.

Krafft, M. & Götz, O. (2011). *Der Zusammenhang zwischen Kundennähe, Kundenzufriedenheit und Kundenbindung sowie deren Erfolgswirkungen.* Wiesbaden: Gabler Verlag. https://doi.org/10.1007/978-3-8349-6618-6_7.

Laiderman, J. (2005). A structured approach to B2B segmentation. *Journal of Database Marketing and Customer Strategy Management, 13*(1), pp. 64–75. https://doi.org/10.1057/palgrave.dbm.3240279.

Laudon, K. C., Laudon, J. & Schoder, D. (2010). *Wirtschaftsinformatik: Eine Einführung.* München: Pearson Studium.

Lauer, T. (2019). *Change Management: Grundlagen und Erfolgsfaktoren.* Berlin: Springer-Verlag GmbH. https://doi.org/10.1007/978-3-662-59102-4.

Leußer, W., Hippner, H. & Wilde, K. D. (2011). *Kundeninformationen als Basis des CRM.* Wiesbaden: Gabler Verlag. https://doi.org/10.1007/978-3-8349-6618-6_24.

Li, L. & Mao, J. (2012). The effect of CRM use on internal sales management control: An alternative mechanism to realize CRM benefits. *Journal of Information and Management, 49*, pp. 269–277. https://doi.org/10.1016/j.im.2012.09.005.

Lucke, D. (1995). *Akzeptanz: Legitimität in der „Abstimmungsgesellschaft".* Wiesbaden: Springer Fachmedien. https://doi.org/10.1007/978-3-663-09234-6.

Manz, U. (1983). *Zur Einordnung der Akzeptanzforschung in das Programm der sozialwissenschaftlichen Begleitforschung. Ein Beitrag zur Anwenderforschung im technisch-organisatorischen Wandel.* München: V. Florenz.

Mathena, J., Yetter, A. & Hostetler, H. (2009). *Success with Microsoft Dynamics CRM 4.0: Implementing Customer Relationship Management.* New York: Springer-Verlag. https://doi.org/10.1007/978-1-4302-1605-6.

Mayring, P. (2016). *Einführung in die qualitative Sozialforschung: Eine Anleitung zu qualitativem Denken.* Weinheim: Beltz Verlag.

Meffert, H., Pohlkamp, A. & Böckermann, F. (2010). *Wettbewerbsperspektiven des Kundenbeziehungsmanagements im Spannungsfeld wissenschaftlicher Erkenntnisse und praktischer Exzellenz.* Wiesbaden: Gabler Verlag. https://doi.org/10.1007/978-3-8349-8745-7.

Migdadi, M. M. (2020). Knowledge management, customer relationship management and innovation capabilities. *Journal of Business & Industrial Marketing, 36*(1), pp. 111–124. https://doi.org/10.1108/JBIM-12-2019-0504.

Moser, M. A. (2021). Impacts of Customer Relationship Management (CRM) on Development of Corporations. Doctoral dissertation. Sopron: University of Sopron, Alexandre Lamfalussy Faculty of Economics.

Narayandas, D. & Rangen, V. K. (2004). Building and sustaining buyer–seller relationships in mature industrial markets. *Journal of Marketing, 68*(3), pp. 63–77. https://doi.org/10.1509/jmkg.68.3.63.34772.

Neumann, A. K. (2014). *CRM mit Mitarbeitern erfolgreich umsetzen: Aufgaben, Kompetenzen und Maßnahmen der Unternehmen.* Wiesbaden: Gabler Verlag. https://doi.org/10.1007/978-3-658-05991-0.

North, K. (2021). Die Wissenstreppe. In K. North (ed.), *Wissensorientierte Unternehmensführung,* pp. 33–69. Wiesbaden: Springer Gabler. https://doi.org/10.1007/978-3-658-32771-2_3.

Palmatier, R. W., Kumar, V. & Harmeling, C. M. (2018). *Customer Engagement Marketing.* Cham: Springer Nature. https://doi.org/10.1007/978-3-319-61985-9.

Perna, A. & Baraldi, E. (2014). *CRM Systems in Industrial Companies: Intra- and Inter-Organizational Effects.* New York: Palgrave Macmillan. https://doi.org/10.1057/9781137335661.

Picot, A. & Reichwald, R. (1987). *Bürokommunikation: Leitsätze für den Anwender.* München: CW-Publikationen.

Rai, A. K. (2013). *Customer Relationship Management: Concepts and Cases.* Delhi: PHI Learning Private Ltd.

Reichwald, R. (1978). *Zur Notwendigkeit der Akzeptanzforschung bei der Entwicklung neuer Systeme der Bürotechnik (Band 1).* München: Hochschule der Bundeswehr.

Rengelshausen, O. (2000). *Online-Marketing in deutschen Unternehmen: Einsatz – Akzeptanz – Wirkungen.* Wiesbaden: Deutscher Universitätsverlag. https://doi.org/10.1007/978-3-663-08808-0.

Rigby, D. K. & Ledingham, D. (2004). CRM done right. *Harvard Business Review, 82*(11), pp. 118–129.

Robra-Bissantz, S. & Lattemann, C. (2019). *Digital Customer Experience: Mit digitalen Diensten Kunden gewinnen und halten.* Wiesbaden: Springer Fachmedien. https://doi.org/10.1007/978-3-658-22542-1.

Rogers, E. M. (2003). *Diffusion of Innovations.* New York: Free Press. https://doi.org/10.1007/978-3-658-09923-7_9.

Schifferer, S. & von Reitzenstein, B. (2018). *Tools und Instrumente der Organisationsentwicklung: Erfolgreiche Umsetzung von Organisationsprojekten.* Berlin: Springer-Verlag GmbH. https://doi.org/10.1007/978-3-662-55560-6.

Schreyögg, G. (2016). *Grundlagen der Organisation: Basiswissen für Studium und Praxis.* Wiesbaden: Gabler Verlag. https://doi.org/10.1007/978-3-658-13959-9.

Schüller, A. M. (2007). *Ist CRM noch zu retten?* Retrieved on August 10, 2019, from http://www.marketing-boerse.de/Fachartikel/details/Ist-CRM-noch-zu-retten/7979/.

Schulze, J. (2002). *CRM erfolgreich einführen.* Berling and Heidelberg: Springer Verlag. https://doi.org/10.1007/978-3-642-56138-2.

Schumacher, J. (2005). *Outsourcing von CRM-Prozessen: Voraussetzungen, Chancen, innovative Einsatzmöglichkeiten im elektronischen B2B-Markt.* Wiesbaden: Deutscher Universitätsverlag. https://doi.org/10.1007/978-3-322-82164-5.

Schumacher, J. & Meyer, M. (2004). *Customer Relationship Management strukturiert dargestellt – Prozesse, Systeme, Technologien.* Berlin and Heidelberg: Springer-Verlag. https://doi.org/10.1007/978-3-642-17107-9.

Selchert, M. (2004). Ermittlung des Erfolgs von CRM-Systemen. *Controlling, 16*(2004), pp. 27–34. https://doi.org/10.15358/0935-0381-2004-1-27.

Seyr, B. F. (2015). Die drei Dimensionen des Wissensmanagements: Empirische Studie anhand des 3-D-Modells zur Selbstevaluation von Organisationen. *Journal of Economy & Society, 2015*(1–2), pp. 3–27. https://doi.org/10.21637/GT.2015.1-2.01.

Seyr, B. F. & Hoffer, T. (2020). Measuring, visualizing, and controlling intangible assets in knowledge management. *Journal of the Knowledge Economy,* 08/2020, pp. 1–15. https://doi.org/10.1007/s13132-020-00676-8.

Sperl, F. (2016). *Customer Relationship Management: Profitabilitätsorientierte Bindung von Wohnungsmietern.* Wiesbaden: Springer Gabler. https://doi.org/10.1007/978-3-658-11547-0.

Stauss, B. & Seidel, W. (2002). Customer Relationship Management (CRM) als Herausforderung für das Marketing. *Thexis Fachbericht für Marketing, 1,* pp. 10–13.

Stein, A. D., Smith, M. F. & Lancioni, R. A. (2013). The development and diffusion of customer relationship management (CRM) intelligence in business-to-business environments. *Journal of Industrial Marketing Management, 42*(6), pp. 855–861. https://doi.org/10.1016/j.indmarman.2013.06.004.

Stender, M., Göbel, S. & Schulz-Klein, E. (2003). Fokus auf Projektorganisation und Change-Management: Tipps für den CRM-Erfolg. *Computerwoche, 39*(2003), pp. 34–35.

Stokburger, G. & Pufahl, M. (2002). *Kosten senken mit CRM: Strategien, Methoden und Kennzahlen.* Wiesbaden: Gabler Verlag. https://doi.org/10.1007/978-3-322-86706-3.

Swift, R. S. (2001). *Accelerating Customer Relationship: Using CRM and Relationship Technologies.* New York: Prentice Hall Inc.

Torggler, M. (2007). *Einsatz von CRM systemen: Aufbau, Funktionalität, Auswahl, Perspektiven.* Wiener Neustadt: University of Applied Sciences Wiener Neustadt.

Trommsdorff, V. (2011). *Konsumentenverhalten.* Stuttgart: Kohlhammer.

Varajão, J. & Cruz-Cunha, M. M. (2016). Main motivations for CRM adoption by large Portuguese companies: A Principal Component Analysis. *Procedia Computer Science, 100*(2016), pp. 1269–1279. https://doi.org/10.1016/j.procs.2016.09.165.

Walter, S. & Schmidt, M. (2004). *Kundenkarte und CRM im Handel.* 2. Auflage. Wiesbaden: Springer Gabler Verlag. https://doi.org/10.1007/978-3-322-89094-8_3.

Wilde, S. (2011). *Customer Knowledge Management: Improving Customer Relationship through Knowledge Application.* Berlin and Heidelberg: Springer-Verlag. https://doi.org/10.1007/978-3-642-16475-0.

WKO – Wirtschaftskammer Österreich. (2019). *Verpackungsindustrie Statistiken.* Retrieved on November 17, 2020 from https://www.wko.at/branchen/industrie/.

Zahay, D., Peltier, J. W. & Krishen, A. (2012). Building the foundation for customer data quality in CRM systems for financial services firms. *Journal of Database Marketing and Customer Strategy Management, 19*(1), pp. 5–16. https://doi.org/10.1057/dbm.2012.6.

3. Accelerated knowledge exchange in times of crisis – Lessons from COVID-19 pandemic

Neha Jain

Abstract: Knowledge exchange and technology transfer are powerful tools for sharing and upscaling technologies that are relatively new to the market as well as those that are state-of-the-art. As the COVID-19 pandemic gripped the world in the year 2021, there was an urgency to share the latest fact-based information about the spreading pandemic as well as to prevent the spread of misinformation. The pandemic showed that it was not a problem limited to one region but a global one and therefore required prompt collective global response. Following a case study methodology, this study aims to highlight the efforts put in by the global organizations like WHO and others in bringing together the scientific, social, and economic communities to have a strengthened collective response in combating the COVID-19 pandemic. The scientific community put down the barriers and came together to share the latest scientific information on a real time basis. Several multinational organizations came together to accelerate the sharing of intellectual property with the goal of upscaling production and equitable sharing of treatments, vaccines, and test-kits in the fight against COVID-19 pandemic. With this study, the author aims to highlight the significance of collective global response in knowledge sharing and technology transfer. This global crisis has only revealed, once again, the significance of collective and collaborative scientific response against protectionist research, utilizing the global scientific resources to their full capacity while avoiding duplicate efforts. Looking ahead, the lessons learnt from accelerated knowledge sharing during COVID-19 pandemic could be useful in addressing the challenges of the future at a global level.

3.1 Introduction

Exchange of knowledge across boundaries is the cornerstone of innovation (Jensen & Szulanski, 2004). The flow of knowledge in the right direction facilitates commercialization of technologies, leading to increased growth and development. Knowledge exchange, however, can be obstructed by different barriers and transferring knowledge across these barriers requires focused efforts to streamline the knowledge flow (Park & Mense-Petermann, 2014). The Novel Corona Virus, also known as coronavirus, and the disease caused thereby, COVID-19 has posed an unprecedented challenge across the globe, including the EU, in the year 2020 (European Commission, 2020). The challenges are real not only in the health and economic fields, but also in the social and academic fields. The till now unknown disease, with a high infectious rate and unknown cure (WHO, 2020a) has demanded quick response in all spheres of life.

At the time of starting this study, as of 23 May 2020, over five million cases of COVID-19 had been reported globally with no confirmed cure (WHO, 2020b). Looking back after more than a year, globally, as of 5:22 pm CEST, 20 August 2021, there had been 209,876,613 confirmed cases of COVID-19, including 4,400,284 deaths, reported to World Health Organization (WHO). As of 20 August 2021, a total of 4,562,256,778 vaccine doses had been administered (WHO, 2021a).

In order to promote focused action, based on transparent information, as well as to collaborate global action in combating the disease as well as in finding a cure, the academic community across the globe, including in the EU, has undertaken several measures to minimize the barriers in the flow of knowledge. This study looks at these measures, adopted across universities, multinational corporations (MNCs), research institutions as other such bodies. Following an online search from official sources of institutions such as the World Health Organization (WHO), the European Union (EU), multiple universities and other relevant institutions, this study compiles the measures for promoting knowledge exchange in times of COVID-19 pandemic. The study later reflects on the possible effects of extending these accelerating measures beyond the pandemic for an overall accelerated knowledge exchange and innovation.

3.2 Research questions

This study aims to answer the following two research questions:

1. How was knowledge exchange accelerated in the scientific community in times of COVID-19 crisis?
2. What are the risks and benefits of extending the knowledge exchange accelerating measures beyond the COVID-19 pandemic?

3.3 Research methodology

This study follows case study methodology. Case study as research methodology offers the benefit that complex issues may be analysed in depth in their real-life settings (Crowe, Cresswell, Robertson, Huby, Avery & Sheikh, 2011). COVID-19 placed several mobility restrictions on the persons across the globe. Travel and personal meetings became increasingly restricted. The Internet as a tool for working from home, studying from home and pursuing research from home gained more acceptance than ever before (Engle, 2020). Even the national and international organizations, realizing the role of online communication, used this platform for updating the current situation, measures and scenarios. This limitation offered the opportunity that online information was often updated at a fast speed. Using this opportunity, the author collected and studied the information available from the official online sources and interpreted them to answer the selected research questions guiding this study. The case study that serves as the data source for this study include is the WHO, strengthened by information from other international organizations like the United Nations Educational, Scientific and Cultural Organization (UNESCO), World Intellectual Property Organization (WIPO), and the World Trade Organization (WTO).

3.4 Scientific contribution

This study offers twofold scientific contribution. Firstly, this study addresses the response to an ongoing global crisis as and when it happened and acted based on the actual information. MNCs, start-ups, national governments, universities, all have accelerated their efforts to be at the newest status of information to be able to act and react timely. Secondly, this study aims to highlight the significance of knowledge exchange in today's times and draw the lessons from this crisis that can be useful for the institutions and firms looking at accelerated innovation based on accelerated exchange of knowledge across different boundaries.

3.5 Knowledge exchange and its relevance in the modern world

Knowledge exchange may refer to methods used to share, replicate or scale-up the available knowledge across institutions, companies, governments or even individuals (International Bank for Reconstruction and Development / The World Bank, 2015). Diffusion of knowledge and technology across borders has been studied as a cornerstone of growth for organizations operating internationally (Teece, 2003). Be it companies or governments, identification of relevant knowledge and exchange thereof contribute to the design of policies fostering diffusion and absorption of knowledge which in turn lead to innovation and growth (Hoekman & Javorcik, 2006a). Diverse industries, be it agriculture, health, information technology today are working on leveraging the benefits of exchange of knowledge across borders (Bright, 1979; Chandra, Bhattacharjee & Bhowmick, 2018; Fu & Zhang, 2011). Especially when considering developing economies, knowledge and technology transfer has been a cornerstone for fighting diseases, promoting agriculture, driving innovation, pushing industrialization, thereby creating overall welfare for the society (Hoekman & Javorcik, 2006; Krattiger, 2004).

Knowledge is transferred by different modes like trade, foreign direct investment (FDI), licensing, joint venture, mergers and acquisitions (Hoekman & Javorcik, 2006a). Sharing of knowledge is vital to equitable growth and overall development of the global community (Krattiger, 2004). Successful knowledge exchange is linked to several factors like willingness to share and learn, knowledge absorption capability, available resources, to name a few (Bright, 1979; Hawkins, 1972; Kumar, 2003).

One of the aims of knowledge exchange is to reduce knowledge stickiness, which happens when the knowledge cannot diffuse and therefore cannot be applied for the purposes that promoted its development in the first place (Blackman & Benson, 2012).

On a macroscopic level, knowledge exchange takes a broader role for the policymakers by supporting innovations that create value at the time and location where needed (UNCTAD, 2014). With the Director General of WHO urgently requesting the global community to come together and lift barriers for knowledge sharing and transfer technology for equitable vaccine and treatment against COVID-19, knowledge exchange remains as relevant in today's world as it ever was in the past (WHO, 2021d).

3.6 COVID-19 pandemic and its implications

The COVID-19 pandemic had far reaching effects on diverse aspects of the society. The social-distancing measures that were undertaken in order to reduce the spread of the pandemic, like quarantine, social distancing, working and learning from home, etc. impacted the major portion of the global population. The front-line workers working in system relevant sectors like healthcare, were forced to work in difficult everyday conditions faced with the threat of the COVID-19 disease. Already in the initial phase of the pandemic in April 2020, employment dropped 3 % below the baseline, cost of imports increased by 25 %, tourism and related industries saw a slowdown of over 50 %, overall consumption in daily services dropped by over 25 % (Maliszewska, Mattoo & Van der Mensbrugghe, 2020). Figure 1 shows the GDP growth in some of the countries with most experiencing negative growth.

International travel and transport became difficult to non-existent for changing periods of times across the globe. The industries across the world were forced to adapt themselves to the continuously changing global environment, faced by increasing shortage of manpower and resources (WHO, 2020c). The supply chain disruption initiated by the COVID-19 crisis deepened over 2021 with no short-term solution in sight (Saul, Xu & Sun, 2021).

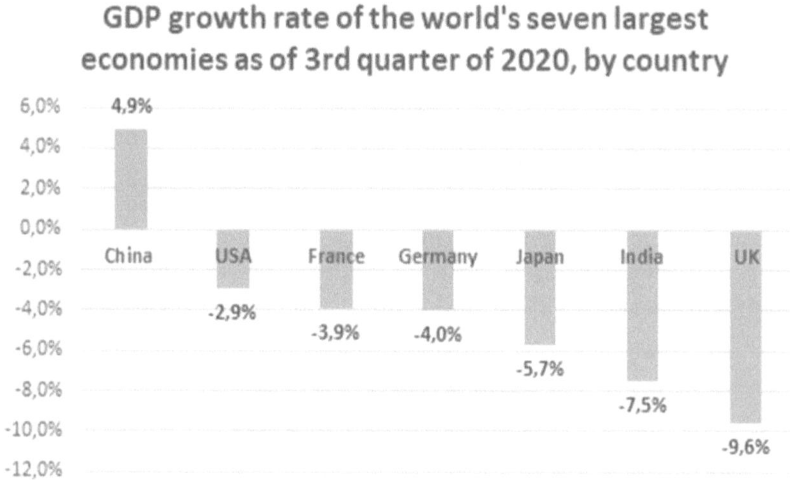

Fig. 1: GDP growth rate of the world's seven largest economies as of 3rd quarter of 2020, by country

Source: Statista (2020)

3.7 Need for knowledge exchange in combating COVID-19 pandemic

As COVID-19 pandemic gripped the global community in 2020, the first reaction was of uncertainty followed by desperation. At first, no one could assess the extent of damage this pandemic would do to the social and economic community, but one thing was certain, this was a global problem requiring collective global response. The unprecedented situation that the COVID-19 pandemic created globally necessitated a consolidated response from regional and global networks and organizations. Collecting reliable data, spreading fact-based information, promoting tools to adapt the socio-financial system to the social restrictions and working on a solution to combat the disease were some of the challenges that the global community was faced with.

3.8 Addressing the first research question: How was knowledge exchange accelerated in the scientific community in times of COVID-19 crisis?

This section highlights three broad areas where the global community has made efforts to accelerate the knowledge exchange during the COVID-19 pandemic. From creating general awareness to sharing scientific information to avoid duplicate work to developing a vaccine, the efforts have all been taken with the common goal of combating the pandemic. Figure 2 shows these three areas where knowledge exchange was accelerated in times of the COVID-19 pandemic.

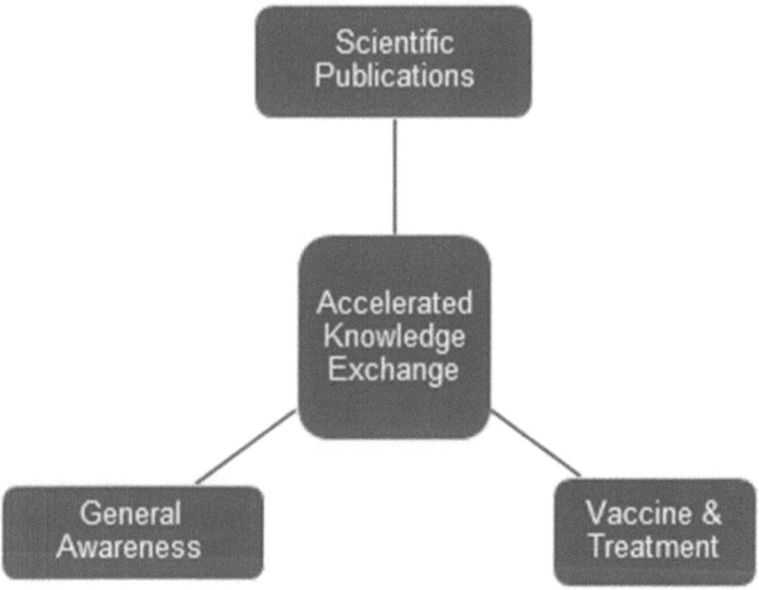

Fig. 2: Three areas focusing on accelerated knowledge exchange with the goal of curbing the COVID-19 pandemic
Source: created by author

3.8.1 Accelerated knowledge exchange for promoting general awareness about COVID-19 disease

The first step in combating the pandemic was to spread fact-based information and avoid fake news from taking a hold in the hearts and minds of the global population. In order to avoid misinformation from spreading, organizations like WHO came forward to proactively spread the actual fact-based news about the disease, symptoms, preventive measures, and the status of ongoing developments to the global population as a whole. The key aspect was to ensure an equitable circulation of fact-based information across all global regions without bias (WHO, 2021b). This proactive information sharing approach was also supposed to fill in any gap in awareness that was created when the right information could not be passed down by the national or regional authorities in some areas across the globe with the desired speed. With physical contact being restricted, social media became a prominent tool in spreading the know-how in a simple understandable way to the general population (WHO, 2021b). One continuous challenge throughout this pandemic has been to control the spread of infodemic (WHO, 2021c) – over exposure to false or misleading information that may hamper the public health response, that causes uncertainty and leads to incorrect health behaviours or even cause civil unrest. Through free info campaigns, global organizations like WHO have put in extra effort to inform the general public about the harm such misinformation could do, offering tips to follow reliable official sources of information and checking the sources before forwarding unvalidated information (WHO, 2021c). With 132 entities signing the Cross-Regional Statement on Infodemic in the Context of COVID-19, the importance of reliable support from media, and other communication channels was endorsed by the United Nations as well as the majority of the world leaders (UN, 2020).

3.8.2 Accelerating global knowledge exchange in the scientific community by promoting open access publications

As the COVID-19 disease started spreading across the world, and the efforts to understand and combat the disease started taking shape, it was understood by the scientific community that time was of utmost essence to lodge a strong collaborative response against the pandemic. Fact based information to create awareness, promote scientific development and avoid duplicate efforts had to be transmitted in real time to keep the speed of response prompt. Promoting open access scientific publications, especially with regards to the research being done in connection with COVID-19 was a key step in this direction (UNESCO, 2020). Studies have shown that the social and scientific impact increases when researchers use open access platforms for publishing their research (Antelman, 2004; Breugelmans et al., 2018; Piwowar et al., 2018; Zhang & Watson, 2017). With the aim to promptly convert medical science to policies and general practices, several publishing entities came together to promote open access and allow accelerated exchange of knowledge (SAGE, 2020; Oxford Academic Journal, 2020; Springer Nature, 2020).

Open access to scientific publication may have a higher impact (Antelman, 2004) but an increased quantity of open access scientific literature is not without its challenges. One of the first challenges is to ensure a certain quality to the publications available under open access. Open access literature shows a higher readership indicating a faster dissemination of information (Björk, 2017; Zhang & Watson, 2017). Therefore, it is all the more important to ensure a high quality of the open access scientific literature. This has social and scientific impacts. On the social side, high quality of open access literature would increase trust in the effort of the scientific community and policymakers and reduce spread of misinformation. On the scientific side, it supports the scientific community across the globe to build on the existing knowledge thereby avoiding duplicate work. Open access, with the fast spread of information in times of COVID-19 pandemic, has shown the power of real-time knowledge exchange (Lee & Haupt, 2021) and the global trends show that open access is here to stay and will gain more acceptance in the coming times (Björk, 2017; Kiley, 2020; OECD, 2020; Lee & Haupt, 2021).

3.8.3 Accelerating knowledge exchange for development of vaccine, tests and treatments in combating COVID-19 pandemic

The scientific community set to work immediately as more information came in about the coronavirus. The search for a treatment or a cure started at a fast pace. Vaccines were considered to be one of the forerunners as a candidate for social medication and disease prevention (EMA, 2021). The initial phase of the development of a vaccine against coronavirus was shadowed by uncertainty as there was little or no information available on the long-term effects of the disease (Sharma, Sultan, Ding & Triggle, 2020) and therefore there was a risk of how the vaccine would affect the high-risk and low-risk population around the world (Forman, Shah, Jeurissen, Jit & Mossialos, 2021).

However, the challenges did not stop at the development of a vaccine. Once a vaccine was developed, the next challenges were to upscale the production, share the know-how and distribute the vaccines throughout the global logistic chain to cover the needs of the global suffering population (Haque & Pant, 2020). Global organizations like WHO (2021d) and UNESCO (2020) urged the global scientific community and policymakers to share knowledge and technology in order to reduce vaccine inequality across the globe. The unequal distribution of vaccine in combating the coronavirus was seen to hamper the economic recovery from the COVID-19 crisis (WHO, 2021e). Studies have shown that the part of the global population that is socially and economically more vulnerable had lower access to the vaccines (Schmidt, 2020; Tatar, Shoorekchali, Faraji & Wilson, 2021), than the rest of the world.

Sensing the challenges that the pandemic could bring for the global community, already in 2020, together with the Member States, WHO launched the COVID-19 Technology Access Pool (C-TAP) with the view to share knowledge and boost equitable access to health products against COVID-19 disease (WHO, 2020d). As more information on the disease was available with passing time, vaccines emerged as one of the possible tools in the fight against the pandemic. The aim of bringing the knowledge on vaccines against the coronavirus to the farthest corners of the globe, including the socially and financially vulnerable segments of the world, laid the foundation for joint consortium and vaccine technology transfer hubs. One of such consortiums working towards equitable COVID-19 vaccine access, COVAX, promoted global research, development, technology transfer, manufacturing, and price negotiation of vaccines (GAVI, 2020). COVAX aimed to make the vaccines against COVID-19 disease available to the low- and middle-income regions of the world. Led by GAVI, CEPI and WHO and with UNICEF acting as the key delivery partner, as of 25 August 2021, COVAX had shipped over 215 million doses of vaccines across 138 countries, including Ghana, Lebanon, to name a few (UNICEF, 2021).

Further to the COVAX consortium, with the aim of bringing the vaccine technology and production closer to the remotest areas, a technology centre hub in South Africa had been initiated, with WHO Member States, including France taking a key role in the technology transfer (WHO, 2021f). With a view to strengthen the vaccine technology in Asia, Vietnam set up a joint venture with USA, Japan and Russia in 2021 (Vir, 2021). AstraZeneca, a company with one of the first few COVID-19 vaccines to receive emergency official approval in the world, in its effort to expand access to vaccines for the global population, made a license agreement with the Serum Institute of India to reach the low- and middle-income population (AstraZeneca, 2020). Latin American countries Argentina, Mexico and Brazil partnered with Chinese COVID-19 vaccine manufacturers like Sinovac, Sinopharm and CanSino to transfer the vaccine technology, starting with a detailed trial phase (Bridge Beijing, 2021).

The events highlighted above show the way knowledge exchange and technology transfer is being used for capacity building of the vaccination drive against COVID-19 disease. A global problem requires a global response and knowledge exchange across borders is currently playing a significant role in speeding up the global response against the coronavirus.

3.9 Addressing the second research question: What are the risks and benefits of extending the knowledge exchange accelerating measures beyond the COVID-19 pandemic?

Knowledge exchange is critical for a collaborative response to combat the pandemic but free knowledge exchange without any check on quality and rules for transfer could have detrimental effects.

Open access publications get wider readership, but the risk of predatory publications cannot be ignored (Björk, 2017). With a clear guideline around the open access publications coupled with a sound quality check, the spread of false information could be controlled, and the fact-based research could enjoy wider readership (Antelman, 2004; Lee & Haupt, 2021).

Another factor that has gained attention in the fight against the coronavirus is the need for sharing of intellectual property (IP) rights and the knowledge and technology surrounding the efforts against the coronavirus. The overall system surrounding the management of IP is focused on consumer benefit and promoting healthy competition (WIPO, 2020). IP offers motivation to the companies to innovate and offers a broader product choice to the consumers (Greenhalgh & Rogers, 2006). With anyone able to copy the newest technologies without a thorough set of rules in place, the innovative companies would lose motivation to invest in research and product development (Maskus, 2000). Competition law and IP, therefore, go hand in hand, promoting innovation and technological development and ensuring healthy competition (Correa, 2007; Whish & Bailey, 2015).

Considering the speed of innovation needed for combating the COVID-19 pandemic, it was imperative that knowledge and technology could flow easily from its source to the point of application. Several measures were taken like sharing licenses, initiating technology transfer hubs but the challenge of equitable vaccine distribution was not an easy one to solve. On October 2, 2020, a proposal requesting a waiver of intellectual property rights related to the prevention, containment or treatment of Covid-19 under the agreement on trade-related aspects of intellectual property rights, also known as TRIPS agreement (WTO, 1995) was submitted to the WTO by a group of 32 countries including India and South Africa (WTO, 2020) This proposal initiated a lot of discussion in the international community about the scope of the TRIPS agreement and the need for IP in innovation and development for the developing countries. Hilty, Carls, Lamping, Batista, Kim & Slowinski (2021), however argue that a complete waiver from all technologies directly or indirectly related to coronavirus would affect several patents in diverse fields and would discourage the companies investing in cutting-edge technologies from innovating. Additionally, article 31 of the TRIPS agreement (WTO, 1995, p. 333) already allows WTO member countries to grant compulsory licenses under selected circumstances. If it is found that the refusal of a patentee to grant a license is unjustified, a state could grant production permits swiftly (WTO, 1995).

The challenges notwithstanding, the need for knowledge and technology exchange to allow swift action against coronavirus is urgent and the pros and cons have to be balanced in the interest of the society. A protectionist knowledge management, especially in times of a pandemic, could jeopardize the efforts put in by multiple stakeholders internationally and could prolong the suffering of the society. An uncontrolled sharing of knowledge, however, could promote the spread of misinformation, negatively affect the quality, and create confusion among the scientific community. It is therefore important to have such discussions, share information, and find a balanced approach to the technology transfer together with IP management.

3.10 Conclusion and discussion

The COVID-19 pandemic, with its highly infectious nature posed a global challenge, affecting the national governments, international institutions and the global population at different levels, be it the national and global economy, the health infrastructure, employment, etc. In order to streamline and consolidate the global response to this crisis, and to minimize double efforts in combating this pandemic, the institutions at different levels undertook several measures to accelerate the knowledge exchange. These measures show that innovation may be speeded up by eliminating barriers in the flow of knowledge. The times for knowledge stickiness and knowledge protectionism are long gone and any rapid response to a global issue requires bringing the knowledge from its source of creation to the point of application, without which the generated knowledge fails to serve its purpose. Licensing, joint ventures, IP waivers, open access to scientific knowledge, the routes may be diverse, but the goal is the same. Combating misinformation, creating general awareness, applying existing scientific knowledge for the good of the global population, these are the strengths of the knowledge exchange that were revealed in this pandemic. The author recommends expanding these measures beyond the COVID-19 pandemic to help promote the knowledge economy, boost innovation and accelerate recovery not only after combating COVID-19 but long beyond this crisis.

Abbreviations

C-TAP	COVID-19 Technology Access Pool
CEST	Central European Summer Time
COVAX	COVID-19 Vaccines Global Access
COVID-19	Coronavirus Disease
GAVI	Global Alliance for Vaccines and Immunizations
GDP	Gross Domestic Product
IP	Intellectual Property
MNC	Multinational Corporation
SARS CoV-2	Severe Acute Respiratory Syndrome Coronavirus 2
TRIPS	Agreement on Trade Related Aspects of Intellectual Property Rights
UN	United Nations
UNCTAD	United Nations Conference on Trade and Development
WHO	World Health Organization
WIPO	World Intellectual Property Organization
WTO	World Trade Organization

References

AstraZeneca (2020). *AstraZeneca takes next steps towards broad and equitable access to Oxford University's potential COVID-19 vaccine.* Available at: https://www.astrazeneca.com/media-centre/articles/2020/astrazeneca-takes-next-steps-towards-broad-and-equitable-access-to-oxford-universitys-potential-covid-19-vaccine.html. [Accessed 25 August 2021].

Antelman, K. (2004). Do open-access articles have a greater research impact? *College & Research Libraries*, 65(5), 372–382.

Björk, B. (2017). Open access to scientific articles: A review of benefits and challenges. *Internal and Emergency Medicine*, 12(2), 247–253.

Blackman, D. & Benson, A. M. (2012). Overcoming knowledge stickiness in scientific knowledge transfer. *Public Understanding of Science*, 21(5), 573–589.

Bridge Beijing (2021). *China and Latin America: COVID-19 Vaccine Collaboration and the Way Forward.* Available at: https://bridgebeijing.com/blogposts/china-and-latin-america-covid-19-vaccine-collaboration-and-the-way-forward/. [Accessed 25 August 2021].

Bright, S. (1979). Technology transfer to developing nations: A pragmatic approach to industrialization. *Loyola of Los Angeles International and Comparative Law Annual*, 2, 123.

Breugelmans, J. G., Roberge, G., Tippett, C., Durning, M., Struck, D. B., & Makanga, M. M. (2018). Scientific impact increases when researchers publish in open access and international collaboration: A bibliometric analysis on poverty-related disease papers, *13*(9).

Chandra, P., Bhattacharjee, T. & Bhowmick, B. (2018). Does technology transfer training concern for agriculture output in India? A critical study on a lateritic zone in West Bengal. *Journal of Agribusiness in Developing and Emerging Economies*, 8(2), 339–362.

Correa, C. (2007). Intellectual property and competition law: Exploration of some issues of relevance to developing countries. Issue Paper, (21).

Crowe, S., Cresswell, K., Robertson, A., Huby, G., Avery, A., & Sheikh, A. (2011). The case study approach. *BMC Medical Research Methodology, 11*(1), 1–9.

European Commission (2020). Press Release. *COVID-19: Commission Sets out European Coordinated Response to Counter the Economic Impact of the Coronavirus.* Available at: https://ec.europa.eu/commission/presscorner/detail/en/ip_20_459. [Accessed 23 May 2020].

EMA (2021). *Treatments and Vaccines for COVID-19.* Available at: https://www.ema.europa.eu/en/human-regulatory/overview/public-health-threats/coronavirus-disease-covid-19/treatments-vaccines-covid-19. [Accessed 12 August 2021].

Engle, S., Stromme, J., & Zhou, A. (2020). Staying at home: Mobility effects of covid-19. *Available at SSRN 3565703.*

Forman, R., Shah, S., Jeurissen, P., Jit, M. & Mossialos, E. (2021). COVID-19 vaccine challenges: What have we learned so far and what remains to be done? *Health Policy*, 125(5), 553–567.

Fu, X. & Zhang, J. (2011). Technology transfer, indigenous innovation and leapfrogging in green technology: The solar-PV industry in China and India. *Journal of Chinese Economic and Business Studies*, 9(4), 329–347.

Gavi (2020). Covax explained. Available at: https://www.gavi.org/vaccineswork/covax-explained. [Accessed 25 August 2021].

Greenhalgh, C. & Rogers, M. (2006). The value of innovation: The interaction of competition, R & D and IP. *Research Policy*, 35(4), 562–580.

Haque, A. & Pant, A. B. (2020). Efforts at COVID-19 vaccine development: Challenges and successes. *Vaccines*, 8(4), 739.

Hawkins, E. F. (1972). Technology transfer to developing regions: A corps of engineers/IHD project. Eos, *Transactions American Geophysical Union*, 53(10), 901–904.

Hilty R., Carls S., Lamping M., Batista P. H. D., Kim D. & Slowinski P. R. (2021). 10 *Arguments against a Waiver of Intellectual Property Rights*. Blog. University of Oxford, Faculty of Law. Available at: https://www.law.ox.ac.uk/business-law-blog/blog/2021/06/10-arguments-against-waiver-intellectual-property-rights. [Accessed 30 August 2021].

Hoekman, B. M. & Javorcik, B. K. S. (2006). *Global Integration and Technology Transfer* (illustrat ed.). Washington, DC: World Bank. https://doi.org/10.1596/978-0-8213-6125-2.

International Bank for Reconstruction and Development / The World Bank, 2015. *The Art of Knowledge Exchange. A Result-Focused Planning Guide for Development Practitioners*. Available at: https://openknowledge.worldbank.org/bitstream/handle/10986/17540/843970WP0art0o0Box0382140B00PUBLIC0.pdf?sequence=18&isAllowed=y [Accessed 20 September 2020].

Jensen, R. & Szulanski, G. (2004). Stickiness and the adaptation of organizational practices in cross-border knowledge transfers. *Journal of International Business Studies*, 35(6), 508–523.

Kiley, R. (2020). *Three lessons COVID-19 has taught us about Open Access publishing*. Available at: https://blogs.lse.ac.uk/impactofsocialsciences/2020/10/06/39677/. [Accessed 25 August 2021].

Krattiger, A. F. (2004). Technology transfer to developing countries and technology diffusion: The future role of institutions in capacity building, regulations, IPRs and funding. *Handbook of Plant Biotechnology*. Wiley Online Library. https://doi.org/10.1002/0470869143.kc071

Kumar, N. (2003). *Globalization, Foreign Direct Investment and Technology Transfers: Impacts on and Prospects for Developing Countries*. Hoboken: Taylor and Francis. https://doi.org/10.4324/9780203193624

Lee, J. J. & Haupt, J. P. (2021). Scientific globalism during a global crisis: Research collaboration and open access publications on COVID-19. *Higher Education*, 81(5), 949–966.

Maliszewska M., Mattoo A., Van der Mensbrugghe D. (2020). The potential impact of COVID-19 on GDP and Trade A preliminary assessment. World Bank Group. *East Asia and the Pacific Region Office of the Chief Economist & Macroeconomics, Trade and Investment Global Practice April 2020*. Available at: https://documents1.worldbank.org/curated/en/295991586526445673/pdf/The-Potential-Impact-of-COVID-19-on-GDP-and-Trade-A-Preliminary-Assessment.pdf. [Accessed 21 August 2021].

Maskus, K. E. (2000). Intellectual property rights and economic development. *Case Western Reserve Journal of International Law*, 32, 471.

OECD (2020). OECD Policy Responses to Coronavirus (COVID-19). *Why Open Science Is Critical to Combatting COVID-19*. Available at: https://www.oecd.org/coronavirus/policy-responses/why-open-science-is-critical-to-combatting-covid-19-cd6ab2f9/. [Accessed 23 August 2021].

Oxford Academic Journal (2020). *Access to OUP Resources on COVID-19, Other Coronaviruses, and Related Topics*. Available at: https://academic.oup.com/journals/pages/coronavirus. [Accessed 25 August 2021].

Park, K. & Mense-Petermann, U. (2014). Managing across borders: Global integration and knowledge exchange in MNCs. *Competition & Change*, 18(3), 265–279.

Piwowar, H., Priem, J., Larivière, V., Alperin, J. P., Matthias, L., Norlander, B. & Haustein, S. (2018). The state of OA: A large-scale analysis of the prevalence and impact of open access articles. *PeerJ*, 6, e4375.

SAGE (2020). *Coronavirus (COVID-19) Research*. Available at: https://journals.sagepub.com/coronavirus. [Accessed 25 August 2021].

Saul J., Xu M. & Sun Y. (2021). *Global supply chains buckle as virus variant and disasters strike. Reuters Business*. Available at: https://www.reuters.com/business/global-supply-chains-buckle-virus-variant-disasters-strike-2021-07-23/. [Accessed 21 August 2021].

Schmidt, H. (2020). Vaccine rationing and the urgency of social justice in the Covid-19 response. *Hastings Center Report*, 50(3), 46–49.

Sharma, O., Sultan, A. A., Ding, H. & Triggle, C. R. (2020). A review of the progress and challenges of developing a vaccine for COVID-19. *Frontiers in Immunology*, 11, 2413.

Springer Nature (2020). *Coronavirus (COVID-19) Research Highlights. Find Free Access to the Latest COVID-19 Research Papers and Articles*. Available at: https://www.springernature.com/gp/researchers/campaigns/coronavirus. [Accessed 25 August 2021].

Statista (2020). *Impact of the Coronavirus Pandemic on the Global Economy – Statistics & Facts*. Available at: https://www.statista.com/topics/6139/covid-19-impact-on-the-global-economy/. [Accessed 22 August 2021].

Tatar, M., Shoorekchali, J. M., Faraji, M. R. & Wilson, F. A. (2021). International COVID-19 vaccine inequality amid the pandemic: Perpetuating a global crisis? *Journal of Global Health*, 11.

Teece, D. J. (2003). *Essays in Technology Management and Policy: Selected papers of David J. Teece*. World Scientific.

UN (2020). *Cross-Regional Statement on "Infodemic" in the Context of COVID-19*. Available at: https://onu.delegfrance.org/IMG/pdf/cross-regional_statement_on_infodemic_final_with_all_endorsements.pdf. [Accessed 21 August 2021].

UNCTAD (2014). *Transfer of Technology and Knowledge Sharing for Development, Science, Technology and Innovation Issues for Developing Countries*. Available at: https://unctad.org/system/files/official-document/dtlstict2013d8_en.pdf. [Accessed 23 August 2021].

UNESCO (2020). Open access to facilitate research and information on COVID-19. Available at: https://en.unesco.org/covid19/communicationinformationr esponse/opensolutions. [Accessed 12 March 2021].

UNICEF (2021). *COVID-19 Vaccine Market Dashboard. An Interactive Tool for Partners, Manufacturers, and Countries to Follow the Developments of the COVID-19 Vaccine Market with Up-to-Date Information*. Available at: https:// www.unicef.org/supply/covid-19-vaccine-market-dashboard. [Accessed 25 August 2021].

Vir (2021). *Vietnam Signs COVID-19 Vaccine Technology Transfer Contracts with US, Japan, and Russia*. Available at: https://vir.com.vn/vietnam-signs-covid-19-vaccine-technology-transfer-contracts-with-us-japan-and-russia-86115. html. [Accessed 25 August 2021].

Whish, R. & Bailey, D. (2015). *Competition Law* (8th ed.). Oxford: Oxford University Press.

WHO (2020a). *Coronavirus. Overview*. Available at: https://www.who.int/hea lth-topics/coronavirus#tab=tab_1. [Accessed 23 May 2020].

WHO (2020b). *WHO Coronavirus Disease (COVID-19) Dashboard*. Available at: https://covid19.who.int/. [Accessed 23 May 2020].

WHO (2020c). *Impact of COVID-19 on People's Livelihoods, Their Health and Our Food Systems. Joint Statement by ILO, FAO, IFAD and WHO*. Available at: https://www.who.int/news/item/13-10-2020-impact-of-covid-19-on-people's-livelihoods-their-health-and-our-food-systems. [Accessed 10 March 2020].

WHO (2020d). *COVID-19 Technology Access Pool*. Available at: https://www.who. int/initiatives/covid-19-technology-access-pool. [Accessed 25 August 2021].

WHO (2021a). *WHO Coronavirus (COVID-19) Dashboard*. Available at: https:// covid19.who.int/. [Accessed 21 August 2021].

WHO (2021b). *Fighting Misinformation in the Time of COVID-19, One Click at a Time*. Available at: https://www.who.int/news-room/feature-stories/det ail/fighting-misinformation-in-the-time-of-covid-19-one-click-at-a-time. [Accessed 21 August 2021].

WHO (2021c). *Let's Flatten the Infodemic Curve*. Available at: https://www.who. int/news-room/spotlight/let-s-flatten-the-infodemic-curve. [Accessed 21 August 2021].

WHO (2021d). *WHO Director-General's Remarks at the 1st International Forum on Vaccine Cooperation – 5 August 2021*. Available at: https://www.who.int/director-general/speeches/detail/who-director-general-s-remarks-at-the-1st-international-forum-on-vaccine-cooperation---5-august-2021. [Accessed 23 August 2021].

WHO (2021e). *Vaccine Inequity Undermining Global Economic Recovery*. Available at: https://www.who.int/news/item/22-07-2021-vaccine-inequity-undermining-global-economic-recovery. [Accessed 25 August 2021].

WHO (2021f). *WHO Supporting South African Consortium to Establish First COVID mRNA Vaccine Technology Transfer Hub*. Available at: https://www.who.int/news/item/21-06-2021-who-supporting-south-african-consortium-to-establish-first-covid-mrna-vaccine-technology-transfer-hub. [Accessed 25 August 2021].

WIPO (2020). *IP and Competition Policy*. Available at: https://www.wipo.int/ip-competition/en/. [Accessed 30 August 2021].

WTO (1995). *Agreement on Trade-related Aspects of Intellectual Property Rights*. Available at: https://www.wto.org/english/docs_e/legal_e/27-trips.pdf. [Accessed 30 August 2021].

WTO (2020). *Waiver from Certain Provisions of the Trips Agreement for the Prevention, Containment and Treatment of COVID-19*. Available at: https://docs.wto.org/dol2fe/Pages/SS/directdoc.aspx?filename=q:/IP/C/W669.pdf&Open=True. [Accessed 30 August 2021].

Zhang, L. & Watson, E. M. (2017). Measuring the impact of gold and green open access. *The Journal of Academic Librarianship, 43*(4), 337–345.

4. Transferring knowledge – nudging transformation: How suitable is Transformation Nudging for steering change and managing knowledge?

Volker C. Horsthemke

Abstract: Change is all but a new concept to humanity. Each individual copes with it in his/her particular way following a typical course, though, depicted by Kübler-Ross in her transition curve. Systems also have to respond to changing conditions in order to secure their survival. According to systems theory a system reacts to change following a sequence of variation, selection, and retention, ultimately preserving an accidental modification of its routines. In organizations change is often addressed with copying mechanism derived from management including fixing targets, milestones, deadlines, etc. Undoubtedly it has proven right that managing techniques are capable of solving transactional challenges. In transformational processes, on the other hand, management often falls short of reaching desired change in timed schedules. The introduction of nudging into transformation management provides an alternative concept. It mainly wants to address the deliberate transformation of organizational cultures. On top of that there indubitably is a connection between transformation and knowledge. This very connection has brought about the genesis of Transformation Nudging as a result of an implementation of knowledge management in a company. This paper aims at showing how purposeful knowledge transfer in the scope of Transformation Nudging can be supportive for bringing about change and managing knowledge at once.

4.1 Introduction

The acquisition of knowledge during childhood and adolescence is dominated by the concept of passing prearranged information from a teacher to a pupil. Knowledge usually is practised in exercises and, finally, tested in examinations. Main utensils are lectures, books, presentations, audio or video files, etc. Learning arrangements for adults more often focus on expanding knowledge through experience since adults validate new information largely based on their interest, their own subjective processing, and the assessment of practical applicability. It is rather more often tested in action than in exams whether acquired knowledge stands up to its fitting with the respective prevailing culture or requirements.

Besides, children, adolescents and adults tend anyway to decide for themselves whether they ought to consider new information valuable and worthy to apply. Society or organizations decide whether an individual with his/her approach is evaluated suitable for the system's respective particular purpose.

The both of the before mentioned approaches towards processing information and turning it into applicable knowledge are stable parts of our learning routine. Especially during the years of infancy, though, children more frequently employ a third style of learning. This method is deeply rooted in human nature because it secures our survival. It is based on replicating the behaviour of others in their own societal environment (DiSalvo, 2014, p. 264).

Even though the learning system changes with each individual's evolution from mainly imitating other's behaviour to a more coordinated studying the human being stays capable of realizing his/her own unawareness of information (Schuster, 2007, p. 5). An individual is able to recognize information as relevant if it makes a difference for him/her (Bateson, 1987, pp. 39–40). Information remains irrelevant, however, as long as a recipient is not going to put it into a context (Rehäuser & Krcmar, 1996, p. 4). With a context the difference will finally really make a difference for the receiver (Simon, 2013, pp. 58–59). As a result, the latter will be able to incorporate this context into his/her own experience and with that turning information into knowledge (Willke, 2011, p. 33).

Centred in the understanding that a management of knowledge – while having to take place within the human being (Horsthemke, 2017, p. 133) – mainly is a means to improve the competitivity of an organization via increasing the efficiency and efficacy of the usage of knowledge (Kilian, Krismer, Loreck, & Sagmeister, 2007, p. 16), the question remains which is the best way to transfer new knowledge into practical application within an organization.

4.2 Research question and approach

Assuming that organizational knowledge only becomes evident and organizationally effective through observable deployment by people (Kilian, Krismer, Loreck & Sagmeister, 2007, p. 16) it may not surprise that prevailing systems of learning fall short when transformational processes within organizations are mainly based on the presentation of information. Based on the observations made in the scope of a distinct scientific study (Horsthemke, 2017) and further observations in practice the following article elaborates on how the efficacy of transformational processes could be improved bearing in mind that humankind needs a context to apply new knowledge.

To create new insight regarding the above-mentioned research question the theoretically elaborated approach of Transformation Nudging (Horsthemke, 2021) as well as its impact on change and knowledge transfer were examined by the author in two separate ethnographic single case studies. In both occasions the researcher was also the responsible manager at the same time. The fact that he, consequently, was obliged to follow the decisions made by the leadership of the respective companies had an effect on the development of the actions. The results of both observations were related afterwards in order to draw a combined conclusion.

The two investigated corporations provided the theoretical backgrounds upon which Transformation Nudging was studied in practice, i.e. the Kübler-Ross-Transition-Curve (Elisabeth Kübler-Ross Foundation, 2021), the Prosci ADKAR model (Hiatt, 2006), and Leading Simple (Grundl & Schäfer, 2018; Grundl, 2019).

Qualitative research tries to profoundly investigate phenomena via instruments like interviews or observation (Marczyk, DeMatteo, & Festinger, 2005, p. 17). A qualitative ethnographic single case study draws its conclusions from the observation of one single phenomenon (Brüsemeister, 2008, p. 55) in an existing context in the present (Yin, 2003, p. 13) where the author him-/herself is interactive part of the observed environment (Szabo, 1998, p. 62). It aims at critically reflecting and assessing diverging interpretations (Hammersley & Atkinson, 2007, p. 4) in order to develop questions and hypothesis for further research or to explore causal relations (Yin, 2003, pp. 5–6). In the scope of this investigation it, accordingly, is expected to gain new insight into the practical application of Transformation Nudging and its effect on the process of steering change and transferring knowledge.

4.3 Transformation nudging

Traditional change management in the understanding of this essay stands for a rigid command and control in the sense of setting up a project including project plan, team, structure, work packages, milestones, a fixed deadline for the project's end, etc. (Personio, 2019). The systemic approach shall mean the acknowledgement of change as an autopoietic sequence of variation, selection, and retention (Simon, 2013, pp. 83–84) with which a system processes an intrusion into its stability leading it to accept or refuse change (Simon, 2011, p. 107). Moreover, it shall be deemed putative that it cannot be predetermined which change will be retained by a system (Simon, 2011, p. 105) nor that the change kept is the best change (to the benefit of the system) (Simon, 2013, p. 84).

In a scientific study (Horsthemke, 2017) a specific approach of a systemic implementation of a system of knowledge management in a company was investigated. Interventions were placed in order to stimulate natural demand for reshaping knowledge management. As no governing top down approach was established it was consented that the interventions might result in isolated projects or actions at first. They were to be linked and aligned in a separate second step. Knowledge managers acted as systemic organizational consultants. Hence, scope, range, devices, and procedures differed according to the respective arrangement between client and consultant. Consequently, a variety of differing knowledge management islands developed.

In a further study it was explored whether the insights from the before mentioned implementation of knowledge management carry a generalizable suitability for conveying change in organizational contexts. Three different approaches were derived: cultural disruption, transformation nudging, and cultural genesis (Horsthemke, 2021, p. 27). Cultural disruption is closest to a change management of command and control, whereas, cultural genesis is basically an autopoietic, free, and largely accidental creation of a new organization comparable to a start-up organization connected to a parent organization which hardly interferes, though (Horsthemke, 2021, pp. 27–28). Although a command-and-control-change-management is the more common approach, the both of the before mentioned approaches are already well established ways to convey transformation. Transformation Nudging, on the other hand, could provide an alternative mode.

Transformation Nudging is based on Thaler and Sunstein's (2017) Nudging approach. Nudging is about subtly inducing people to alter their action (Bendel, 2019) acknowledging that behaviour may or may not change. While Transformation Nudging recognizes that transformation cannot be predetermined or tightly managed, it assumes, though, that transformation – based on the concept of Nudging – can at least be influenced. Transformation Nudging, hence, means a series of interventions placed to trigger a system to change, but permitting to alter a transformation's direction whenever the course it has taken has led to an undesired outcome (Horsthemke, 2021, p. 23).

Following the thoughts of sociological systems theory, a system exists by differentiating itself against its environment (Just, 2016, p. 16). The latter, on the other hand, has an impact on the system and can cause it to modify (Just, 2016, p. 17). A system exists because of the communication between its elements (Just, 2016, p. 17). An organization is a system that consists of people joining in order to achieve a common goal (Lieb, 2011, p. 78). As such an organization is autopoietic, i.e. it creates and sustains its system's elements by itself (Just, 2016, p. 17). People are the elements who produce an organization. An organization tends to assure its own survival in the first place (Simon, 2011, pp. 27–28). Transformation Nudging, in consequence, is an intended impact aiming at changing an organizational system, the observation of the system's autopoietic selective process of alteration, and the deliberate decision to keep a change or to impact the organization again in order to cause a further modification (Horsthemke, 2021, pp. 23–24). Transformation Nudging stops when the sum of transformative sub processes has led to a situation judged to be acceptable by the leading body of the transformational process (Horsthemke, 2021, p. 24).

4.4 Framework for the analysis

In order to evaluate the effectiveness of Transformation Nudging in practice two classical approaches should be taken into consideration:

1. **The ADKAR Model** (Hiatt, 2006, pp. 1–3)
   The ADKAR Model by Prosci is considered to be an effective tool for managing change at an individual level that also provides guidance at the organizational level. It aims at describing change as a natural order of how an individual experiences change. This change lifecycle consists of
   - **A**wareness of the need for change
   - **D**esire to support and participate in the change
   - **K**nowledge of how to change
   - **A**bility to implement required skills and behaviours
   - **R**einforcement to sustain the change

     Change – according to this understanding – becomes only effective for an individual after having gone through all of the before described stages. In order to transform itself an organization, in consequence, needs at least a critical mass of individuals having embraced and reinforced their own specific change.
2. **The Kübler-Ross-Transition-Curve** (Orridge, 2009, pp. 5–9; Elisabeth Kübler-Ross Foundation, 2021)

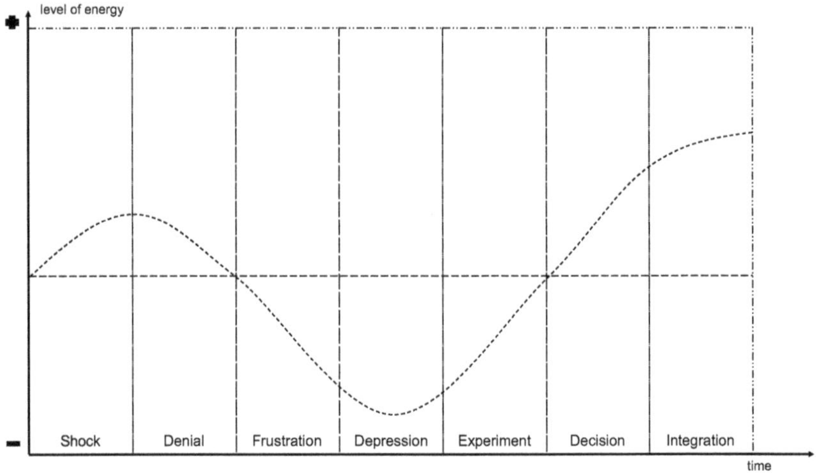

Fig. 1: The Kübler-Ross-Transition-Curve

Own illustration based on the Kübler-Ross-Transition-Curve (Elisabeth Kübler-Ross Foundation, 2021)

According to the Kübler-Ross-Transition-Curve (KRTC) any change affects an individual in a similar way (cf. Fig. 1).

In order to cope with change s/he will go through the same seven transition phases:

- **Shock**: feeling of being overwhelmed, unable to reason, understand, or make plans
- **Denial**: trying to reject change, continuing to do things the way they have been done before (business as usual), temporary retreat from reality
- **Frustration**: recognizing that things do not work out anymore as they did in the past, and with copying routines failing feeling incompetent and frustrated
- **Depression**: acknowledging that things are different, but not knowing how to cope with the new situation feeling depressed and without energy
- **Experiment**: gradually engaging with the new situation, trial and error to explore new coping mechanisms, first successes lead to slowly gaining back confidence
- **Decision**: learning how to cope with the new situation, feeling more competent and more positive

- **Integration**: new copying mechanisms are integrated into own routine leading to necessary change in behaviour and action, feeling of confidence and competence fully re-established based on new habits.

Combining the logics of ADKAR and the KRTC it becomes apparent that any process of organizational transformation needs the system's individuals to change. As the human being, on top of that, tends to explain his/her experience through their own perception and assessment (Maturana, 1997, p. 68), change shall be designed to address the human being and what s/he needs to alter his/her behaviour first and foremost (Berner, 2010, p. 241). Consequently, no individual shall be exempt. Therefore, the following interdependencies shall apply:

- Commitment and exemplary function of leadership: leaders themselves have to be the driver of any change, they shall set an example and motivate others to embrace change (Bär, Krumm, & Wiehle, 2007, p. 87)
- Continuity rather than rapid fire of actions: change must rather be a continuous process than a solitary project detached from business routines (Berner, 2010, pp. 41–42, 64)
- Sense and sensibility: people need to understand why transformation is necessary (Berner, 2010, p. 87). Sense in this case shall be distinctive as people have different approaches towards processing information and developing sense. Therefore, coaching the integration of change into the routines shall be adopted rather than enforcement and sanctioning of not following an expected behaviour (Berner, 2010, pp. 88–89)
- Resources: necessary resources shall be planned and provided (Berner, 2010, p. 41)
- Systems and integration: new (IT-)systems and processes shall be incorporated into the new routines in such way that they substitute the old ones (Berner, 2010, p. 215).

4.5 Fostering change by usage of transformation nudging

As has been depicted in the previous chapter people tend to experience any kind of change similarly by going through the seven steps of the KRTC. Part of this process is a counterproductive period of fighting the change through the stages of shock, denial, frustration, and depression. Albeit consuming a lot of energy change factually is not going to happen during that time. The ADKAR-Model, on the other hand, postulates that change can be facilitated by applying the model's five steps from awareness through to reinforcement in a kind of managed transition (cf. Fig. 2). It is assumed that an individual will alter his/her view, behaviour, and action if addressed properly. It is assumed that intrinsic desire

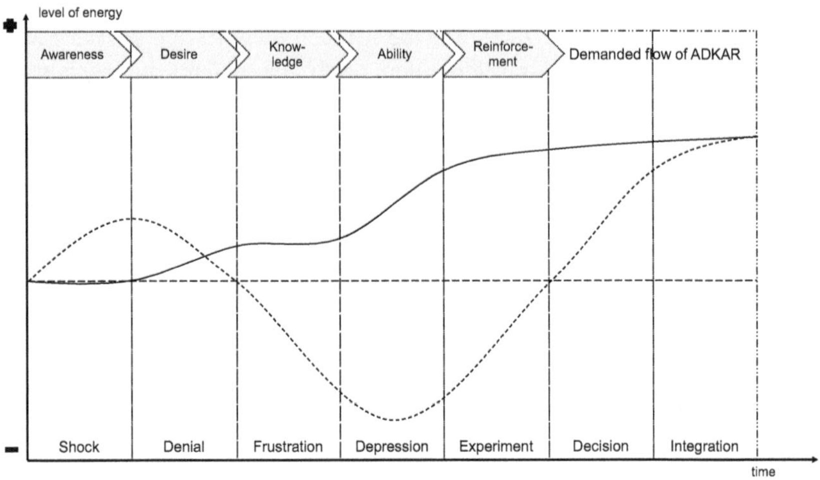

Fig. 2: The ADKAR-Model within the Kübler-Ross-Transition-Curve and its demanded influence

Own illustration based on the Kübler-Ross-Transition-Curve (Elisabeth Kübler-Ross Foundation, 2021) and the ADKAR-Model (Hiatt, 2006)

to change can be stimulated by making a person aware of the irrevocable necessity to adapt to new conditions. This desire shall motivate this person to actively wanting to acquire the needed knowledge and to put into practice.

In organizations change typically is a compulsion either caused by an external incident or an internal choice. Yet, organizations tend to be sluggish, i.e. they try to avoid radical change for the sake of maintaining their stability in order to avoid any change that could put their existence into danger (Hannan & Freeman, 1984, pp. 60–61, 67). Consequently, the need to adapt to change seldomly becomes evident to the organization's members immediately.

Assuming that having to go through each stage of the KRTC is inevitable ADKAR would ignore that awareness in any case will be followed by shock and denial rather than desire if people are confronted out of the blue with interventions meant to create awareness (cf. Fig. 3). They still would oppose change as a result of seeking to ignore it which finally would lead to dysfunctional routines and frustration. ADKAR's next step of knowledge would only ignite after the individual having gone through depression and the exhausting experience of not being able to address the new requirements with old routines. Just after that and rather by compulsion than desire the individual would be willing to acquire the necessary knowledge which would ensure his/her survival in the transitioning organization. As the required knowledge shall already be prepared and available, applying ADKAR, at least, should smoothen the phases of experimentation and decision of the KRTC significantly. The latter, again, would coincide with ADKAR's steps "Ability" (to implement the required skills and behaviours) and their "Reinforcement" (as new practice). Herewith, the

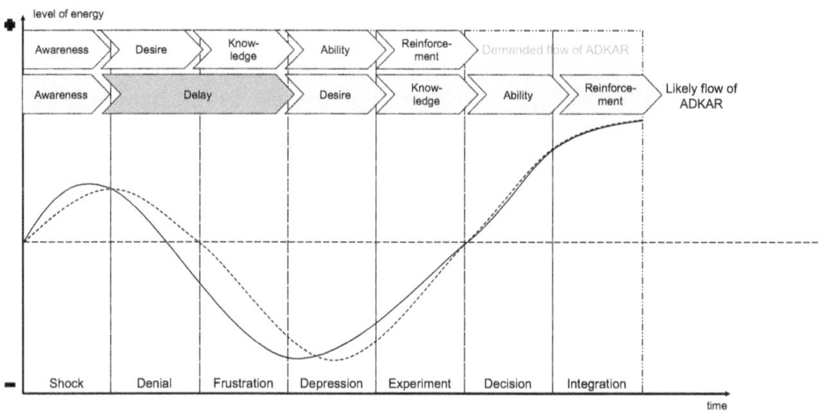

Fig. 3: The ADKAR-Model within the Kübler-Ross-Transition-Curve and its likely influence

Own illustration based on the Kübler-Ross-Transition-Curve (Elisabeth Kübler-Ross Foundation, 2021) and the ADKAR-Model (Hiatt, 2006)

KRTC's last step of integration would also have been reached. Now the individual is fully functional again, confident and motivated. Change – on the individual level – has taken place.

As any given organizational change depends upon its individuals to change the questions may be raised how transformational processes could be steered in an organizational context. As has been shown before, even if ADKAR is applied as a tool of transformation management, each person tends to react to change individually. Is it possible to really control this by applying a rigid change management? While this is a valid question it shall not be investigated here to full extend. In this article solely shall be explored whether Transformation Nudging could be an approach suitable for supporting transformation, especially capable of flattening the KRTC. Against this background it is presupposed that

Transformation Nudging positively influences transformational penetration. It is assumed that the following demands as vital prerequisites for a successful transformation have been met (Horsthemke, 2021, pp. 25–26):

- the top management of the organization has committed to a shared goal and has opted for Transformation Nudging as means to carry the change – accepting its idiosyncrasy of rather trying to influence than wanting to command and control the transformational process
- technical, financial, and human resources are provided and available
- Transformation Nudging's main elements are sensemaking and facilitation of interventions into the system. These interventions are planned, carried out and, subsequently, supported by transformation coaches
- a joint body of transformation coaches is responsible to collaboratively evaluate the combined effect of the interventions and decide whether and how to evolve Transformation Nudging.

Embedded in the KRTC and the ADKAR-Model Fig. 2 shows the envisaged effect of Transformation Nudging on a transformational process. It starts with a series of impulses before the actual change is scheduled to set in. While the impulses are not expected to have any immediate effect, they are meant to raise "Awareness" without the usual abrupt and harsh confrontation with a necessity to change instantly. They shall be designed to display new opportunities rather than perils. The awaited outcome is that sufficient momentum for an intrinsic "Desire" to change will have been generated in a critical mass of individuals who at the same time also would intuitively take on a role as multiplier. As a result, the state of shock should not only be smoothened, it should even have been created an appeal to voluntarily seek the acquisition of the required "Knowledge" pre-prepared and provided by transformation coaches. These coaches, additionally, support the willing in translating knowledge into the specific practice (Ability)

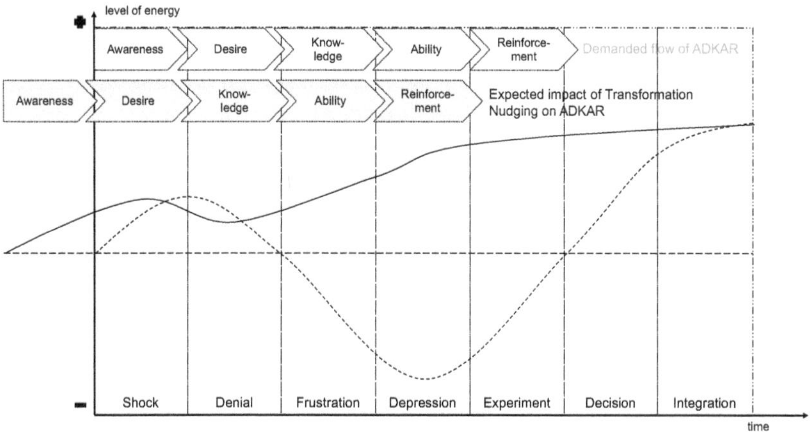

Fig. 4: Expected influence of Transformation Nudging on flattening KRTC
Own illustration based on the Kübler-Ross-Transition-Curve (Elisabeth Kübler-Ross Foundation, 2021) and the ADKAR-Model (Hiatt, 2006)

and provide guidance in integrating the changed processes into new routines (Reinforcement). With Transformation Nudging, henceforth, it shall be possible to moderate the effects of shock, denial, frustration, and depression.

In order to reflect on the practicability of this approach two examples shall be provided. Although they were designed and carried out with different characteristics the both of them embrace Transformation Nudging.

In order to change its leadership practices from a traditional, hierarchical top-down-management to a participative leadership style of empowerment and self-actuation an internationally active automotive supplier chose to steer the change the same way the final leadership should work. A team of motivated experts was put together. They were responsible for creating the respective interventions that should foster the transformation. The very transformational processes started with the top management themselves. While not every intervention had a positive outcome – some even turned out to be counterproductive – those impulses that were assessed beneficially did not only trigger a new thinking, they also had a lasting positive effect on the members of the top management. This finally led to an intrinsically motivated change in their behaviour. As a result of the positive experience the top management was even eager to share their new insight actively with their teams and with that turned into natural multipliers. They deliberately shared their experience and supported their team members with their own transition. With that the team members turned into natural multipliers themselves, too.

A team of motivated transformational experts had been assembled to develop tools from the interventions. They were provided for the whole organization basically simultaneously. Local adaptations happened intuitively in action. Instead of making the use of the instruments mandatory events that invited to join in were organized in all parts of the organization. Defined groups of people – leadership and change managers in general – were expected to participate in the before mentioned events, though. The group of transformational experts who were responsible for the transformation also offered coaching services for those who desired guidance. New self-motivated experts from basically all divisions joined the experts voluntarily. Interventions were intensified and continuously placed all over the company. By providing exchange among the experts experiences were shared and developed. That led to a natural evolution of the instruments and the transformational process on the whole as well as the development of a shared mindset. Rather than defining an expected end to the process with a deadline or milestones the progress was assessed in the scope of an employee survey which was scheduled to take place every other year. From this assessment the next steps for the transformational process were to be derived.

In the second example a manufacturer of measuring instruments also aimed at implementing a new leadership style. The main intervention that aimed at reshaping the existing leadership style(s) was an unabridged model provided by an external consultancy[1]. The main difference to the first example described before was the mandatory character of the whole transformational process. Each intervention was designed in a pre-arranged sequence. It started with the input of the above-mentioned complete leadership model which consisted of four training sessions in the course of several months. During the sessions the model and its instruments were trained. The training itself already largely differed from other trainings as it focused on self-reflection rather than conveying new input and practicing it in exercises. Each participant's attitude and behaviour was mirrored with the model in order to detect opportunities for personal development. Between the trainings online courses and additional exercises had to be done. This way, students were able to intensify the knowledge by studying and doing exercises.

---

1 The model itself shall not be treated, analysed, judged, or assessed in the scope of this paper. Instead, it shall be described how the company composed the follow-up.

As a major challenge of training in general is to make sure that new knowledge is transferred into practice the company's department of people development designed and organized a supplementary series of interventions. These were a fixed sequence of workshops followed by a team coaching, a group reflection, an online test and a learning transfer survey. The workshops had the objectives of developing a shared understanding of the studied material and of developing strategies of how to effectively integrate the new knowledge in each individual's routines. Each workshop group had a mentor who had already experienced benefits from changing his/her behaviour and actions. The group members themselves supported each other in developing coping strategies for individual challenges. This way also the distinctiveness of each participant's situation became transparent. At the end of a workshop each participant had created his/her own milestones for transferring knowledge into practice. In order to ensure that the positive impetus of the workshop was not washed away after returning to daily business the group had to organize team coaching sessions. By a set of questions provided by the transformation coach, the group self-responsibly cross-checked the success of their coping strategies. They provided support to each other if something had not worked out well. To make sure that the process would not stop here, the teams reflected their lessons learnt after the series of team coaching sessions. On top of that, with a delay of a couple of weeks each participant received an online questionnaire to test his/her theoretical knowledge. After that and with an additional delay of various weeks the participants and their superiors were asked to assess how change had materialized in practice. If necessary, further steps were derived from that analysis by the decision body of the transformational change process.

Both processes differ quite a bit. As the second example was greatly pre-organized it could be even questioned whether it qualifies for Transformation Nudging. In the opinion of the author of this paper it does. Although predetermined in sequence and character, each intervention just was meant to create a nudge. Each participant decided for him-/herself how to process the information and their insight. There was no intention to reward or punish. Furthermore, at the end of each intervention and in line with the basic idea of Transformation Nudging it was decided how to continue.

4.6 Conclusion

While the idea of nudging stems from marketing and sales, the idea of Transformation Nudging originated from a specific way of implementing knowledge management in an organization in order to change the handling of knowledge. Thus, transformation nudging is expected to be both, an alternative way of steering transformation and knowledge management in the stricter sense. The aim of this paper, therefore, was to validate whether Transformation Nudging could be a means of transferring knowledge into practice. The KRTC and the ADKAR-model provided a framework for the assessment. Two examples showed how the basic concept of Transformation Nudging was differently used in practice, with the first one being very close to the original idea of nudging and the second one focusing on knowledge transfer.

In order to, firstly, explore the effects of Transformation Nudging on transformational processes the author applied it on KRTC and ADKAR being the assumption of the unavoidable reaction of an individual towards change and a means of steering change processes, respectively. The examination showed that by gradually familiarizing individuals with the need for change rather than abruptly confronting them with it Transformation Nudging is likely to ease the effects of a change process on the organization's individuals. The KRTC's stages of shock, denial, frustration, and depression shall be moderated. Although it still can be argued whether ADKAR or similar approaches really are capable of managing change, the analysis showed that ADKAR at least can be supportive. It is unquestionable that knowledge (K) is needed to empower people to handle change (Ability and Reinforcement). Therefore, if necessary knowledge is provided ex ante right after a nudge, i.e. when desire to change starts to surface, also the KRTC phases of experimentation and decision can be smoothened. Desire, then, does derive from positive yearning rather than incriminating compulsion. Furthermore, experimentation is rather a playful testing of diverse fitting options than a fatiguing random trial and error within the unknown. Henceforth, it can be concluded that Transformation Nudging is capable of diminishing undesired aspects of transformational processes.

Finally, the examples chosen from real life application showed the diversity of Transformation Nudging, especially with respect to its capability to transfer knowledge into practice. Both examples used different approaches. While the largely uninhibited application of Transformation Nudging displayed that knowledge is intuitively being managed by merely using Transformation Nudging as tool to manage change, it also turned out that a rigid knowledge management can be eased be implanting aspects of Transformation Nudging. Although there was a compulsory part that maintained its burden the inserted nudges facilitated sensemaking and prove of practical applicability. In the light of the KRTC shock, denial, and frustration could not be avoided, as a result of multiple coaching and practical transfer that was jointly reflected, they were shortened, though. By providing a tool set the phase of experimentation was trimmed, too.

Having originated from knowledge management it was depicted that Transformation Nudging is to be considered to be both, a valid alternative to change management and an instrument for transferring knowledge into practice.

References

Bär, M., Krumm, R. & Wiehle, H. (2007). *Unternehmen verstehen, gestalten, verändern – Das Graves-Value-System in der Praxis.* Wiesbaden.

Bateson, G. (1987). *Geist und Natur: eine notwendige Einheit.* Frankfurt a. M.

Bendel, O. (2019). *Nudging – Definition: was ist "Nudging"?* (Gabler Wirtschafslexikon, Editor) Retrieved June 1, 2020, from https://wirtschaftslexikon.gabler.de/definition/nudging-99919/version-369156

Berner, W. (2010). *Change! 15 Fallstudien zu Sanierung, Turnaround, Prozessoptimierung, Reorganisation und Kulturveränderung.* Stuttgart.

Brüsemeister, T. (2008). *Qualitative Forschung Ein Überblick.* Wiesbaden.

DiSalvo, D. (2014). *Was Ihr Gehirn glücklich macht … und warum Sie genau das Gegenteil tun sollten.* Heidelberg.

Elisabeth Kübler-Ross Foundation. (2021). *Elisabeth Kübler-Ross Foundation.* Retrieved June 1, 2021, from https://www.ekrfoundation.org/5-stages-of-grief/change-curve/

Grundl, B. (2019). *Verstehen heißt nicht, einverstanden sein – Wie Sie respektiert werden, Freunde gewinnen und Stress meistern.* Berlin.

Grundl, B. & Schäfer, B. (2018). *Leading Simple – Führen kann so einfach sein.* Offenbach.

Hammersley, M. T. & Atkinson, P. (2007). *Ethnography – Principles in Practice.* London.

Hannan, M. T. & Freeman, J. (1984). Structural Inertia and Organizational Change. *American Sociological Review, 49*(2), 149–164.

Hiatt, J. M. (2006). *ADKAR: A Model for Change in Business, Government and Our Community.* Loveland.

Horsthemke, V. C. (2017). *Zur Implementierbarkeit eines Systems des Wissensmanagements im Unternehmen* (Repositorium der Zeppelin Universität, Ed.) Retrieved March 19, 2019, from Repositorium der Zeppelin Universität: https://repositorium.zu.de/frontdoor/deliver/index/docId/21/file/Zur+Implementierbarkeit+eines+Systems+des+Wisssensmanagements+im+Unternehmen_Dissertation+ZU_Volker+C.+Horsthemke.pdf

Horsthemke, V. C. (2021). Wissensmanagement ist Wandel: Was man aus der Einführung eines Wissensmanagements im Unternehmen über die Steuerbarkeit von Veränderung lernen kann. In B. F. Seyr (ed.),

Multidisziplinäre Perspektiven im Innovations- und Wissensmanagement (Vol. 2.). Berlin u. a.

Just, A. (2016). *Systemische Beratung – Kommunikation durch Skizzieren – Fallbeispiele aus der Schulsozialarbeit.* Münster u. a.

Kilian, D., Krismer, R., Loreck, S. & Sagmeister, A. (2007). *Wissensmanagement – Werkzeuge für Praktiker.* Wien.

Lieb, H. A. (2011). *Methodik zur Integration motivationspsychologischer Erkenntnisse in Qualitätsmanagementsysteme.* Dissertation zur Erlangung des Grades eines Doktors der Philosophie, Rheinisch-Westfälische Technische Hochschule Aachen, Philosophische Fakultät, Aachen.

Marczyk, G., DeMatteo, D. & Festinger, D. (2005). *Essentials of Research Design and Methodology.* Hoboken (NJ).

Maturana, H. R. (1997). *Was ist erkennen?* München.

Orridge, M. (2009). *Change Leadership – Developing a Change-Adept Organization.* Surrey, Burlington.

Personio. (2019). *Organisationsentwicklung: So wird Ihr Unternehmen fit für den Wandel.* (Personio GmbH, Ed.) Retrieved May 22, 2020, from www.personio.de: https://www.personio.de/blog/organisationsentwicklung/

Rehäuser, J. & Krcmar, H. (1996). *Wissensmanagement im Unternehmen* (Vol. Wissensmanagement). (G. Schreyögg, Ed.) Berlin u. a.

Schuster, H. G. (2007). *Bewusst oder unbewusst?* Weinheim.

Simon, F. B. (2011). *Einführung in die systemische Organisationstheorie.* Heidelberg.

Simon, F. B. (2013). *Einführung in Systemtheorie und Konstruktivismus.* Heidelberg.

Szabo, E. (1998). *Organisationskultur und Ethnographie.* Wiesbaden.

Thaler, R. T. & Sunstein, C. R. (2017). *Nudge – Wie man kluge Entscheidungen anstößt.* Berlin.

Willke, H. (2011). *Einführung in das systemische Wissensmanagement.* Heidelberg.

Yin, R. K. (2003). *Case Study Research – Design and Methods.* Thousand Oaks.

5. Performance management of educators in the Netherlands with regards to the OKR framework

Daan Linnartz, Vincent Pijnenburg & Patrick Szillat

Abstract: Purpose: Literature provides theoretical, conceptual Strategic Human Resource Management (SHRM) frameworks. However, the papers do not include a case study where the Dutch Secondary Education (SE) is examined. Of course, problems in the SE are described by government documents, but no practical analysis on the progress of SHRM within the SE has been conducted. The dissertation at hand fills this gap by providing a methodology that can be used to combine the best practices from industry's Performance Management (PM) to the Dutch SE's SHRM.

Methodology: Theoretically, the study triangulates three different types of research: using grounded theory, eight in-depth interviews have been conducted and analysed (1). By means of a literature analysis concerning PM, industry's theoretical best practices are identified (2). A document study is conducted to gain a thorough understanding concerning the nation-wide implementation of policies related to the SHRM model in Dutch SE (3).

Findings: The results show that there is no well-structured, annual performance-oriented process in place. The SHRM model remains conceptual, but little tools of SHRM have been found implemented in Dutch SE. This makes the process subjective, unstandardized, and hence fails to enhance performance. At the hand of the Objectives and Key Results (OKR) framework an improved model is proposed. The improved model ensures that PM best practices are incorporated in the existing SHRM model.

5.1 Introduction

The National Education Agreement of 2013 shares the policy makers' vision on the future of the Dutch Secondary Education system (hereinafter: SE system). The Netherlands strive for "*excellent education*" and state the ambition to belong to the top-five countries in the world in terms of SE performance (Bussemaker et al., 2013, p. 1). However, in various reports of the state secretary and other bodies of the central government, the SE-council, Inspection of Education, and experienced professionals voiced in the Dutch media, concerns are shared. For one instance, the 2019 report of the Inspection of Education highlights issues with student motivation, quality of education and quality of teachers. Moreover, 20 % of the school administrators do not have a proper overview of the quality of education in their schools, are they able to improve it (Inspectie van het Onderwijs, 2019). Ultimately, the primary threat for the SE system is considered to be the existing teacher shortage (Ministry of Education Culture and Science, n.d.) that is prognosticated to increase to roughly 1,500 FTE in 2028. The Ministry of Education announced that the annual budget for the education sector will be upped to roughly half a billion euros and that the budget to fight the teacher shortage will increase with more than 10 % (Ministry of Education Culture and Science, 2020), which indicates the severity of the problems.

To structurally improve the situation of the Dutch SE, attention is focussed towards Strategic Human Resource Management (hereinafter: SHRM) (Bussemaker et al., 2013). Research concludes that high-performing teachers are a prerequisite and driver for a high-performing education system (Barber & Mourshed, 2007). Accordingly, the Dutch government puts effort in the "*professionalization*" of SE teachers (Ministry of Education Culture and Science, n.d.). Under the umbrella of professionalization is a variety of activities set-out to push and support the teachers to continuously develop themselves (Raijmakers, 2020).

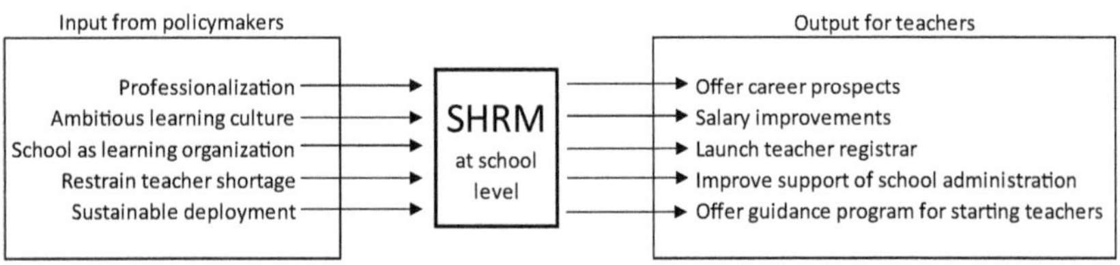

Fig. 1: SHRM as nexus (Authors' illustration)

Figure 1 not only depicts SHRM as the nexus of government policy on the one hand and concrete actions towards teachers on the other hand, it also gives insight in how the top-level policy cascades top down. This decentralization of policy execution is given shape in the last years. The government pleads for a bottom-up flow of initiatives shaped by development-driven teachers that find themselves accountable to, and simultaneously supported by, their school administration. In other words, the decentralization introduces responsibility for policymaking, policy execution and monitoring of execution at school-level, including both teachers and school administration (OECD, 2010; OCW & VO-Council, 2013). A letter of the Minister of Education, Culture and Science in 2019 to the teachers in the Dutch Secondary Education sector revealed that the status of Strategic Human Resource Management in Dutch Education System is "*unsatisfactory*" (Engelshoven & Slob, 2019).

The general topic of Strategic Human Resource Management has had a great history in the Industrial Sector. Especially on the topic of performance-oriented management, innumerable developments have been realized. Peter Drucker published *The Practice of* Management (1954) in which he introduced the management theory Management by Objectives (hereinafter: MBO), which serves as a basis for all performance-oriented management theories (Aplin, Schoderbek & Schoderbek, 1979). MBO was a novelty; a two-way management philosophy that due to the bottom-up characteristics completely reshaped the employer-employee relationship. Abdallah & Elhoss quote Drucker (1954) to define MBO as a: "*management model that aims to improve the performance of an organization by clearly defining objectives that are agreed by both management and employees*" (Abdallah & Elhoss, 2019, p. 15). More recent developments gave the world the Objectives and Key Results framework (hereinafter: OKR), which is being used by e.g. Google, Amazon and many other Silicon Valley giants (Niven & Lamorte, 2016). OKR is defined by Niven & Lamorte as: "*a critical thinking framework and ongoing discipline that seeks to ensure employees work together, focusing their efforts to make measurable contributions that drive the company forward*" (2016, p. 11). Similar to MBO, the goal of OKRs framework is to accelerate performance by centralizing goal-setting.

The research at hand aims to understand the essence and shortcomings of Strategic Human Resource Management system, and how this can be improved and applied in Dutch SE by using the knowledge gained of the developments of SHRM from the Industry.

5.2 Literature review

5.2.1 Performance management

Cardy & Leonard (2015) state that performance is the behaviour (1) and (lack of) achievements (2) that are being realized by the worker and that are relevant to the job or the workplace in general. To both the worker and the firm it is important to establish performance, as it directs and clarifies the worker in what he should be doing, as it serves as a base for incentives for the firm.

Torrington et al. (2014) define PM as "*a continuous process of identifying, measuring, and developing the performance of individuals and teams and aligning performance with the strategic goals of the organization*". The literature on the subject of performance and Performance Management (hereinafter: PM) is vast; the early forms of measuring performance – called Performance Appraisal systems – originated in the industry after WWI (Barrett, 1967). PM as an outcomes-based management practice has gained significance ever since, as the broad majority of businesses today have some sort of PM System (hereinafter: PMS) implemented (Cascio, 2006). In this period, PM has developed from the act of carrying out annually Performance Appraisals (hereinafter: PAs) to an ongoing continuous process that is in direct connection with the business strategy.

The Performance Management Process (hereinafter: PMP) is shaped by a sequence of stages that typically contain goal setting, performance monitoring, PA and feedback, and improved performance – or a variance of these stages (Gruman & Saks, 2011). The PMP is an ongoing and cyclical process (e.g. Pulakos, 2004; Armstrong, 2000; Aguinis, 2008) that concerns PA (1) and employee development (2) (for a well explained PMP the reader is referred to Torrington et al., 2014). As it serves these two connected – but not by definition mutually supporting, and even possibly counteracting – objectives, the process must be constantly balanced. Moreover, Cardy & Leonard (2015) specifically state that the entire process needs to be valued for PM to be successful. Poorly implemented PMPs lead to decreased performance and development (Wiese & Buckley, 1998; Cardy & Leonard, 2004; Aguinis, 2013).

Throughout the process, many interactions between manager and employee take place. As is typical for today's HR practices, PMP is not a top-down management activity, but a process that needs commitment from everyone involved and requires two-way communication (Cardy & Leonard, 2004). This is shifting attention on to soft skills. E. g. feedback can be given, but it should also be accepted by the receiver for it to make an impact.

5.2.2 Outcomes-based management in the public sector

Whereas PM is typically applied in the Industry Sector, Public Management deals with the managerial actions in public organizations (e.g. government, public sector, non-profit organizations) with the aim to improve the quality and services delivered by these organizations.

Public sector administration saw itself reinvented in the period around the 1980s. The phenomena of stagnated economic growth, and an increase in world trade and international competition resulted in shifting paradigms. With this, New Public Management was shaped (Hood, 1995). A crucial paradigm shift was moving away from a process-based management style in a regulated environment, towards an outcome-based management style where managers hold more discretionary power. With outcomes-based management – which, by reason, ultimately led to the centralization of performance management practices within the public sector – a large body of research has been conducted on what Knies

& Leisink dub the "*HRM-performance chain*" (Knies & Leisink, 2014). This relatively new strand of research seeks to answer how HR practices lead to enhanced performance, which is called "unlocking the black box" of HRM-performance linkage (Knies & Leisink, 2014; Torrington et al., 2014; Marin-Garcia & Martinez Tomas, 2016). The link between aspects of public management and the performance of public services has been verified by many (see for example Andrews, Boyne & Walker, 2006; O'Toole & Meier, 2011; Meier & O'Toole, 2016).

5.3 SHRM in the Dutch secondary education

In the introduction the central role of SHRM was explained. Country-level policies need to be implemented and converted into specific actions (output) for teachers. This conversation takes place on school level, resulting in SHRM being the nexus of policy making and implementation. In the previous subsection it has been explained that outcome-based management led to a focus on the public sector's version of performance management: the HRM-performance chain.

The Dutch government enrolled the AMO-model as a tool for the HRM-performance linkage. The acronym stands for the three elements Individual Ability (A), Motivation (M) and the Opportunity to participate (O), which together construct employee performance (Marin-Garcia & Martinez Tomas, 2016). The conceptual value of these three elements has been well-demonstrated by Wright & Boswell (2002), after which the theory has been widely accepted in HRM literature and further developed (Appelbaum et al., 2000; Boxall, 2003; Boselie, Dietz & Boon, 2005; Marin-Garcia & Martinez Tomas, 2016) to ultimately the AMO-model. "*According to the model, people perform well when they have the capabilities, they have the adequate motivation, and their work environment provides opportunities to participate*" (Marin-Garcia & Martinez Tomas, 2016, p. 1042).

The version of the model that is applied in the Dutch SE has been developed by Knies & Leisink (2017), see Fig. 2. The researchers present the AMO-model as "the heart" of HR practices (see Knies & Leisink, 2019, p. 18). By literature review one can conclude that the AMO framework is indeed at the heart of the HR value chain (Jiang et al., 2012; Torrington et al., 2014). See for example Marin-Garcia & Martinez Tomas (2016) who conceptualize HRM and demonstrate the integral part that the AMO-model takes in. The applied AMO-model in the Dutch education sector pinpoints the importance of institutional goal-setting, behavioural goal-setting, and HR-practice design. However, the ultimate question is how the AMO aspects can be shaped to create the desired behaviour.

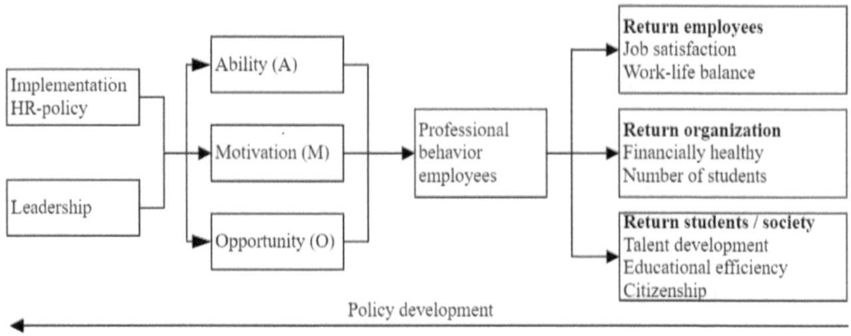

Fig. 2: AMO-model (Knies & Leisink, 2017)

5.4 Research gap

Ultimately, the literature review contains a review of literature on PM, public management, and the AMO-model applied in the Dutch SE. These topics are related to each other as is modelled in Fig. 3. The literature provides conceptual frameworks to be applied in real life, yet do not include a case study of any kind. Of course, issues in the Dutch SE are described in government documents, but no study on the progress of SHRM within the SE has been found. The strand of research concerning PM could possibly add value to the implementation and adherence of SHRM in the Dutch SE. By Torrington et al. (2014) it became clear that the literature about PM and PMS took a more pragmatic approach, resulting in a PMP that offers practical handles for the implementation of a theoretic model. The paper at hand intends to fill the gap in this manner by providing a new model (dotted box below in Fig. 3) that can be used to combine the best practices from industry's PM (black boxes) to the Dutch SE's SHRM (white box). Herewith, this project is a contribution to the related disciplines, as it combines the two different fields within a real-life situation.

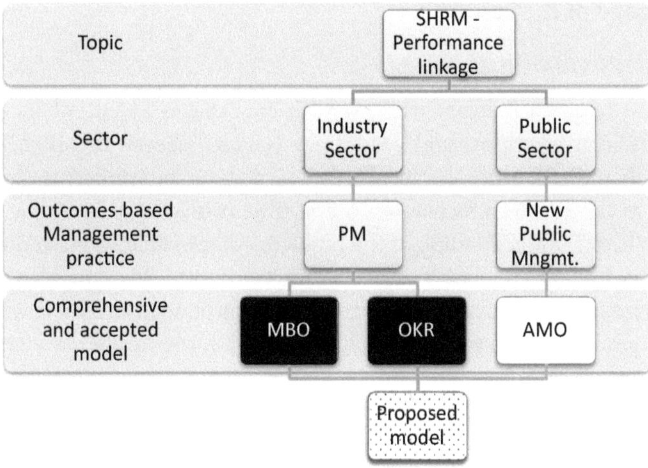

Fig. 3: Research gap modelled (Authors' illustration)

5.3. Research design

5.3.1 Research question

The literature review shows that the AMO-model is theoretically validated but subject to problems that occur in practice. It was found that PM offers a more practical approach to the management of performance because of its cyclical nature and pragmatic additions to the theoretic model. This forms the theoretical premise for the following empirical research question:

In what way can the Strategic Human Resource practices of the Dutch Secondary Education system be improved using the best practices of Performance Management?

In light of this research question, a number of sub questions have been developed:

- *What is the status of the SHRM AMO-model in the Dutch SE, and how is the implementation and execution experienced by the teachers?*
- *What are the indicators for a successful Performance Management Process?*
- *What industrial frameworks can add value to the theoretical AMO-model, and which framework is the best fit for the Dutch SE?*
- *How will this improve the current system?*

5.3.2 Scope of the research

5.3.2.1 Type of research

Qualitative research involves working with data that is not numbers but text, interviews, conversations, and recordings (Guest, Namey & Mitchell, 2013; Wollenweber, 2019). More specifically, the research can be typified as exploratory research as the research focuses on a first-time in-depth analysis that aims to provide a better understanding of the problem and possible solution directions; and not on finding conclusive answers (Yousaf, n. d.). This type of research is characterized by inductive reasoning, for which grounded theory is well applicable. "*A grounded theory is one that is inductively derived from the study of phenomena it represents*" (Corbin & Strauss, 2008). Hence, grounded theory focuses on the discovery of theoretical ideas from the data, rather than having these specified beforehand. This implies an iterative process in which data is analysed before the data collection phase is finished. Grounded theory is both a method to categorize the discovered theory (1) as a coding approach (2) (Gibbs, 2012).

5.3.2.2 Population qualification

Because the pedagogic role of the educator on VMBO level is considered significantly bigger than on HAVO-VWO level, this affects the vocation of the lecturer (Veugelers & Schuitema, 2010). For homogeneity reasons, the scope of the research is limited to the HAVO-VWO level. There are two groups that could serve as the research population; the school administration (1) and the teachers (2). However, the school administration is involved with the implementation of SHRM, which gives them more insight (1) and more responsibility (2). As a result, they are presumably prone to the social desirability bias as they will try to prove the accomplishments of their implementations (Favero et al., 2016). Secondly, there is a difference between intended SHRM and perceived SHRM (Knies & Leisink, 2014). Consequently, in pursuit of high research validity, the researcher will solely question teachers in the Dutch SE.

5.3.2.3 Sampling design

Nonprobability sampling is subjective sampling (OECD, 2004). This is useful when the population is large with a wide geographical spread, and the researcher is not part of the population and therefore has limited access to the population (Etikan, Musa & Alkassim, 2016). Due to the exploratory character of the research, probability sampling is not per se more valuable than nonprobability sampling. Further research will have to prove to which extent the findings deviate depending on the population sample.

The limited access of the researcher possibly affects the reliability of the research (Scott, 2019). This is consequential to convenience sampling, in which some practical criteria are leading, e. g. geographical proximity, availability and willingness to participate (Etikan et al., 2016). The paper at hand for example, contains interviews with teachers from 10 different SE's in the North-Brabant province. To increase the research reliability, purposive sampling methods are applied. Maximum Variation Sampling is used to increase the degree of heterogeneity. For example, both HAVO and VWO teachers are questioned, only one participant per school is questioned.

Additionally, the use of grounded theory goes hand in hand with theoretical sampling, as the data collection and data analysis take place simultaneously. Hence, the sampling approach is led by the developing theory of the researcher (Gibbs, 2012). For example, additional process defining questions in the initial interviews, focus on teachers with a longer tenure and/or a higher seniority.

5.3.3 Data collection

Qualitative research is by definition subjective; it depends how the researcher sees the world. A statement can be interpreted in multiple ways, depending on the background and knowledge of the person that analyses that statement (Gibbs, 2012). The paper at hand describes an exploratory research, which typically goes hand in hand with a broad and general questioning (Guest et al., 2013). This aligns with grounded theory, that stipulates the researcher to be as objective as possible. Charmaz (2006, p. 163) adds to this that it is important for the researcher to not bring in theoretic ideas during the interviews, but that these are kept for the data analysis.

Throughout the iterative process of data collection and data analysis, the researcher looks for a certain degree of saturation – where new information does not provide further insights in a certain category or topic. In Charmaz's words: "*systematic application of grounded theory will lead to multiple levels of analysis, progressively becoming enhanced abstract and analytic.*" (Charmaz, 1983, p. 125). Because of this, the researcher is able to funnel down throughout the data collection phase. This is needed as the applicability of the data for the data analysis has to be taken into consideration in the data collection. Ultimately, the aim of the research is to compare PM practices to the SHRM model. The literature prescribes that this requires at least semi-structured forms of inquiry (Guest et al., 2013) that facilitates data comparison. In order to keep the interview structure as prescribed by Charmaz, different kinds of data collection are required in this research. This will provide an opportunity to increase the research validity. This method is called triangulation, see Fig. 4.

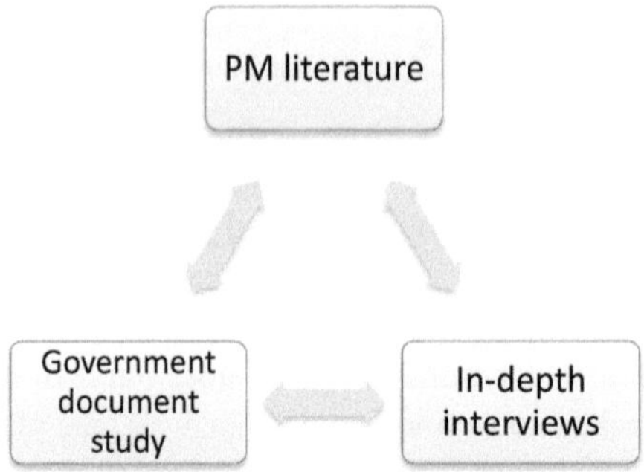

Fig. 4: Triangulation of collected data (Authors' illustration)

Triangulation refers to "*the use of multiple methods or data sources in qualitative research to develop a comprehensive understanding of the studied phenomenon*" (Patton, 1999). In other words, it helps to remove any biases that arise from a single method or source. Triangulation does not always lead to a higher consistency of results, but inconsistencies can be explained if the researcher has a holistic understanding of the phenomenon (Mathison, 1988). In Fig. 4, *Government document study* describes the document study carried out on the existing policy making documents, newspapers and broadcasts, recordings and studies concerning nation-wide implementation of policies related to the SHRM model. *PM literature* comprises of an in-depth literature analysis concerning PM best practices. The PMP of Torrington et al. (2014) can be expanded by pinpointing specifics that make a PMP successful; bringing to surface the industry's best practices (Gruman & Saks, 2011). *In-depth interviews* are conducted with SE teachers to get a better understanding of the perceived implementation of SHRM.

5.3.4 Empirical data analysis

Literature describes that arranging, labelling (or: coding), and interlinking are key for structuring qualitative data (Baarda, Goede & Teunissen, 2009). As stated in subsection 5.3.2.1, grounded theory is also a coding approach. Charmaz defines two iterative phases: an initial phase of open coding followed by a phase of selective coding (Charmaz, 2006). Open coding is done on word, line, sentence or segment level and gives the researcher codes of data that are closely related to the text itself. The codes can be bundled in code groups – or: categorized. With this step the codes become more abstract, which makes selective coding possible. In selective coding the researcher builds the narrative around a set of core categories. Data analysis alternates these two phases. The researcher should keep an open mind to be able to understand when a topic has reached a saturation point, or when there are gaps in the data (Charmaz, 2006, p. 48). Finding the right degree of conceptualization is important. Gibbs (2012) explains the problem of having too many codes, which makes it increasingly difficult to get an overview and interlink codes. For this, similar activities are bundled under the same code; e.g. "*teacher aware of individual education strategy*", "*teacher aware of independence* strategy" etc. are conceptualized to "*teacher aware of strategy*". As the data collection and analysis phases progresses and the level of situation increases, segment-by-segment coding is useful for confirming working theories.

5.3.5 Research overview

Through the preliminary literature research, it is understood that whilst PM and New Public Management come from a different origin, both are considered outcomes-based management practices in the field of the SHRM-performance linkage. The AMO-model that is applied in the Dutch SE provides mostly a theoretic basis. Following the guidelines of grounded theory, a qualitative research will be performed. The empirical research takes place in the form of open-ended structured interviews, as extensively described in the previous subsection. Furthermore, extensive literature on the best practices of PM and government involvement (i. e. policies and plans) will be carried out. The findings of the analyses will be bundled in a topic-coverage overview that visualizes the gaps of the current SHRM-model.

In order to present a new model, a comparison of the findings needs to be made. Multi-criteria decision-making (hereinafter: MCDM) is a term for a set of methods that aids in making decisions in cases characterized by multiple criteria and objectives (Zeiler, 2008). MCDM proves to be very helpful in the valuation of qualitative data (Wang et al., 2009). There is a multitude of MCDM methods, which all have a different background. Originated from the morphology field, the Pugh decision-matrix allows concept selection and is hence applicable as a base model for the paper at hand. Two comprehensive performance oriented management philosophies are involved in this research; MBO and OKR. Based on a set of criteria that are subject to weighing factors, these concepts are being scored on each criterion, which will give a total weighed score that gives insight in the best-fit concept (Siers, 2004; Lugo, 2012).

The weighing of each criteria and the application of scoring is performed at the hand of the information gathered by extensive literature research. The method serves as a tool to enable the researcher to be as objective as possible. However, it should be mentioned that this process is, as part of an exploratory, qualitative research, susceptible to bias and lacking rigor (Anderson, 2010). The aim of this approach is to increase the research's repeatability, and the reader should realize that although the presented results are of a highly probable nature they by no means constitute an absolute truth.

5.4 Findings

In the data analysis, the codes were analysed individually and thereafter grouped and linked together. Afterwards, these findings are compared with the best practices from PM literature and policies of the central government, so that the current SHRM system can be evaluated. Lastly, with the input of the interviews, the importance of the gaps in the current SHRM system have been valued. E. g. it became apparent that separation of PA and PR is not recommended in the Dutch SE as salary and promotion discussions do not take place in these meetings.

It was established that the central government prefers giving control to the individual schools when it comes to implementing SHRM. However, one could raise the question why there are no tools shared with the schools to do so. The only tool that was shared was the teacher registrar. Yet practical management tools that could benefit school administrations and team leaders in the execution of the SHRM, like e.g. knowledge about SMART goal-setting, are not being shared to that level. This is partly a cascading problem. It has been found that the strategic goals are not cascading down to section level and individual level, keeping them too ambiguous for teachers to work with, and team leaders to monitor. Research supports these findings, as Knies & Leisink (2017; 2019) state that the vision document that contains the four-year plan is often a multitude of ambitions and strategic focal points, written in management language that does not connect to the daily practice. The research at hands adds to this topic that a lack of goal-setting, possibly partly consequential to the lack of cascading objectives, impacts performance development significantly. Some teachers have shared that they set goals for themselves, but that there are no processes in place to accelerate performance. This starts with goal-setting, as the lack of this affects all the other stages of a performance oriented SHRM; precise monitoring of performance, performance evaluation and long term development prove difficult without goal setting.

Furthermore, there is a strongly noticeable difference between initiatives launched by the central government, and initiatives that require high school involvement. This forebodes a fundamental paradox within the SHRM set-up within the Dutch SE: The central government pushes – by means of professionalization – for teacher development whereas the school administrations prioritize a well-functioning teacher in the classroom. The position of the school is seemingly understandable as they have to deal with the teacher shortage every day. However, as a result, many initiatives are carried out to some extent, but not fully and without follow-up; thereby failing to contribute to performance development, while contributing to a high workload pressure. Partly because of this reason teachers who teach courses with a shortage will not be able to get a second certification (Raijmakers, 2020; Swinkels, 2020), teachers do not receive the guidance that they are looking for (Bonnema, 2020; Raijmakers, 2020), career guidance does not take place (Swinkels, 2020; Wouters, 2020), the additional coaching stops as soon as after one year (Swinkels, 2020; Verhagen 2020; Wouters, 2020), and observations and evaluations take place in a low frequency (Alphen et al., 2010; Raijmakers, 2020; Van der Velden, 2020; Wouters, 2020).

Additionally, performance evaluation meetings take place in a setting that closely relates to PA meetings in a PA system. Performance evaluation meetings are all about evaluation of past performance and not about forward-looking continuous performance development. Moreover, due to the limited observations prior to the performance evaluation meeting, there is little foundation to rate the performance which, as a result, makes it very difficult to allocate the performance to system or person and thus nearly impossible to remove any system barriers.

Ultimately, the role of the central government should be discussed. The government plays an important role in the form of providing funding and long-term strategizing. Not all government initiatives are valued by the teachers. Time and money spent on career prospects and teacher registrar are perceived as purposeless. To illustrate, the revocation of the teacher registrar, after many years of investing in the implementation, showcases the ineffectiveness of these governmental programs (VO-Council, 2019). Concerning government efforts on the topic of salary development, such conclusion cannot be made. As became apparent in the literature and during the interviews, salary development in the education sector is slow. However, as Scheepens states, this is more an issue in primary education than for teachers in the secondary education (2020).

The findings of the analyses are bundled in a topic-coverage overview that visualizes the gaps of the current SHRM-model, see Fig. 5. It is visualized which topics in the SHRM literature in fact have an impact on the PM of Dutch SE (according to the educators) and to what extent. In light of these findings, one can conclude that the application of PM theory in the SHRM within Dutch SE adds value. In the following section a practical model will be proposed.

BEST PRACTIE	RECOGNIZED AS PART OF SHRM BY TEACHERS	PRACTICE ABSENCE HAS NEGATIVE IMPACT?
PM literature		
Strategic awareness	☑	
Function PMS / SHRM is determined	☒	YES
Cascading of objectives & goal-setting	☒	YES
Frequent observation & feedback (formal)	☒	YES
Frequent observation & feedback (informal)	☑	
Openness to feedback	☑	
PA separated from performance review	☒	NO
Progressive evaluation with performance allocation and removal of system barriers	☒	YES
Employee-manager relationship	☑	
Government policy		
professionalization	☑	
Strategic awareness	☑	
Teacher guidance program	☑	
Salary developments	☒	NO
Career prospects	☒	NO
Teacher registrar	☒	NO
Unmentioned		
Reducing workload pressure	☒	YES

Fig. 5: Overview of findings (Authors' illustration)

5.5 Comparative frameworks

The data from Fig. 5 serves as the input for the Pugh-decision matrix. Since the goal is not to replace the existing system, only the best practices that have been recognized as pitfalls and that have a negative impact on the performance are selected.

5.5.1 Model set-up

5.5.1.1 Weighing factors

In the process of applying weighing factors the criteria are cross-paired and allocated a 0 or 1 based on importance. The scores are then summed up and based on this summation given a weighing score of 1, 2 or 3. Based on this process, *cascading of objectives & goal-setting* has been allocated as the most important criteria and as such has given the highest weighing factor (3). *Frequent formal observation & feedback* and *Reducing workload pressure* were have been given a weighing factor 2. *Function PMS is determined* and *Progressive evaluation with performance allocation and removal of system barriers* are weighed with weighing factor 1.

In the following subsections scoring will be allocated to the fit of MBO and OKR for each of the criteria. Following the method described by Siers (2004), the minimum score is 1 and the maximum score 4. A small scale is used to stay away from accuracy pretension. The use of an even-numbered scale urges the researcher to avoid averages.

5.5.1.2 Function PMS is determined

Founder of MBO, Peter Drucker states that even the smallest public service institutions has a greater diversity and complexity than a conglomerate, with more incompatible objectives and less tangible output than industry companies. Because of this, these organizations need objectives and concentration of efforts on goals and results (Drucker, 1976). "*MBO should always result in changing the allocation of effort, the assignment of people and the jobs they are doing*" (Drucker, 1976). This implies that MBO follows a hard version of PM, in which the organizational development and performance enhancement always has the highest priority (Armstrong, 2006).

For OKR too, the end goal is to accelerate performance. However, performance is considered merely a distal outcome of a PMP (Gruman & Saks, 2011), and is thus considered too narrow to serve as a sole focus. The OKR framework is a "*critical thinking framework*". Niven & Lamorte (2016) believe that by iteratively setting and updating OKRs on every level of the organization, the performance of organization and employees will accelerate. However, as employees can set their own OKRs, the framework could well as support a more employee development-oriented process. Ultimately, theorists state that it is very unlikely that a PMP will serve different purposes (Pulakos, 2004; Aguinis, 2013). MBO is characterized by more limitations than OKR, however, that the purpose of the system is therewith significantly clearer. **Scoring: MBO: 4, OKR: 2.**

5.5.1.3 Cascading of objectives & goal-setting

The two management philosophies are both focused on goal-setting. Kleber (1972) praises the effectiveness of MBO in a production or sales environment. For vocations where the output is tangible (e.g. number of units produced, amount of sales made) MBO is the natural way of management. However, Kleber also acknowledges that in areas in which output is more abstract (e.g. in R&D, education, NGOs, government), it is difficult to implement a successful MBO system. Nevertheless, he argues, MBO should still be desirable as output indicators directs the management attention on the purpose of the vocations, thereby preventing the professionals in these areas to wander off in (ineffective) activity. For this reason, Kleber sets a common practice that enables MBO to fit with any area. Kleber argues that operational goals should be established based on strategic goals and that implementation of MBO works best top-down. This belief is shared by Drucker, who pleads for top-down decision making (Drucker, 1976, p. 18).

OKR starts with the setting of Mission OKRs (MOKRs). MOKRs are the OKR way to pen down a mission statement. Niven & Lamorte (2016) state that it is needed to align OKRs to the mission to assure that the work that is done on the short term is adding value to the long-term purpose of the organization. Under the name of vertical connecting, OKRs flow down the levels within the organization. The process specifically contains facilitation of OKRs by lower levels. As Niven & Lamorte (2016) state: "*Lower-level parties look upon preceding steps and ask: How can we influence those OKRs? What can we do and measure at our level to drive both our and their success?*". Zhou & He (2018) praise the awareness of company focus that OKR creates. Because this top-down and bottom-up mix, the employee is aware of the organizational direction and feels committed to the organization, which ultimately leads to increased motivation. Not all objectives are equally achievable. Therefore, it is valuable to look at the merit of the progress and not merely focus on objective achievement (Cardy & Leonard, 2015). For comparison and evaluation purposes, three requirements should be taken into account: the level of difficulty of the objectives (1), the gradations to which extent an objective has been achieved (2), factors that may have had an influence on whether objectives have been achieved (3). Niven and Lamorte (2016) emphatically oppose to the use of binary KRs. Binary KRs are those where the outcome is either *achieved* or *not achieved*. The reason for this is straightforward; when an employee realizes the goal is out of reach, the motivation to go for it takes a hit. Henceforth, the authors stress for a Key Results metric, by applying scoring. Proposed is a point system; scoring 1.0 when an extremely ambitious outcome has been realized, 0.7 for a difficult-to-achieve outcome, 0.3 for business as usual, and 0 when no progress has been made. It is not expected that the goals are always obtained completely. In fact, this indicates that the set goal was too easy.

Some controversy exists concerning connecting OKRs to the individual level. While doing so could increase awareness, comprehension and commitment, it could well be perceived as a top-down managerial exercise (Klau, 2013; Niven & Lamorte, 2016). It could be that SMART goal-setting is preferable. Even though SMART goal-setting is often related to MBO, Drucker never mentioned this or anything else about how a well-defined goal should look like (Seyna, 1986).

Conclusively, both systems use top-down cascading of objectives to ensure focus in activities. However, OKR actively applies a bottom-up involvement as well, creating room for personal initiatives and development, whereas Drucker did not (Niven & Lamorte, 2016). It is then the nature of the organization, and the degree of hierarchy therein, that determines how goal-setting takes place. Especially in the Dutch SE this bottom-up aspect is needed; as is pushed for by the central government. Concerning goal-setting OKR is far more advanced than MBO, which lacks a "*how-to-do-it book*" (Seyna, 1986). On individual level goal-setting both systems cannot seem to compete with the SMART-tool. **Scoring: MBO: 3, OKR: 4.**

5.5.1.4 Frequent formal observation & feedback

MBO holds a prominent place for feedback on performance as this feedback forms the basis for decision-making on training needs, assignments and transfers (Wiese & Buckley, 1998). Involvement of the manager here is key, as these feedback moments often take place in PA meetings. Aplin et al. (1979) finds in their research of over 130 managers, that 60 % did not receive enough feedback to do their job adequately, even though MBO is enrolled in all the organizations of the surveyed mangers. The authors state that in formal MBO, systems reviews – and thus feedback sessions – often take place on an annual basis. Furthermore, interim reviews are scheduled semi-yearly, or at most quarterly. Grove wanted to apply MBO when he was the CEO at Intel (1987–1998) (Niven & Lamorte, 2016). However, he made some crucial modifications. One of these alterations was that goal-setting – and consequently feedback and evaluation – should take place monthly, or at least quarterly instead of annually.

With regards to OKR, Doerr introduces monthly check-ins at the hand of the concept of CFRs, standing for bidirectional conversations between manager and employee, feedback among peers, and recognition of contributions. CFRs are used as communication stimuli in combination with OKRs and are a part of what Doerr coins continuous PM. According to Doerr, continuous PM ensures alignment and transparency, imperatives crucial for the success of both employer and employee. Struggling employees will receive advice whenever they need it, instead of solely at the end of a period. Therefore, continuous PM does not only raise the individual's performance, morale and development, but with that also boosts the performance of the company. The question whether continuous performance management can be applied within the Dutch SE is valid. The issues of teacher shortage and a high perceived workload pressure are currently already affecting the time that team leaders have for observation and feedback sessions. Nevertheless, with CFRs, OKR offers a more structured process, and the tools that can pragmatically applied, which is an essential addition in comparison with the AMO-model. **Scoring: MBO: 2, OKR: 3.**

5.5.1.5 Progressive evaluation with performance allocation and removal of system barriers

As explained in subsection 5.5.1.2, MBO theory connects the management system to organizational decision-making. This includes rewards and salary (Drucker, n.d.). PM literature finds this is dangerous as it impacts the setting in which the performance evaluation takes place. Pink (2009) concludes that extrinsic rewards (e.g. monetary incentives) negatively impact intrinsic motivation, which, as is known from the AMO literature, influences a whole array of aspects. Moreover, it supports short-term thinking. Niven & Lamorte (2016) coin *sandbagging*, which means to under-promise and over-deliver. When incentives are directly linked to performance, employees will try to negotiate easy to accomplish goals for their own benefit. Not only is this in a direct way harmful for the performance, it moreover jeopardizes the perceived fairness of the process, which is a prerequisite of PM (Pulakos, 2004).

There is a second aspect in which OKR differs from MBO. The evaluation of performance according to the MBO means evaluating if the set goals have been met (Seyna, 1986). This is something that Grove changed in his time as CEO of Intel. He realized that goal achievement should just be one of the metrics to determine employee performance (see also Niven & Lamorte, 2016). This approach allows the employee and manager to have a discussion to allocate the performance, which is in line with PM literature concerning the actor/observer bias (e.g. Cardy & Leonard, 2015). Additionally, Klau (2013) states that OKR is a method for grading yourself looking backwards, and setting new objectives looking forward, pointing out the progressive nature of evaluation meetings. As this approach was so blatantly missing in the current SHRM system, OKR provides a big improvement on this aspect. **Scoring: MBO: 1, OKR: 3.**

5.5.1.6 Reducing workload pressure

Both management systems follow the path of top-down cascading objectives. This makes the company objectives clearer in all layers of the organization, and therewith determines the focus. Driving focus is important, as a lack of focus either has a paralyzing effect, in which no-one undertakes anything, or, it invites initiatives without assessment whether they contribute to the end goal or not (Grove, in Niven & Lamorte, 2016). Fed by the bottom-up enablement strategy that the government lays out in the Dutch SE, the latter is applicable. Cascading of objectives helps to prevent this (Drucker, n.d.). Additionally, OKR supplies for another method to keep responsibilities tracked and in-sync. The way to do so, is to connect OKRs horizontally. This means connecting OKRs with dependent and depending stakeholders. This is applicable in case of a dependent Key Result (1); which is when one team has a defined Objective, but one of the Key Results linked to this Objective is depending on another team; or in case of a shared OKR (2); when multiple teams are working on the same Objective. Klau (2013) explains that within Google, the OKRs are made publicly. With regards to Raijmakers (2020) who stated that communication over-sections does not take place, and Verhagen (2020), who berates the lack of communications structure on process changes, one can see the relevance of this methodology. **Scoring: MBO: 2, OKR: 4.**

5.5.2 Proposed model

5.5.2.1 Pugh Matrix

Figure 6 presents the Pugh decision-matrix filled with the scores given in subsection 5.5.1. The scores have been multiplied with the respective weighing factors. As a result, it is found that of the two frameworks, the OKR framework is the best fit. Moreover, showing an 81 % overall weighed scoring, OKR seems to be a very good match to fill the gaps of the current SHRM system. OKR rates the maximum value of the criteria that was found to be most important, and it contains tools and methods for many of the other criteria as well. The point of attention focusses on the first criteria: *Function PMS is determined.* The OKR framework appears to be versatile which makes it widely applicable yet less stringent. Because of the latter, the framework scored low on this criteria. Nevertheless, in OKR literature, every stage of the implementation process is well-described; from thinking about the mission and strategy of the organization, the first pilot, creating awareness in the organization to the ramping up of their use in the entire organization. Even the process of actually setting OKRs has a methodology: the mnemonic acronym CRAFT – Create, Refine, Align, Finalize, Transmit – offers guidance in this process. In other words, strategizing will always be the work of the people in the organization. The OKR framework offers them a guide into translating strategies into practice.

Criteria	Weighing factor	MBO	OKR		Ideal
Function PMS is determined	1	(4) 4	(2) 2		(4) 4
Cascading of objectives & goal-setting	3	(3) 9	(4) 12		(4) 12
Frequent formal observation & feedback	2	(2) 4	(3) 6		(4) 8
Progressive evaluation with performance allocation and removal of system barriers	1	(1) 1	(3) 3		(4) 4
Reducing workload pressure	2	(2) 4	(3) 6		(4) 8
Total weighed score		**22**	**29**		**36**
Total weighed score in percentage		**61%**	**81%**		**100%**

Fig. 6: Applied Pugh decision-matrix (Authors' illustration)

5.5.2.2 Applied OKR SHRM process

Ultimately, the various factors are being brought together in the form of a OKR oriented SHRM process, see Fig. 7. The process describes the cycle that starts with the context (i.e. the plans and policies of the central government) and strategy of the school administration. The strategic objectives cascade down the organization to teacher level, supporting the school organization with the right tools for a successful PMP. MOKRs are being set and OKRs are vertically connected from administration to team leader and section level to teacher level. Teacher experience and knowledge are depicted in the third flow cycle as Teacher know-how.

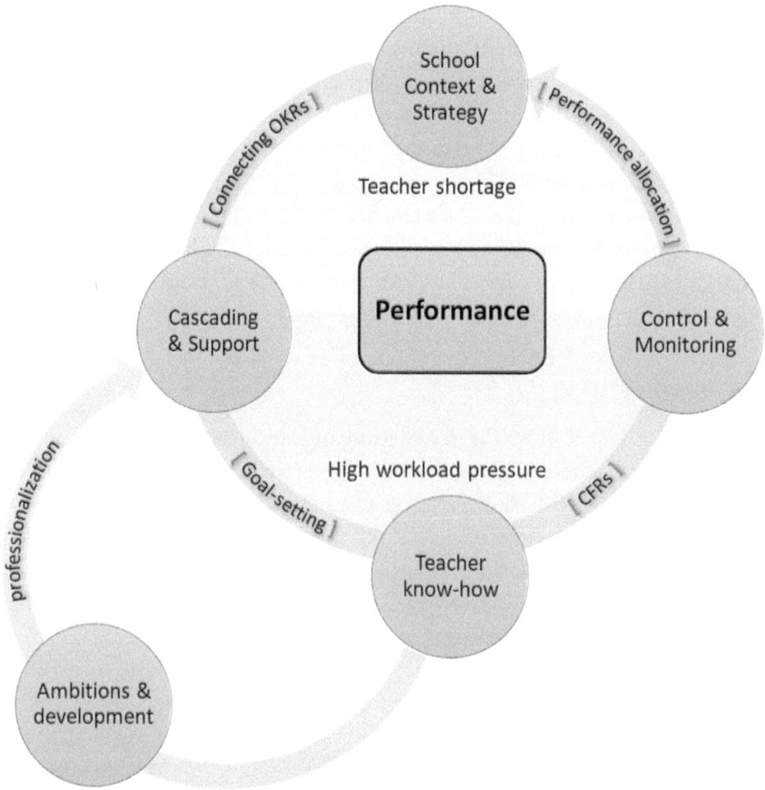

Fig. 7: OKR oriented SHRM process (Authors' illustration)

Because of the autonomy and authority of teachers, they should be regarded as a separate entity in the cycle. The freedom that teachers have in their classroom is important, but this is not the same as full autonomy, what the teachers currently seem to have. Controlling and monitoring (e.g. by regular observations and formal feedback sessions) will help the teachers to develop themselves and accelerate performance. Teachers' feedback to school strategy and processes will come, via the team leaders and sections, back to school administration and serve as an input for strategizing. This takes place by (1) monthly OKR check-ins (or CFRs), and by (2) performance allocation and the subsequent removal of system barriers. The entity "ambitions & development" visualizes the professionalization loop. Currently, teachers lack support of team leaders / school administration. Development should be incorporated because of its importance for both teachers and the school, and because focus on development has a positive effect on performance. The external context is characterized by teacher shortage (which predominantly affects the strategizing of government and high school administration) and high workload pressure (which is the number one issue for teachers and team leaders). Connecting OKRs aid to fight the high workload pressure to some extent as it enables teachers to share their best practices (Bosch et al., 2013). Nevertheless, these impacting factors need to be taken into account throughout the PMP, in order to prevent a multitude of programs with no adequate follow-up.

5.6 Conclusion

SHRM plays a key role in the translation of nation-wide policy to concrete actions towards teachers. The decentralization of SHRM policy execution has as consequence that SHRM takes place on the school level. As such, it was found that there are significant differences per school in the shape and status of SHRM. Nevertheless, some topics, amongst the teacher shortage and high workload pressure, affect the SHRM nationwide. Furthermore, a government document study was conducted to get insights in the drivers that shape the SHRM model in the Dutch SE.

The researcher conducted in-depth interviews with teachers from different secondary education schools. In these interviews the teachers were asked what SHRM activities they have encountered and what their opinion concerning these activities is. It was found that the SHRM process is ill-defined, lacks structure and misses practical tools for implementation, for example a high degree of ungoverned teacher initiatives. As a result, teachers take on a multitude of different roles besides teaching, often based on their own interest. Inter-sectional communication does not take place in a structured way. Additionally, observations and formal feedback sessions with the team leader often take place once a year. Teachers deem this insufficient for a valid evaluation. Consequentially, negative feedback in performance evaluation meetings is not supported and the perceived value of evaluation meetings is low. As a result, the SHRM process fails to deliver and does not steer performance forward.

Through literature research a set of PM best practices has been gathered. The findings from the PM literature research and government document study were compared with the outcomes of the in-depth interviews. Through this process the gaps of the current model could be identified:

- The function of the PMS should be determined;
- Cascading of objectives and goal-setting should take place;
- Formal observations and feedback should take place frequently;
- Evaluation should be conducted progressively;
- Workload pressure should be reduced.

These were then listed as criteria to which the industrial frameworks MBO and OKR were matched with. It was found that the OKR framework is complementary to the gaps of the current model, scoring an 81 % coverage, and is thus the best model to serve as an addition to the current AMO-model in place. It is expected to bring a more performance-oriented, structured, forward looking process. Ultimately, a new model was proposed, integrating the existing AMO-model with the OKR framework.

5.7 Limitations and further research directions

This research describes the first empirical analysis that investigates the applicability of PM practices in the Dutch SE. The findings cannot be stated without limitations. Firstly, as the research is a qualitative research, it will face reliability issues (Anderson, 2010). One can foresee that the small sample size will impact the statistical reliability of the study. In order to pursue a high reliability, theoretical research formed a firm part of the research in the form of triangulation. The researcher sought to relate and compare situations and findings with theories from other larger-scale studies. Secondly, the exploratory character implies that the findings point towards causality and other natures of relationships amongst the various topics within the research scope (Charmaz, 2006). Yet, these relationships are indications and not quantified. It is recommended to conduct further quantitative research on the various findings this paper offered. Thirdly, the proposed model is well-underpinned, and the use of concepts has been applied throughout to validate the model. Nevertheless, PM and SHRM literature clearly states that the context in which an HR system is applied determines the value of the model. E.g. Gulick noted the importance of context on the effectiveness of management in place, noting the influence of time and place, and size and stability of organizations (Meier, 2010, p. 289). Consequently, a conceptual model should always be applied to the given situation. Coinciding with the critique on the contingency approach (Grundy, 1998; Torrington et al., 2014), it will be challenging to find the best way to bring this model into practice, as the context is constantly changing. Specifically, in the Dutch SE, two major topics – a systematic teacher shortage and a systematic high workload pressure – put pressure on the entire system. This already affects the current system in place. Moreover, as already stated in Section 5.3.5, it should be mentioned that qualitative research is susceptible to bias and lacking rigor (Anderson, 2010). The research method selected urges the researcher to be as objective as possible (Charmaz, 1983). As the research was to be applied within a certain scope, and additionally literature analysis had to be conducted to determine said scope, a constant trade-off was made to stay within the boundaries of the research while simultaneously intending not to steer the interviews. Finally, the way the researcher "*looks at the world*" impacts the way the data has been analysed (Charmaz, 2006; Gibbs, 2012;). This said, because of the unavoidable involvement of the researcher in the data gathering phase, the interviewees' response may have been affected.

References

Abdallah, F. & Elhoss, W. (2019). The Impact of Management by Objectives (MBO) on Organizational Outcome in a Digital World: A Case Study in the Aviation Industry: Vol 358. *Digital Econnomy. Emerging Technologies and Business Innovation*. Springer.

Aguinis, H. (2013). *Performance Management*. Boston: Pearson.

Aguinis, H. & Pierce, C. A. (2008). Enhancing the relevance of organizational behavior by embracing performance management research. *Journal of Organizational Behavior: The International Journal of Industrial, Occupational and Organizational Psychology and Behavior*, *29*(1), 139–145.

Alphen, H. van, Drunen, R. van, Hendriks, I. & Veltkamp, C. (2010). *Functiemix in VO*. Amersfoort: CPS Onderwijsontwikkeling en advies

Anderson, C. (2010). Presenting and Evaluating Qualitative Research. *American Journal of Pharmaceutical Education*, *74*(8), 141. https://doi.org/10.5688/aj7408141

Andrews, R., Boyne, G. A. & Walker, R. M. (2006). Subjective and objective measures of organizational performance: An empirical exploration. *Public service performance: Perspectives on measurement and management*, 14–34.

Aplin, J., Schoderbek, C. & Schoderbek, P. (1979). Tough-monded Management by Objectives. *Human Resource Management*, *18*(2).

Appelbaum, E., Bailey, T., Berg, P., Kalleberg, A. L., & Bailey, T. A. (2000). *Manufacturing advantage: Why high-performance work systems pay off*. Cornell University Press.

Armstrong, M. (2006). *A Handbook of Human Resource Management Practice* (10th ed.). London: Kogan Page.

Armstrong, M., & Baron, A. (2000). *Performance management*. Kogan Page Limited.

Baarda, D., Goede, M. D. & Teunissen, J. (2009). Basisboek Kwalitatiefonderzoek, tweede druk. *Groningen/Houten: Noordhoff Uitgevers bv.*

Barber, M. & Mourshed, M. (2007). *How the World's Best-performing School Systems Come Out on Top*. Retrieved from: http://researchgate.net

Barrett, E. W. & Ben-Dov, O. (1967). Application of the lidar to air pollution measurements. *Journal of Applied Meteorology and Climatology*, *6*(3), 500–515.

Bonnema, B. (2020). *Interview by D. Linnartz*. August 20, 2020, Eindhoven.

Bosch, P., Ikkersheim, R., Rutten, F. & Simons, J. (2013). *Voortgezet ondervijs. Ho erg is het?* Universiteit Utrecht.

Boselie, P., Dietz, G., & Boon, C. (2005). Commonalities and contradictions in HRM and performance research. *Human resource management journal, 15*(3), 67–94.

Boxall, P. (2003). HR strategy and competitive advantage in the service sector. *Human Resource Management Journal, 13*(3), 5–20.

Bussemaker, J., Dekker, S., Zijl, J. van, Berg, H. van den, Dittrich, K., Veenstra, J. & Besten, R. den (2013). *Nationaal Onderwijsakkoord: De route naar geweldig onderwijs*. Den Haag: Ministerie van Onderwijs, Cultuur en Wetenschap.

Cardy, R. & Leonard, B. (2004). Performance Management: Concepts. *Skills, and Exercises, ME Sharpe, Armonk, NY, 163.*

Cardy, R. & Leonard, B. (2015). *Performance Management* (2nd ed.). New York: Routledge.

Cascio, W. F. (2006). Managing Human Resources: productivity, quality of work life, profits 7th Edition Tata McGraw-Hill. *Abnormal and Social Psychology*, *62*, 401–407.

Charmaz, K. (1983). The Grounded Theory Method: An Explication and Interpretation. In R. M. Emerson (Ed.), *Contemporary Field Research* (pp. 109–126). Boston: Little Brown.

Charmaz, K. (2006). *Constructing Grounded Theory* (1st ed.). Sage Publications, Inc.

Corbin, J. & Strauss, A. (2008). *Basics of Qualitative Research: Techniques and Procedures for Developing Grounded Theory* (3rd ed.). https://doi.org/10.4135/9781452230153

Drucker, P. (1954). What is a Business? *Practice of Management*, 33–48.

Drucker, P. F. (1976). What Results Should You Expect? A Users' Guide to MBO. *Public Administration Review, 36*(1), 12. https://doi.org/10.2307/974736

Engelshoven, I. van & Slob, A. (2019). *Aan de leraar*. Retrieved from: http://rijksoverheid.nl

Etikan, I., Musa, S. & Alkassim, R. (2016). Comparison of Convenience Sampling and Purposive Sampling. *American Journal of Theoretical and Applied Statistics*, *5*(1), 1. https://doi.org/10.11648/j.ajtas.20160501.11

Favero, N., Meier, K. J. & O'Toole, L. J. (2016). Goals, Trust, Participation, and Feedback: Linking Internal Management with Performance Outcomes. *Journal of Public Administration Research and Theory*, *26*(2), 327–343. https://doi.org/10.1093/jopart/muu044

Gibbs, G. (2012). *Grounded Theory, Coding and Computer-assisted Analysis* (2nd ed.). Bristol, UK: Policy Press.

Gruman, J. A. & Saks, A. M. (2011). Performance Management and Employee Engagement. *Human Resource Management Review*, *21*(2), 123–136. https://doi.org/10.1016/j.hrmr.2010.09.004

Grundy, T. (1998). Strategy implementation and project management. *International Journal of Project Management*, *16*(1), 43–50.

Guest, G., Namey, E. & Mitchell, M. (2013). *Collecting Qualitative Data: A Field Manual for Applied Research*. Los Angeles: Sage Publications.

Hood, Christopher. (1995). The "New Public Management" in the 1980s: Variations on a Theme. *Accounting, Organizations and Society*, *20*(2–3), 93–109. https://doi.org/10.1016/0361-3682(93)E0001-W

Inspectie van het Onderwijs. (2019). *De staat van het Onderwijs 2019*. Retrieved from: http://onderwijsinspectie.nl

Jiang, K., Lepak, D. P., Hu, J. & Baer, J. C. (2012). How Does Human Resource Management Influence Organizational Outcomes? A Meta-analytic Investigation of Mediating Mechanisms. *Academy of Management Journal*, *55*(6), 1264–1294. https://doi.org/10.5465/amj.2011.0088

Klau, R. (2013). How Google Sets Goals: OKRs. *Startup Lab Workshop*. Retrieved from https://www.youtube.com/watch?v=mJB83EZtAjc

Kleber, T. (1972). The Six Hardest Areas to Manage by Objectives. *Personnel Journal*, (August), 571–575.

Knies, E. & Leisink, P. (2014). Leadership Behavior in Public Organizations: A Study of Supervisory Support by Police and Medical Center Middle Managers. *Review of Public Personnel Administration*, *34*(2), 108–127. https://doi.org/10.1177/0734371X13510851

Knies, E. & Leisink, P. (2017). *De staat van strategisch personeelsbeleid (hrm) in het VO*. Universiteit Utrecht.

Knies, E. & Leisink, P. (2019). *Werk maken van strategisch hrm*. Universiteit Utrecht.

Lugo, J. (2012). Pugh Method: How to Decide between Different Designs? Retrieved from https://sites.nd.edu/jlugo/2012/09/24/pugh-method-how-to-decide-between-different-designs/

Marin-Garcia, J. & Martinez Tomas, J. (2016). Deconstructing AMO Framework: A Systematic Review. *Intangible Capital, 12*(4). Retrieved from https://www.intangiblecapital.org/index.php/ic/article/view/838/574

Mathison, S. (1988). Why Triangulate? *Educational Researcher, 17*(2), 13–17. https://doi.org/10.3102/0013189X017002013

Meier, K. J. (2010). Governance, Structure, and Democracy: Luther Gulick and the Future of Public Administration. *Public Administration Review, 70* (December), 284–291.

Merriam-Webster (n.d.). "Deduction" vs. "Induction" vs. "Abduction." Retrieved from Merriam-Webster website: https://libguides.newcastle.edu.au/researchmethods#

Ministry of Education Culture and Science (2009). *Regeling versterking van functiemix leraren VO in de Randstadregio's*. Retrieved from http://docplayer.nl/53074249-Regeling-versterking-van-functiemix-leraren-voortgezet-onderwijs-in-de-randstadregio-s.html

Ministry of Education Culture and Science (n.d.). *Lerarentekort voortgezet onderwijs*. Retrieved from https://www.rijksoverheid.nl/onderwerpen/werken-in-het-onderwijs/aanpak-tekort-aan-leraren/lerarentekort-voortgezet-onderwijs

Ministry of Education Culture and Science (2020). *Bijna een half miljard extra naar onderwijs*. Retrieved from https://www.rijksoverheid.nl/onderwerpen/werken-in-het-onderwijs/nieuws/2020/04/24/bijna-een-half-miljard-extra-naar-onderwijs

Niven, P. & Lamorte, B. (2016). *Objectives and Key Results*. Hoboken: Wiley.

OCW & VO-Council (2013). *Klaar voor de toekomst! Samenwerken aan onderwijskwaliteit; Sectorakkoord VO 2014-2017*. Retrieved from http://vo-raad.nl

OECD (2004). *Non-probability Sample*. Retrieved from https://stats.oecd.org/glossary/detail.asp?ID=5143

OECD (2010). *PISA 2009 What Makes a School Succesful? – Recources, Policies and Practices* (Volume IV). Retrieved from https://www.oecd.org/pisa/pisaproducts/48852721.pdf

O'Toole Jr, L. J. & Meier, K. J. (2011). *Public management: Organizations, governance, and performance*. Cambridge University Press.

Patton, M.Q. (1999). Enhancing the quality and credibility of qualitative analysis. *Health Sciences Research, 34*, 1189–1208.

Pink, D. H. (2009). *Drive: The Surprising Truth About What Motivates Us*. New York City: Riverhead Books.

Pulakos, E. D. (2004). *Performance Management*. Alexandria: SHRM Foundation.

Raijmakers, V. (2020). *Interview by D. Linnartz*. August 28, 2020, Eindhoven.

Scheepens, G. (2020). *Interview by D. Linnartz*. September 1, 2020, Eindhoven.

Scott, A. (2019). *Research Validity and Reliability*. Retrieved from https://www.youtube.com/watch?v=QN2oh2ZnFBs

Seyna, E. J. (1986). MBO: The Fad that Changed Management. *Long Range Planning, 19*(6), 116–123. https://doi.org/10.1016/0024-6301(86)90104-4

Siers, F. J. (2004). Methodisch ontwerpproces. In Volgens H. H. van den Kroonenberg (Ed.), *Methodisch ontwerpen* (pp. 875–896). Groningen: Noordhoff Uitgevers.

Swinkels, E. (2020). *Interview by D. Linnartz*. 18 August 2020, Eindhoven.

Torrington, D., Hall, L., Taylor, S. & Atkinson, C. (2014). Resource management. In *Human Resource Management* (9th ed.). https://doi.org/10.1017/CBO9781139062381.069

Velden, van der, M. (2020). *Interview by D. Linnartz*. September 3, 2020, Eindhoven.

Veugelers, W. & Schuitema, J. (2010). Grenzen aan de pedagogische taak van de docent: een verdeling van taken binnen de school en tussen school, ouders, jeugdzorg en politie. *Pedagogische Kwaliteit* (80).

Verhagen, T. (2020). *Interview by D. Linnartz*. 28 August 2020, Eindhoven.

VO-Council (2019). *Verplichte lerarenregister in ijskast*. Retrieved from https://www.vo-raad.nl/nieuws/verplichte-lerarenregister-in-ijskast

Wang, J. J., Jing, Y. Y., Zhang, C. F. & Zhao, J. H. (2009). Review on Multi-criteria Decision Analysis Aid in Sustainable Energy Decision-making. *Renewable and Sustainable Energy Reviews, 13*(9), 2263–2278. https://doi.org/10.1016/j.rser.2009.06.021

Wiese, D. S. & Buckley, M. R. (1998). The Evolution of the Process. *Journal of Management History (Archive), 4*(3), 233–249. MCB University Press, 1355-252X

Wollenweber, L. E. (2019). Research Methods. *Research Methods*, 30–31.

Wouters, T. (2020). *Interview by D. Linnartz*. 16 August 2020, Eindhoven.

Wright, P. M. & Boswell, W. R. (2002). Desegregating HRM: A Review and Synthesis of Micro and Macro Human Resource Management Research.

Journal of Management, *28*(3), 247–276. https://doi.org/10.1016/S0149-2063(02)00128-9

Yousaf, M. (n. d.). Explanatory Research Definition, Types, Comparison, Advantages and Disadvantages. Retrieved from Scholarship Fellow website: https://scholarshipfellow.com/explanatory-research-definition-types-comparison-advantages-disadvantages/

Zeiler, W. (2008). *Morphologic Multi Criteria Decision Support for Conceptual Integral Design of Flex(ible En)ergy Infrastructures.* Retrieved from http://researchgate.net

Zhou, H. & He, Y.-L. (2018). Comparative Study of OKR and KPI. *DEStech Transactions on Economics, Business and Management* (eced), 319–323. https://doi.org/10.12783/dtem/eced2018/23986

6. Open innovation by collaborative capabilities: A new vehicle to competitive advantage

Noor ul Ain & Ali Akbar Sohail

Abstract: Innovation has become the key driver to gain and sustain competitive advantage. Traditionally, a large number of companies had followed closed model of innovation. However, in this era of intense competition, the strategies of the closed model have proved to be insufficient. Presently, open innovation is a modern topic in the field of innovation management. This paper aims to provide a thorough understanding of open innovation processes to improve R & D efforts and innovative outcomes of firms and then to illustrate how to overcome the negative effects of open innovation by collaborative capabilities to be more innovative and competitive. In doing so, this paper explores the conceptual underpinnings regarding open innovation processes including the transition from closed to open innovation, several practices to be used and then discussing the role of collaborative capabilities to overcome the negative side of innovation. It is concluded that open innovation has been a worthwhile concept to be applied by various firms under different circumstances. In order to realize the potential benefits of open innovation in the face of environmental uncertainty and fast changing market needs, managers and practitioners need to acknowledge the necessity to develop collaborative capabilities for successful management of open innovation.

6.1 Introduction

Since last few decades, innovation has become the key driver for companies to grow, prosper and sustain competitive advantage and high profitability (Dahlander & Gann, 2010; Thomke, 2001; Zobel, 2017). This trend has shifted the question to focus from "Is innovation important?" to "What are the ways to innovate and how to manage the innovation process?" (Chesbrough et al., 2006; Naqshbandi & Jasimuddin, 2018). The societal and economical changes in the working patterns, improved mobility of knowledge workers (Chesbrough, 2003; Singh, Gupta, Busso & Kamboj, 2019), the shorter product life cycles (Gassmann, Enkel & Chesbrough, 2010; Henttonen & Lehtimäki, 2017), trends of agility, outsourcing and flexibility (Gassmann, 2006), high division of labor due to globalization (Patra & Krishna, 2015), the upsurge of innovative technologies for the collaboration in various geographical distances (Huizingh, 2011;

Jeon & Degravel, 2019), upgraded market institutions to trade ideas (Dahlander & Gann, 2010), high developmental cost of new technologies (Chesbrough, 2007; Lee et al., 2018), are the fundamental forces to cause breakup in the boundaries of innovation processes (Wu, Tsai & Chang, 2011).

Traditionally, numerous companies have followed closed model of innovation (Gassmann, 2006) and the innovation processes were controlled by the company itself and interactions with the external environment were limited (Herzog & Leker, 2010). However, the strategies of the closed model have proved to be insufficient for the effective pursuit of innovation. This is connected with an increase in the acquisition of external technologies to complement the existing core knowledge base of the firms by in-licensing and strategic alliances to obtain the right for the use of external knowledge (Almirall & Casadesus-Masanell, 2010; Beamish & Lupton, 2009; Cassiman & Veugelers, 2006; Teece, 1986). This stimulates the need to open up organizational innovation processes as well as the need for externally and internally developed technologies to create value and competitive advantage for the business (Bae & Chang, 2012; Neto & Rua, 2021).

Due to such developments, Chesbrough in 2003 has coined the term of "open innovation" to describe novel innovation processes with the help of which the firms extensively interact with their external environment, resulting in substantial amount of exploitation and exploration of external knowledge (Chesbrough, 2003; Sing et al., 2019). Open innovation has quickly became a crucial concern for both the researchers and practitioners and it has been extensively discussed in the literature of innovation management over the last decade (Dahlander & Gann, 2010, Lichtenthaler, 2011; Nguyen, Huang & Tian, 2021; Oumlil, Faouzi & Juiz, 2020). Open innovation is defined as "the use of purposive knowledge inflows and outflows for the acceleration of internal innovation along with the expansion of markets for external use of innovation, respectively" (Chesbrough et al., 2006).

According to Chesbrough, internal R & D as a precious strategic asset has been outdated now, as there is a fundamental shift in the ways by which companies generate and bring innovative ideas to the market (Chesbrough, 2003; Nguyen, Huang & Tian, 2021). Open innovation has been regarded as a shift in paradigm from "generating and keeping innovations internally" to "obtaining, integrating and collaborating external knowledge" (Chesbrough & Bogers, 2014). The companies like Procter & Gamble, Cisco or Deutsche Telekom have successfully generated enormous revenues along with improved R & D efficiency by innovations from external sources (Enkel et al., 2009; Chesbrough, Lettl & Ritter, 2018). Proctor & Gamble in 1999, by their "Connect and develop initiative", extended its innovation approach and access external sources (e. g. suppliers, customers and other stakeholders) for innovative ideas (Buecheler, Sieg, Füchslin & Pfeifer, 2010; Rousseau et al., 2016). Additionally, for the organizations that are in search of innovative ideas and new knowledge, crossing organizational boundaries has become a prerequisite to cope up with growing complexity and ferocious competition in the battle of innovation (Chesbrough et al., 2006; Lichtenthaler, 2011; Oumlil, Faouzi & Juiz, 2020).

Open innovation is a two-edged sword (Chesbrough & Bogers, 2014). On one hand, it facilitates the generation of new ideas, acquisition of new technologies and expansion of markets (Jeon & Degravel, 2019). On the other hand, it can increase collaboration costs, loss of innovation expertise and also eradicates the barriers to competition and ultimately can hurt the profits of organization (Enkel et al., 2009; Henttonen & Lehtimäki, 2017).

Laursten and Salter (2006) revealed that due to an increase in the depth and breadth of searching new ideas and knowledge by external sources enhanced performance outcomes can be reached (Hung & Chou, 2013; Zobel, 2017). But still the extant research results have been equivocal (West et al., 2014). Indeed, some research studies demonstrated negative relationship between innovation and performance (Sisodiya et al., 2013; Thornhill, 2006). In the same sense, research has also shown that patents marketability and R & D productivity is negatively influenced by openness (Caputo et al., 2016). Moreover, Du et al. (2014) revealed that R & D projects having science-based open innovation partnerships gained higher financial earnings, but the projects having market-based open innovation partnerships were unable to do so. Hence, extensive use of external sources of knowledge could lead towards performance deterioration and diseconomies (Gassmann et al., 2010; West et al., 2014).

Thus, openness which is adopted for the sake of innovative ideas and knowledge from external sources must account for various collaborative activities such as strategic alliances partnerships, joint ventures, network relations and research associations with a view to collaborate capabilities of various partners (Beamish & Lupton, 2009; Hosseini et al., 2017; Ring & Van de Ven, 1994). Accordingly, to cope with competitive pressures, the use of R & D alliances in order to complement internal R & D activities of the firm has become a frequent practice (Barbosa et al., 2021). At present, external collaboration is viewed and preferred as an appropriate approach for accompanying innovation activities (Lieshout et al., 2021; Powell, Koput & Doerr, 1996).

Therefore, factors such as high technological uncertainty, hyper market competition, increased organizational complexity have highlighted the necessity for innovative ideas and knowledge creation for organizational survival, which consequently made the role of collaboration more essential (Tyler, 2001). The fundamental view point of strategic alliances illustrates the inter-firm collaboration as a method to leverage the expertise of the firm along with acquisition of new and innovative competencies (Lichtenthaler, 2011; Segers, 2015; West et al., 2014). Strategic alliances basically provide interfaces by which various firms collaborate their capabilities and provide interactions with external environment to facilitate the acquisition of valuable external knowledge and innovative ideas (Dyer & Singh, 2004; Teece, 1992). Thus, the fundamental key to a firm's ability to innovate lies in the question how well the firm is able to incorporate, reconfigure and build internal and external capabilities in order to cope with fast changing environments (Hosseini et al., 2017; Teece, Pisano & Shuen, 1997). Collaborative capabilities are described as organizational processes with the help of which new knowledge is acquired and generated from external knowledge sources and combined with the internal R & D efforts (Kogut & Zander, 1992). Therefore, it is proposed that collaboration capabilities may act as meta-capability facilitating the integration and synthesis of both external and internal knowledge in this dynamic and complex environment (Battistella & Nonino, 2012). Moreover, collaboration capabilities act as a significant source for competitive advantage because these are rare, valuable, socially complex and inimitable competencies (Barney, 1991).

6.2 Research goals, research question and methods

On the basis of above arguments, the primary aim of this research was to provide a thorough understanding of open innovation processes to improve the R & D efforts and innovative outcomes of the firm and then to illustrate that how to overcome the negative effects of open innovation by collaborative capabilities to be innovative and effectively sustaining organizational competitive advantage. Therefore, this piece of research contributes to the existing literature by providing new insights regarding what "being open" means for an organization, consideration of which would make the firms better able to integrate innovative ideas from external sources and consequently firms could develop new innovative capabilities. At last, this study provides novel insights about the influence collaborative capabilities to combat the deleterious effects of open innovation. Finally, research limitations and future research avenues regarding the phenomenon are elaborated. This research addressed the following research question:

> *How the processes of open innovation can be effectively applied in the organization by collaborative capabilities in order to create or sustain a competitive advantage?*

The research methods are based on literature analyses combined with a hermeneutical approach.

6.3 Transition from a closed to an open model of innovation

Conventionally, large companies managed their innovation processes with the help of internal research and development departments (Herzog & Leker, 2010). Consequently, R & D departments were considered as valuable strategic assets by which competitive advantage could be achieved and sustained (Almirall & Casadesus-Masanell, 2010; Van de Vrande et al., 2009). Furthermore, huge investments and capabilities required for R & D have made it more difficult for other firms to enter in the market, thus creating barriers to entry (Bae & Chang, 2012). Likewise, large organizations internally explored, advanced, and commercialized technologies to take advantage of the innovation not only by improved products, processes and services, but also by radical innovations (Dries et al., 2014).

This kind of innovation process is called closed innovation, in which the knowledge and innovative ideas are explored and commercialized internally, and it has dominated the field of innovation for a long time (Chesbrough, 2003). The closed innovation model has been described by Henry Chesbrough (2003), as shown in Fig. 1. There are large numbers of projects in the research area of companies in the form of funnel-shaped waterproof membrane boundaries. But only a few projects have been shifted towards the development area (Chesbrough, 2003). Thus, illustrating that in the closed model of innovation, only few developments have become successful and then released to the market (Boscherini, 2012).

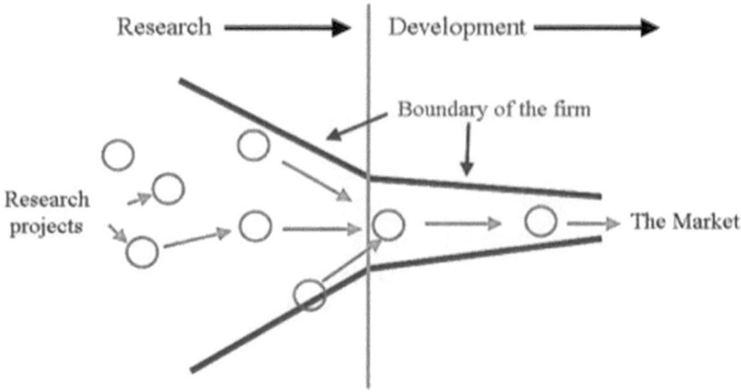

Fig. 1: Closed innovation model (Chesbrough, 2003)

At present, the context of innovation has been changed (Zobel, 2017). This is because performing internal research and development activities are often inadequate to generate innovative outcomes to be competitive (Hung & Chou, 2013). Thus, the development of new ideas, resources, expertise and technologies are needed for the creation of such an environment in which innovative outcomes can be generated by internal and external knowledge flows of the organization (Fey & Birkinshaw, 2005). Now, companies are needed to exchange ideas and knowledge with external sources such as suppliers, customers, stakeholders and even competitors to gain knowledge and ideas from these sources for the creation of innovative outcomes by information exchange (Ahmed et al., 2018; Lee et al., 2018).

The transition from a closed to a more open innovation model has been attributed to substantial alterations in the external competitive environment, for instance the intense global competition, increased uncertainty and dynamics, fast changing innovative advancement in technology and globalization of business markets (Bianchi et al., 2011; Patra & Krishna, 2015). Chesbrough (2003) has described the new paradigm for innovation, called "open innovation model", which is shown in Fig. 2. In the model of open innovation, the boundaries of the organization are considered to be more porous, thus enabling the knowledge and ideas from external sources to move easily inside as well as outside of the organization at different stages of innovation process (Jeon & Degravel, 2019).

In Netherlands almost 605 SMEs in the service sector have focused on the discovery of open innovation practices due to market issues such as to provide better customer services and to discover new market opportunities and segments (Van de Vrande et al., 2009). To do so, almost 31 % of companies have made joint ventures, 61 % of companies have integrated customers for the generation of ideas, acquiring innovative knowledge, attainment of additional resources, establishing industry standards and intensifying social networks with a view of reducing costs and sharing risk (Hoffmann & Schlosser, 2001). Additionally, a multiple case study of 13 SMEs was conducted by Henttonen and Lehtimäki (2017) in forestry sector in Finland. The study revealed that open innovation has been used by SMEs with a purpose of commercialization instead of research and development. Thus, open innovation goes beyond the battle of closed innovation model implying that there are various degrees of openness involving multiple external and internal technology sources and commercialization channels, thus open innovation can be done at various stages of the innovation cycle at varying degrees (Dahlander & Gann, 2010; West & Gallagher, 2006).

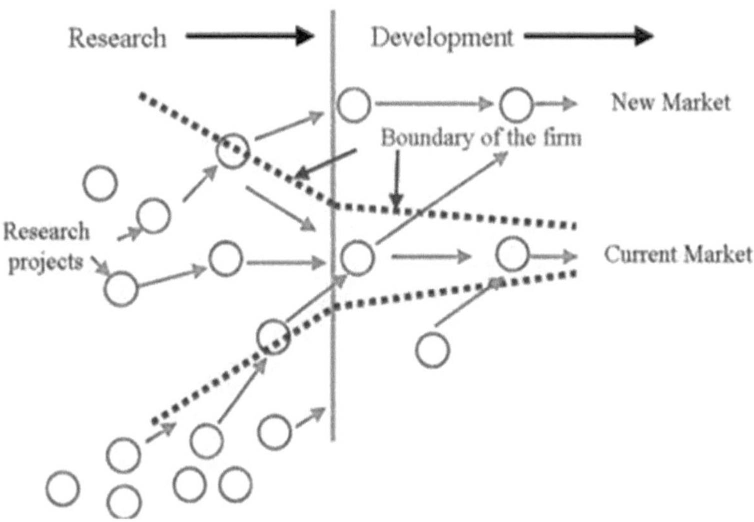

Fig. 2: Open innovation model (Chesbrough, 2003)

6.3.1 Open innovation definition

Chesbrough (2003) has captured two extremes of innovation (closed and open) and emphasized that for the purpose of technology advancement, the need is to use both internal and external ideas and paths to market. In 2006, Chesbrough et al. stated open innovation as "the purposive use of knowledge outflows and inflows to increase the pace of internal innovation along with the expansion of markets for the use of innovation externally, congruently" (Chesbrough, Vanhaverbeke & West, 2006). Moreover, external knowledge retention is also used by firms for maintaining the external knowledge over time, which is beyond the boundaries of organization (Lichtenthaler & Lichtenthaler, 2009). Therefore, open innovation could also be defined as "systematically carrying out exploration, exploitation and retention of knowledge within and beyond the boundaries of an organization during the course of the innovation process" (Lichtenthaler, 2011).

6.3.2 Classification of openness

The concept of open innovation is a relatively rich and ambiguous concept. A clear understanding of this concept is necessary for the development of effective frameworks of open innovation. The first vagueness which must be cleared is that open innovation must not be considered as a dichotomy (closed versus open), instead it should be viewed as a continuum having varying degrees of openness at one end and entirely closed at the other (Dahlander & Gann, 2010; Trott & Hartmann, 2009). Accordingly, the innovation processes can be positioned from the most open to the closest ones. Furthermore, the concept of open innovation is not only for the high technology industries but can be applied to low-tech industries as well for better functioning of such industries (Chesbrough, 2003). Although there is a wide range of activities associated with open innovation these can be broadly classified into two categories on the basis of the type of technology and the nature of knowledge flow, namely *technological exploitation* also called *outbound open innovation*, and *technological exploration* also known as *inbound open innovation* (Van de Vrande et al., 2008).

However, Gans and Stern (2003) emphasize that opening the company's borders to the external sources involves a high degree of risk. It fundamentally involves the risk of losing autonomy and difficulty in the commercialization of their internal innovative ideas due to trading of ideas (Gans & Stern, 2003). On the other hand, the technological exploitation comprises of the activities for the product development via out-licensing its technology (Lichtenthaler & Ernst, 2006). Texas Instruments, Dow Chemical and IBM are very famous examples which generate large profits (more than 50 % of their revenues) due to licensing of their innovations. Lichtenthaler (2009) demonstrated in his study of 136 industrial companies that opening boundaries of an organization on the road to the exploitation of technology often leads to positive organizational outcomes and higher profits. However, in case of large companies, technological exploration is seen as more fruitful and important than technological exploitation because of the fact that companies are scared of firming up their potential competitors due to their sold patents (Chesbrough & Brunswicker, 2013). Additionally, the decision regarding either to exploit the existing technological knowledge or to explore the new external knowledge for the generation of innovation would depend upon the type of innovation (i. e. process or product), and level of investment, uncertainty and involved risk (Chiaroni et al., 2011; Santamaría et al., 2010).

6.3.3 Inbound vs. outbound innovation

Inbound open innovation focuses on inward transfer of technology. It states the process of searching and assimilating the external knowledge by collaborating and networking with other organizations, for instance customers, universities, partners, suppliers, and other stakeholders for the development of innovative products and services along with in-house use of in-licensing (intellectual property licenses) (Chesbrough, 2007). By inbound open innovation, firms leverage the discoveries of others by the use of open innovation strategies which ultimately influence the internal R & D productivity of organization (Cassiman & Veugelers, 2006). Outbound open innovation denotes outward transfer of technology and it suggests exclusive commercialization of technology or in addition to its internal application in the form of out-licensing (Chesbrough & Crowther, 2006). The process of inbound open innovation basically states the use of external knowledge internally, whereas outbound open innovation denotes the outside exploitation of core knowledge of organization (Lichtenthaler & Ernst, 2006). This concerns three fundamental processes of knowledge including knowledge exploitation, retention and exploration which can be accomplished either internally or outside from the boundaries of organization (Lichtenthaler & Lichtenthaler, 2009).

There are multiple activities in both the outbound and inbound open innovation as Bianchi et al. (2011) have reported three such outbound and inbound activities including: (1) in and out licensing agreements, (2) supply and purchase of scientific and technical services, (3) non-equity strategic alliances. Moreover, empirical evidences from various studies have constantly reported that comparatively more inbound activities are performed by companies than outbound (Bianchi et al., 2011; Cheng & Huizingh, 2010; Chesbrough & Crowther, 2006), and found that these firms were not fully successful to capture the actual potential benefits of these activities (Van de Vrande et al., 2009, Chesbrough, 2003). For instance, only 10 % of the available technologies have been utilized by Procter & Gamble (Huston & Sakkab, 2006). Thus, for gaining substantial benefits, the combination of both exploration and exploitation is recommended, thereby integrating both the outbound and inbound open innovation (Gassmann et al., 2010).

6.3.4 Open innovation and performance

Another interesting issue regarding open innovation is its effects on firm performance. Tomlinson (2010) states that there is a positive impact of vertical collaboration on the innovative performance, but here the crucial point in such collaboration is the strength of these ties instead of their mere existence. However, a curvilinear relationship has been found by Laursen and Salter (2006) between performance and open innovation, implying that firm performance is offended by too much open innovation (Bigliardi et al., 2020), suggesting that not all activities of open innovation are equally beneficial for firm effectiveness (Caputo et al., 2016; Dahlander & Gann, 2010). Therefore, there could be a chain of effects of open innovation, ranging from immediate strategic consequences to the long-term one. For instance, outbound open innovation has strategic benefits including improving the technological position of the firm and getting access into the new markets (Lichtenthaler, 2007; Nagaoka & Kwon, 2006). Moreover, outbound open innovation could generate positive effects on the immediate (short term) profits but may have negative consequences on the long-term profits (Drucker, 2014; Helm et al., 2019).

Furthermore, even after adopting the open innovation processes, firms are unable to enhance the performance. Therefore, it is important to identify and scrutinize the causes of failure that either the firm has implemented open innovation approach imperfectly or open innovation was not the right approach for that particular firm (Vanhaverbeke et al., 2008). Keupp and Gassmann (2009) revealed the transaction costs related to the use of knowledge from external sources and considerations of intellectual property as the crucial factors which could negatively affect the achievability of better performance by open innovation.

6.4 Processes of open innovation

Two processes for open innovation have been suggested by Huizingh (2011) while moving towards open innovation: first, the fundamental transition process which leads towards open innovation, i.e. the opening up of previously closed processes of innovation; second, practices to be adopted for open innovation.

6.4.1 On the way to open innovation

The process of transition shows the details of steps involved from closed to open innovation by which the innovation process is opened up by the firm. Open innovation generally starts by outsourcing agreements with service organizations, backed by new strategic means of innovation (Gassmann et al., 2010; Rousseau et al., 2016). The research study of Chiaroni et al. (2011) in four Italian firms recognized that open innovation implementation involves a three stage process namely moving, unfreezing and institutionalizing, by which the changes are needed to be made in four dimensions of organizations, i. e. organizational structures, networks, knowledge management systems and evaluation processes, when moving from closed to open innovation (Urbinati et al., 2020).

6.4.2 Practices of open innovation

The second process comprises the open innovation practices how open innovation should be implemented. Managers need to take several new decisions when moving towards open innovation in exploiting and exploring the activities of innovation. Hereby the basic decisions are concerning the following questions: in what ways, how, when, with what purpose and with whom the organization should collaborate to acquire external knowledge and technology?

The external sources should include all stakeholders, i. e. customers, suppliers, research institutions, direct and indirect competitors, and other firms in different industries either having solutions to particular company's problems that can increase the innovative outcomes of the company or these can also exploit different solutions and technologies which are developed by the company (Chesbrough et al., 2018). The time period for such collaborations may vary depending upon the purpose of collaboration. For instance, these can be ended after a significant period, e. g. when developing a new technology jointly, but they may be repeated for some other technologies by involving other organizations (Huizingh, 2011). Moreover, different collaborations might have different initiators depending upon the purpose of knowledge acquisition and consisted of different departments of the firm, not just the R & D (Bissola et al., 2017). Van de Vrande et al. (2009) distinguished between the processes of technology exploitation and technology exploration and suggested various practices such as the use of inter-organizational networks in innovation processes, IP licensing to and from other organizations, customers and employees involvement, outsourcing of R & D and venturing.

Another model proposed by Fetterhoff and Voelkel (2006) discusses five stages for innovation processes including pursuing opportunities, assessing the creativity and market potential of such opportunities, engaging potential partners for development, commercializing the innovation to capture value and advancing the offerings of innovation (Ettabaa et al., 2019). Wallin and von Krogh (2010) describe the creation of effective governance tools as a crucial phase to manage the projects of open innovation. This phase includes various important governance issues such as the selection of partners, assessment of their contributions, profits and losses distribution, intellectual property ownership, conflict management and team based decision making (Wallin & von Krogh, 2010). Moreover, another very crucial and time consuming practice in open innovation is establishing partnerships. Here the fundamental question to think about is either partnership should be managed by the firms themselves or with the help of a third party. An intermediated network model has been proposed by Lee et al. (2010), in which the network is organized by an intermediary to build and maintain trustworthy links between network organizations. Collective research centres can also be used as intermediary for building absorptive capacities between different client firms in order to facilitate the process of open innovation (inbound and outbound) (Bissola et al., 2017; Spithoven et al., 2010).

6.5 Open innovation as a source of competitive advantage

6.5.1 General remarks

Moving from closed to open innovation has become a prerequisite to create innovative outcomes (Bae & Chang, 2012; Neto & Rua, 2021; Sing et al., 2019). The fundamental motive to rely on external knowledge sources is to complement internal R & D efforts, technology advancement and improvement of knowledge related capabilities (Lieshout et al., 2021) in order to create synergies and facilitate organizational learning (Muthusamy & White, 2005). However, the knowledge exploration and exploitation by external sources is quite challenging as it might create exclusive coordination and collaboration challenges such as alignment of conflicting interests of partners. Moreover, innovative knowledge and ideas are mostly tending to be composite and frequently tacit in nature, therefore knowledge acquisition and sharing entails the development of certain organizational mechanisms (Antikainen et al., 2010). Dyer and Singh (2004) conceptualized the above concerns as the *willingness and ability* of partners to integrate and collaborate knowledge based resources effectively. Thus, collaborative capability may provide a significant solution for coordination challenges during knowledge exploration and exploitation in open innovation.

6.5.2 Collaborative capabilities

The presence of particular collaborative capabilities can assist the explanation regarding the question why few firms perform better in the process of open innovation than others. Collaboration capabilities basically facilitate the internal or external acquisition and development of new capabilities and even assist the replacement of the old capabilities (Hosseini et al., 2017). These may be seen as a key part of the transformational capacity of a firm (Garud & Nayar, 1994) which basically refers to the capacity of a firm to constantly redefine its product and services portfolio on the basis of technological opportunities and advancement generated inside the organization (Tyler, 2001).

Thereby, the collaborative capability is described by Knudsen and Nielsen (2010), as a dynamic capability involving interactions between organizational level resources (structural, strategic, physical) and individual level resources (human capabilities and competences). Hence, the collaborative capabilities are significant and worthwhile only if these effectively integrate and influence the mechanisms of an organization to foster open innovation by governing the inter-firm relationships (Cheng & Chen, 2013). Geringer (1991) illustrated that collaborative capabilities consist of forming of pre-alliance procedures for the assessment of fit between strategic objectives (i. e. innovation) and objectives of other partners. Henderson and Cockburn (1994) exemplified that collaborative capabilities consist of the formation of post-alliance procedures signifying the speed of knowledge transfer and developing effective ways for creating synergies among dispersed and complex tacit knowledge resources. Therefore, it is proposed that collaboration capabilities may act as meta-capability facilitating the integration and synthesis of both external and internal knowledge according to the fast changing needs in dynamic and complex environment.

Moreover, research has demonstrated that collaboration has high effects on performance (Miller & Shamsie, 1996). More precisely, collaboration capability seems to be a crucial capability in a network economy to gain competitive advantage. The presence of collaborative capabilities has been studied by many scholars although with various labels i.e. collaborative know-how (Simonin, 1997), combinative capabilities (Kogut & Zander, 1992), alliance capabilities (Heimeriks & Duysters, 2007), meta-capability which leads towards dynamic capabilities (Blomqvist & Seppänen, 2003), relational capability (Dyer & Singh, 2004). All of these studies have suggested that good management of alliance signifies a distinctive capability or resource which has positive impact on performance (Anand & Khanna, 2000). According to resource based view (RBV), there are bundles of resources and capabilities which are distributed among the firms heterogeneously (Wernerfelt, 1984) and with the help of which competitive advantage can be created which is valuable, rare, non-substitutable and inimitable (Barney, 1991). This kind of competitive advantage can be achieved by creating and managing dynamic capabilities (Cheng & Chen, 2013; Eisenhardt & Martin, 2000; Teece, et al., 1997). Moreover, critical resources of the firms as characterized by RBV are; human (i-e firm specific knowledge, expertise and experience), physical (i-e firm specific assets and equipment), and organizational (i-e organizational structure, culture, R & D department), by which value can be captured to attain competitive advantage (Barney, 1986). Just like, Kogut and Zander (1992) coin the term "collaborative or combinative capabilities" in order to define processes of organization by which organizations acquire, combine, synthesize and create new ideas and knowledge from external sources of knowledge to gain competitive advantage. Unsuccessful innovation coalitions and alliances frequently fail just because that these are not collaboratively developed or exploited (Miles et al., 2000). Hence, collaborative capability can be seen as a catalyst for the development of dynamic and technological capabilities of the firm (Blomqvist & Seppänen, 2003; Tyler, 2001), which consequently may become a source of sustainable competitive advantage (Miles et al., 2006).

6.6 Discussion and conclusion

Open innovation has quickly became the important matter of concern for both researchers and practitioners and has been extensively discussed in the literature of innovation management over the last decade. Such as, openness to the external environment for the exploration and exploitation of new ideas improves innovation performance of the firm and it has become a superior practice as compared to in-house, closed and internal focus of generation of innovative ideas (Chesbrough, 2003). Internal R & D as a precious strategic asset has been outdated now, as there is a fundamental shift in the ways by which companies generate and bring innovative ideas to the market (Ahmed et al., 2018; Chesbrough et al., 2006). Moreover, the organizations that are in search of innovative ideas and new knowledge, crossing organizational boundaries has become a prerequisite to effectively cope with growing complexity and ferocious competition in the battle of innovation (Ettabaa et al., 2019).

Therefore, this research aimed to provide a thorough understanding of the open innovation processes to improve the R & D efforts and innovative outcomes of the firm. For doing so, theoretical background regarding open and closed innovation models has been presented and then the concept of innovation is further elaborated by classification of openness in the form of inbound and outbound innovation to clarify certain activities of open innovation. Afterwards, the effects of open innovation on the performance of the firm are discussed to clarify the potential benefits of open innovation. Subsequently, two processes for open innovation as suggested by Huizingh (2011) are discussed to shed light on the conditions and suitable time for opening up the processes for innovation along with an explanation of the ways by which open innovation must be done to enjoy maximum potential benefits. Finally, the role of collaboration capabilities to facilitate the successful adoption of open innovation is elaborated.

In sum, it is concluded that open innovation has been a worthwhile concept to be applied by various firms to achieve organizational objectives. Still, the knowledge gain from external sources only complements the internal R & D efforts therefore these must not be considered as a substitute for the internal capabilities of the firm for the management of open innovation process (Bissola et al., 2017). Thus, the managers and practitioners must acknowledge the necessity to develop collaborative capabilities for the successful management of open innovation and to advance the pace of overall innovation process. The future research can focus on the development of an integrated framework that clearly depicts and facilitates the managers in decision making regarding which open innovation practices needed to be deployed and quantitatively identify the activities where collaborative capabilities are more fruitful to capture maximum value by collaboration during the process of open innovation.

References

Ahmed, S., Halim, H. A. & Ahmad, N. H. (2018). Open and closed innovation and enhanced performance of SME hospitals – A conceptual model. *Business Perspectives and Research*, *6*(1), 1–12.

Almirall, E. & Casadesus-Masanell, R. (2010). Open versus closed innovation: A model of discovery and divergence. *Academy of Management Review*, *35*(1), 27–47.

Anand, B. N. & Khanna, T. (2000). Do firms learn to create value? The case of alliances. Strategic *management journal*, *21*(3), 295–315.

Antikainen, M., Mäkipää, M., & Ahonen, M. (2010). Motivating and supporting collaboration in open innovation. *European Journal of Innovation Management*, *13*(1), 100–119.

Bae, Y. & Chang, H. (2012). Efficiency and effectiveness between open and closed innovation: empirical evidence in South Korean manufacturers. *Technology Analysis & Strategic Management*, *24*(10), 967–980.

Barbosa, A. P. F. P. L., Salerno, M. S., de Souza Nascimento, P. T., Albala, A., Maranzato, F. P. & Tamoschus, D. (2021). Configurations of project management practices to enhance the performance of open innovation R & D projects. *International Journal of Project Management, 39*(2), 128–138.

Barney, J. (1991). Firm resources and sustained competitive advantage. *Journal of Management, 17*(1), 99–120.

Barney, J. B. (1986). Strategic factor markets: Expectations, luck, and business strategy. *Management Science, 32*(10), 1231–1241.

Battistella, C. & Nonino, F. (2012). Open innovation web-based platforms: The impact of different forms of motivation on collaboration. *Innovation, 14*(4), 557–575.

Beamish, P. W. & Lupton, N. C. (2009). Managing joint ventures. *Academy of Management Perspectives, 23*(2), 75–94.

Bianchi, M., Cavaliere, A., Chiaroni, D., Frattini, F. & Chiesa, V. (2011). Organisational modes for Open Innovation in the bio-pharmaceutical industry: An exploratory analysis. *Technovation, 31*(1), 22–33.

Bigliardi, B., Ferraro, G., Filippelli, S., & Galati, F. (2020). The influence of open innovation on firm performance. *International Journal of Engineering Business Management, 12*, 1–14.

Bissola, R., Imperatori, B. & Biffi, A. (2017). A rhizomatic learning process to create collective knowledge in entrepreneurship education: Open innovation and collaboration beyond boundaries. *Management Learning, 48*(2), 206–226.

Blomqvist, K. & Seppänen, R. (2003). Bringing together the emerging theories on trust and dynamic capabilities–collaboration and trust as focal concepts. In *IMP Conference Proceedings. 4th–6th September. Lugano, Switzerland* (1–25).

Boscherini, L., Chiaroni, D., Chiesa, V. & Frattini, F. (2012). How to integrate open and closed innovation. *International Journal of Entrepreneurship and Innovation Management, 16*(3–4), 226–244.

Buecheler, T., Sieg, J. H., Füchslin, R. M. & Pfeifer, R. (2010, August). Crowdsourcing, open innovation and collective intelligence in the scientific method – A research agenda and operational framework. *ALIFE*, 679–686.

Caputo, M., Lamberti, E., Cammarano, A. & Michelino, F. (2016). Exploring the impact of open innovation on firm performances. *Management Decision, 54*(7), 1788–1812.

Cassiman, B. & Veugelers, R. (2006). In search of complementarity in innovation strategy: Internal R & D and external knowledge acquisition. *Management Science, 52*(1), 68–82.

Cheng, C. C. & Chen, J. S. (2013). Breakthrough innovation: the roles of dynamic innovation capabilities and open innovation activities. *Journal of Business & Industrial Marketing, 28*(5), 444–454.

Cheng, C. & Huizingh, K. R. E. (2010, June). Open innovation to increase innovation performance: evidence from a large survey. In *2010. Proceedings of the XXI ISPIM International Conference, Bilbao, Spain,* 6, 9.

Chesbrough, H. (2003). The logic of open innovation: managing intellectual property. *California management review, 45*(3), 33–58.

Chesbrough, H. W. (2007). Why companies should have open business models. *MIT Sloan Management Review, 48*(2), 22–28.

Chesbrough, H. & Bogers, M. (2014). Explicating open innovation: Clarifying an emerging paradigm for understanding innovation. *New Frontiers in Open Innovation. Oxford: Oxford University Press,* 3–28.

Chesbrough, H. & Brunswicker, S. (2013). *Managing open innovation in large firms*. Fraunhofer Verlag.

Chesbrough, H. & Crowther, A. K. (2006). Beyond high tech: early adopters of open innovation in other industries. *R & D Management, 36*(3), 229–236.

Chesbrough, H., Lettl, C. & Ritter, T. (2018). Value creation and value capture in open innovation. *Journal of Product Innovation Management, 35*(6), 930–938.

Chesbrough, H., Vanhaverbeke, W. & West, J. (Eds.). (2006). *Open innovation: Researching a new paradigm*. OUP Oxford.

Chiaroni, D., Chiesa, V. & Frattini, F. (2011). The Open Innovation Journey: How firms dynamically implement the emerging innovation management paradigm. *Technovation, 31*(1), 34–43.

Dahlander, L. & Gann, D. M. (2010). How open is innovation? *Research Policy, 39*(6), 699–709.

Dries, L., Pascucci, S., Török, Á. & Tóth, J. (2014). Keeping your secrets public? Open versus closed innovation processes in the Hungarian wine sector. *International Food and Agribusiness Management Review, 17*(1), 147–162.

Drucker, P. (2014). *Innovation and entrepreneurship*. Routledge.

Du, J., Leten, B. & Vanhaverbeke, W. (2014). Managing open innovation projects with science-based and market-based partners. *Research Policy, 43*(5), 828–840.

Dyer, J. H. & Singh, H. (2004). The relational view: Cooperative strategy and sources of interorganizational competitive advantage. In Jeffrey J. Reuer (Ed.), *Strategic alliances. theory and evidence.* OUP Oxford.

Eisenhardt, K. M. & Martin, J. A. (2000). Dynamic capabilities: What are they? *Strategic Management Journal, 21*(10–11), 1105–1121.

Enkel, E., Gassmann, O. & Chesbrough, H. (2009). Open R & D and open innovation: exploring the phenomenon. *R & D Management, 39*(4), 311–316.

Ettabaa, R., Bouami, D. & Elfezazi, S. (2019, June). Open Innovation from Chesbrough to now: where do we stand today?: An exploratory review of Open Innovation Model. In *2019 International Colloquium on Logistics and Supply Chain Management (LOGISTIQUA)* (pp. 1–7). IEEE.

Fetterhoff, T. J. & Voelkel, D. (2006). Managing open innovation in biotechnology. *Research-Technology Management, 49*(3), 14–18.

Fey, C. F. & Birkinshaw, J. (2005). External sources of knowledge, governance mode, and R & D performance. *Journal of Management, 31*(4), 597–621.

Gans, J. S. & Stern, S. (2003). The product market and the market for "ideas": commercialization strategies for technology entrepreneurs. *Research Policy, 32*(2), 333–350.

Garud, R. & Nayyar, P. R. (1994). Transformative capacity: Continual structuring by intertemporal technology transfer. *Strategic Management Journal, 15*(5), 365–385.

Gassmann, O. (2006). Opening up the innovation process: Towards an agenda. *R & D Management, 36*(3), 223–228.

Gassmann, O., Enkel, E. & Chesbrough, H. (2010). The future of open innovation. *R & D Management, 40*(3), 213–221.

Geringer, J. M. (1991). Strategic determinants of partner selection criteria in international joint ventures. *Journal of International Business Studies*, 41–62.

Heimeriks, K. H. & Duysters, G. (2007). Alliance capability as a mediator between experience and alliance performance: an empirical investigation into the alliance capability development process. *Journal of Management Studies, 44*(1), 25–49.

Helm, R., Endres, H. & Hüsig, S. (2019). When and how often to externally commercialize technologies? A critical review of outbound open innovation. *Review of Managerial Science, 13*(2), 327–345.

Henderson, R. & Cockburn, I. (1994). Measuring competence? Exploring firm effects in pharmaceutical research. *Strategic Management Journal, 15*(S1), 63–84.

Henttonen, K. & Lehtimäki, H. (2017). Open innovation in SMEs: Collaboration modes and strategies for commercialization in technology-intensive companies in forestry industry. *European Journal of Innovation Management, 20*(2), 329 –347.

Herzog, P. & Leker, J. (2010). Open and closed innovation–different innovation cultures for different strategies. *International Journal of Technology Management, 52*(3/4), 322–343.

Hoffmann, W. H. & Schlosser, R. (2001). Success factors of strategic alliances in small and medium-sized enterprises – An empirical survey. *Long Range Planning, 34*(3), 357–381.

Hosseini, S., Kees, A., Manderscheid, J., Röglinger, M. & Rosemann, M. (2017). What does it take to implement open innovation? Towards an integrated capability framework. *Business Process Management Journal, 23*(1), 87–107.

Huizingh, E. K. (2011). Open innovation: State of the art and future perspectives. *Technovation, 31*(1), 2–9.

Hung, K. P. & Chou, C. (2013). The impact of open innovation on firm performance: The moderating effects of internal R & D and environmental turbulence. *Technovation, 33*(10–11), 368–380.

Huston, L. & Sakkab, N. (2006). Connect and develop. *Harvard Business Review, 84*(3), 58–66.

Jeon, R. H. S. & Degravel, D. (2019). Open Innovation, a Tool for Globalization: The Case of South Korean SMEs. *Journal of Management Policy and Practice, 20*(2), 51–74.

Keupp, M. M. & Gassmann, O. (2009). Determinants and archetype users of open innovation. *R & D Management, 39*(4), 331–341.

Knudsen, L. G. & Nielsen, B. B. (2010). Collaborative capability in R & D alliances: exploring the link between organisational-and individual-level factors. *International Journal of Knowledge Management Studies, 4*(2), 152–175.

Kogut, B. & Zander, U. (1992). Knowledge of the firm, combinative capabilities, and the replication of technology. *Organization Science, 3*(3), 383–397.

Laursen, K. & Salter, A. (2006). Open for innovation: The role of openness in explaining innovation performance among UK manufacturing firms. *Strategic Management Journal, 27*(2), 131–150.

Lee, M., Yun, J. J., Pyka, A., Won, D., Kodama, F., Schiuma, G., … & Zhao, X. (2018). How to respond to the fourth industrial revolution, or the second information technology revolution? Dynamic new combinations between technology, market, and society through open innovation. *Journal of Open Innovation: Technology, Market, and Complexity, 4*(3), 21–40.

Lee, S., Park, G., Yoon, B. & Park, J. (2010). Open innovation in SMEs – An intermediated network model. *Research Policy, 39*(2), 290–300.

Lichtenthaler, U. (2007). The drivers of technology licensing: An industry comparison. *California management review, 49*(4), 67–89.

Lichtenthaler, U. (2009). Outbound open innovation and its effect on firm performance: examining environmental influences. *R & D Management*, *39*(4), 317–330.

Lichtenthaler, U. (2011). Open innovation: Past research, current debates, and future directions. *The Academy of Management Perspectives*, *25*(1), 75–93.

Lichtenthaler, U. & Ernst, H. (2006). Attitudes to externally organising knowledge management tasks: a review, reconsideration and extension of the NIH syndrome. *R & D Management*, *36*(4), 367–386.

Lichtenthaler, U. & Lichtenthaler, E. (2009). A capability-based framework for open innovation: Complementing absorptive capacity. *Journal of Management Studies*, *46*(8), 1315–1338.

Miles, R. E., Miles, G. & Snow, C. C. (2006). Collaborative entrepreneurship: a business model for continuous innovation. *Organizational Dynamics*, *35*(1), 1–11.

Miles, R. E., Snow, C. C. & Miles, G. (2000). The Future. org. *Long Range Planning*, *33*(3), 300–321.

Miller, D. & Shamsie, J. (1996). The resource-based view of the firm in two environments: The Hollywood film studios from 1936 to 1965. *Academy of Management Journal*, *39*(3), 519–543.

Muthusamy, S. K. & White, M. A. (2005). Learning and knowledge transfer in strategic alliances: a social exchange view. *Organization Studies*, *26*(3), 415–441.

Nagaoka, S. & Kwon, H. U. (2006). The incidence of cross-licensing: A theory and new evidence on the firm and contract level determinants. *Research Policy*, *35*(9), 1347–1361.

Naqshbandi, M. M. & Jasimuddin, S. M. (2018). Knowledge-oriented leadership and open innovation: Role of knowledge management capability in France-based multinationals. *International Business Review*, *27*(3), 701–713.

Neto, F. M. & Rua, O. L. (2021). Impact of Open Innovation in the Competitive Advantage of Hotels. In *International Workshop Tourism and Hospitality Management* (p. 19).

Nguyen, T. P. T., Huang, F. & Tian, X. (2021). A meta-analysis of the impact of open innovation on performance. *Journal of Management & Organization*, 1–18.

Oumlil, R., Faouzi, H. & Juiz, C. (2020). Uncovering Two Decades of Open Innovation Benefits: A Qualitative Meta-Analysis. *International Journal of Innovation and Technology Management*, *17*(08), 2030006.

Patra, S. K. & Krishna, V. V. (2015). Globalization of R & D and open innovation: linkages of foreign R & D centers in India. *Journal of Open Innovation: Technology, Market, and Complexity*, *1*(1), 7.

Pisano, G., Shuen, A. & Teece, D. (1997). Dynamic capabilities and strategic management. *Strategic Management Journal, 18*(7), 509–533.

Powell, W. W., Koput, K. W., & Smith-Doerr, L. (1996). Interorganizational collaboration and the locus of innovation: Networks of learning in biotechnology. *Administrative science quarterly, 41*(1), 116–145.

Ring, P. S. & Van de Ven, A. H. (1994). Developmental processes of cooperative interorganizational relationships. *Academy of Management Review, 19*(1), 90–118.

Rousseau, M. B., Mathias, B. D., Madden, L. T. & Crook, T. R. (2016). Innovation, firm performance, and appropriation: A meta-analysis. *International Journal of Innovation Management, 20*(03), 1650033.

Santamaría, L., Nieto, M. J. & Barge-Gil, A. (2010). The relevance of different open innovation strategies for R & D performers. *Cuadernos de Economía y Dirección de la Empresa, 13*(45), 93–114.

Segers, J. P. (2015). The interplay between new technology based firms, strategic alliances and open innovation, within a regional systems of innovation context. The case of the biotechnology cluster in Belgium. *Journal of Global Entrepreneurship Research, 5*(1), 1–17.

Simonin, B. L. (1997). The importance of collaborative know-how: An empirical test of the learning organization. *Academy of Management Journal, 40*(5), 1150–1174.

Singh, S. K., Gupta, S., Busso, D. & Kamboj, S. (2019). Top management knowledge value, knowledge sharing practices, open innovation and organizational performance. *Journal of Business Research, 128*, 788 –798.

Sisodiya, S. R., Johnson, J. L. & Grégoire, Y. (2013). Inbound open innovation for enhanced performance: Enablers and opportunities. *Industrial Marketing Management, 42*(5), 836–849.

Spithoven, A., Frantzen, D. & Clarysse, B. (2010). Heterogeneous Firm-Level Effects of Knowledge Exchanges on Product Innovation: Differences between Dynamic and Lagging Product Innovators*. *Journal of Product Innovation Management, 27*(3), 362–381.

Teece, D. J. (1986). Profiting from technological innovation: Implications for integration, collaboration, licensing and public policy. *Research Policy, 15*(6), 285–305.

Teece, D. J. (1992). Competition, cooperation, and innovation: Organizational arrangements for regimes of rapid technological progress. *Journal of Economic Behavior & Organization, 18*(1), 1–25.

Teece, D. J., Pisano, G. & Shuen, A. (1997). Dynamic capabilities and strategic management. *Strategic Management Journal, 18*(7), 509–533.

Thomke, S. 2001. Enlightened experimentation – the new imperative for innovation. *Harvard Business Review*, 79(2), 66–75.

Thornhill, S. (2006). Knowledge, innovation and firm performance in high-and low-technology regimes. *Journal of Business Venturing*, *21*(5), 687–703.

Tomlinson, P. R. (2010). Co-operative ties and innovation: Some new evidence for UK manufacturing. *Research Policy*, *39*(6), 762–775.

Trott, P. & Hartmann, D. A. P. (2009). Why "open innovation" is old wine in new bottles. *International Journal of Innovation Management*, *13*(04), 715–736.

Tyler, B. B. (2001). The complementarity of cooperative and technological competencies: a resource-based perspective. *Journal of Engineering and Technology Management*, *18*(1), 1–27.

Urbinati, A., Chiaroni, D., Chiesa, V. & Frattini, F. (2020). The role of digital technologies in open innovation processes: an exploratory multiple case study analysis. *R & D Management*, *50*(1), 136–160.

Van de Vrande, V., De Jong, J. P., Vanhaverbeke, W. & De Rochemont, M. (2009). Open innovation in SMEs: Trends, motives and management challenges. *Technovation*, *29*(6–7), 423–437.

van Lieshout, J. W., van der Velden, J. M., Blomme, R. J. & Peters, P. (2021). The interrelatedness of organizational ambidexterity, dynamic capabilities and open innovation: a conceptual model towards a competitive advantage. *European Journal of Management Studies*, *26*(2/3), 39–62.

Vanhaverbeke, W., Van de Vrande, V. & Chesbrough, H. (2008). Understanding the advantages of open innovation practices in corporate venturing in terms of real options. *Creativity and innovation management*, *17*(4), 251–258.

Wallin, M. W. & Von Krogh, G. (2010). Organizing for open innovation: Focus on the integration of knowledge. *Organizational Dynamics*, *39*(2), 145–154.

Wernerfelt, B. (1984). A resource-based view of the firm. *Strategic Management Journal*, *5*(2), 171–180.

West, J. & Gallagher, S. (2006). Challenges of open innovation: the paradox of firm investment in open-source software. *R & D Management*, *36*(3), 319–331.

West, J., Salter, A., Vanhaverbeke, W. & Chesbrough, H. (2014). Open innovation: The next decade. *Research Policy*, *43*(1), 805–811.

Wu, L. J., Tsai, C. T. & Chang, P. L. (2011). Dynamic open innovation model of research and development management for enterprise globalization. In *First International Technology Management Conference* (pp. 827–835). IEEE.

Zobel, A. K. (2017). Benefiting from open innovation: A multidimensional model of absorptive capacity. *Journal of Product Innovation Management*, *34*(3), 269–288.

7. Bruderhahnaufzucht für mehr Tierwohl: Verbot des Tötens männlicher Küken, Aufzucht männlicher Küken versus embryonale Früherkennung, Kosten-Nutzenanalyse, Grenzen der Umsetzung

Caspar von der Crone, Horst Lang & Markus Mau

Abstract: Ethik und Tierwohl führen in unserer Gesellschaft zum kritischen Nachdenken. Die tierische Veredlung stellt deshalb zunehmend höhere Anforderungen an Tierschutz, insbesondere im Geflügelsektor. Mit der Änderung des deutschen Tierschutzgesetzes ist die bisher übliche Praxis des Tötens männlicher Küken nach dem Schlupf verboten. Als Alternativen kommen duale Linien, die embryonale Früherkennung und die Aufzucht der männlichen Küken in Betracht. Letztere Variante ist aus ökonomischer Sicht aber alles andere als sinnvoll, denn die Züchtung von Hybriden ist auf eine hohe Legeleistung und nicht auf Fleischansatz ausgerichtet. Das betrifft auch Zweinutzungslinien.

Die Wirtschaft ist gefordert und die Analyse dieser Untersuchung konzentriert sich auf Lösungsansätze im Bereich der Legehennenhaltung. In den zurückliegenden Jahren hat es bereits gravierende Änderungen gegeben, wie zum Beispiel das Verbot der Käfighaltung. Entgegen den Voraussagen von Wirtschaftsbeteiligten hatte das jedoch keinerlei negative Auswirkungen auf das Marktgeschehen. Der Verbrauch ist wieder gestiegen und Vertrauen in das Produkt Ei zurückgekehrt. Dies beruht hauptsächlich darauf, dass Eier, bedingt durch hohe Cholesterinwerte, nicht mehr als gesundheitlich schädigend gesehen werden.

Tierwohl und Tierschutz stehen seit geraumer Zeit im Fokus der Öffentlichkeit. Die Produktionsmethoden wurden angepasst. Bemerkenswert ist die jüngste Initiative der EU-Kommission, nach dem Vorbild Geflügel auch ein Verbot der Käfighaltung bei Schweinen und Kälbern vorzugeben. Hierbei geht es ebenfalls um emotionale Aspekte und nicht um ökonomische Prinzipen. Das bestätigt erneut den großen Einfluss von Nichtregierungsorganisationen (NGOs) auf das Marktgeschehen und die Gesetzgebung. Wirtschaftliche Interessen spielen eine untergeordnete Rolle. Vielmehr geht es darum, dass Tiere artgerecht gehalten werden, letztendlich aber auch um eine Balance zwischen Wirtschaft und Verbrauchern herzustellen. Hierbei kommt es immer wieder zu unterschiedlichen Auslegungen des Begriffs „artgerecht".

Die Analyse im Bereich der Eierproduktion mit der Aufzucht männlicher Küken soll darstellen, dass ein Kompromiss bei den Ansprüchen möglich ist.

7.1 Ausgangssituation

Die Rechtsgrundlagen im Bereich der Eierproduktion haben sich in den letzten Jahren grundlegend geändert. Das führt zu strukturellen Veränderungen. Aus der ursprünglichen Massentierhaltung mit großen Käfiganlagen entstanden kleinere Betriebe mit Boden-, Freiland- und Biohaltung. Die prozentual größten Zuwachsraten verzeichnet der ökologische Bereich. Der Anteil beträgt bereits 15 %, insbesondere in Deutschland, Österreich und den Niederlanden ist die Tendenz steigend. Das Verbraucherverhalten orientiert sich zwar zunehmend in Richtung mehr Tierwohl, dem mit den neuen Haltungsanforderungen zusehends Rechnung getragen wird. Dennoch finden als Tierschutz ausgelobte Eier mit einem Marktanteil von weniger als 2 % bisher kein großes Interesse. Der Mehrwert und die Anforderungen sind für viele Konsumenten nicht transparent, während der ökologische Bereich mit zum Teil weitergehenden Vorgaben weitaus mehr Akzeptanz findet (von der Crone et al., 2018).

7.1.1 Gesetzliche Grundlagen

Die Neufassung des Tierschutzgesetzes verbietet mit Inkrafttreten der letzten Änderung vom 26. Juni 2021 das Töten männlicher Küken ab 2022 (Bundesgesetzblatt, 2021). Zweck dieses Gesetzes ist es, aus der Verantwortung des Menschen für das Tier als Mitgeschöpf dessen Leben und Wohlbefinden zu schützen. Niemand darf einem Tier ohne Grund Schmerzen, Leiden oder Schäden zufügen.

Die Verordnung (EU) 2018/848 des Europäischen Parlament und des Rates vom 30. Mai 2018 und die Durchführungsverordnung (EU) 2020/464 der Kommission vom 26. März 2020, die erst ab 1. Januar 2022 in Kraft treten, regeln die Vorgaben der Aufzucht und Mast von Geflügel im ökologischen Bereich. Erstmals werden damit auch Vorgaben für die Haltung und Aufzucht von Bruderhähnen aufgeführt.

Im konventionellen Bereich gelten für Geflügelfleisch die Vermarktungsnormen mit Durchführungsvorschriften der Verordnung (EG) Nr. 543/2008 der Kommission vom 16. Juni 2008 und für Eier ist die Verordnung (EG) Nr. 589/2008 der Kommission vom 23. Juni 2008 maßgebend. Grundlage ist die Verordnung des Rates über die einheitliche GMO Nr. 1234/2007 vom 22. Oktober 2007.

Die Durchführungsvorschriften zur Verordnung (EG) Nr. 1234/2007 des Rates hinsichtlich der Vermarktungsnormen sind für Eier und Geflügelfleisch maßgebend. Spezifische Anforderungen für die Aufzucht von Bruderhähnen und Kennzeichnungsvorgaben für die Vermarktung gibt es bisher nicht. Die

EU-Kommission überarbeitet allerdings die Rechtsgrundlagen und wird künftig entsprechende Regelungen implementieren.

Das Tierschutzgesetz und die Tierschutz-Nutztierhaltungs-Verordnung beinhalten Vorgaben für das Halten von Nutztieren zu Erwerbszwecken. Es handelt sich um deutsche Verordnungen und diese begründen nationale Bestimmungen, die im Wesentlichen sehr detaillierte Vorgaben für die tierische Erzeugung auf Basis des Tierschutzgesetzes beinhalten. Dazu gehört das flächendeckende Verbot des Kükentötens in Deutschland ab 1. Januar 2022. Ab Januar 2024 müssen die männlichen Küken aufgezogen werden, sofern keine Geschlechtsbestimmung bis zum 6. Tag erfolgt. Damit steht die Geflügelwirtschaft vor einer großen Herausforderung.

Darüber hinaus gelten für die Umsetzung der Bestimmungen spezifische Vorgaben der jeweiligen Verbände und der des Bundesministeriums für Ernährung und Landwirtschaft (BMEL, 2021) zur Umsetzung eines nationalen Tierwohlsiegels.

7.1.2 Untersuchungsziele und Hypothesen

Die Vorgaben des Tierschutzgesetzes beinhalten gravierende Restriktionen. Bisherige Grundsätze verlieren an Bedeutung und es müssen neue Strukturen geschaffen werden. Mit der embryonalen Früherkennung wäre das Problem gelöst, doch stehen die derzeitigen wissenschaftlichen Erkenntnisse im Widerspruch zu den Anforderungen der Tierschutzorganisationen und anderer NGOs. Während z. B. in Frankreich die embryonale Früherkennung ab dem 13. Tag bei sog. Braunlegern kein Problem darstellt, ist das in Deutschland und damit auch in den Niederlanden, die am deutschen Eiermarkt einen Anteil von 50 % haben, nicht vorstellbar. Tierschützer priorisieren wegen des möglichen Schmerzempfinden der Embryonen den 6. Tag oder früher. Mit der Anpassung des Tierschutzgesetzes wird dieser Forderung Rechnung getragen. Als Option werden außerdem die Aufzucht der männlichen Küken (Bruderhähne) oder Zweinutzungslinien favorisiert.

Die bisherigen Verfahren der embryonalen Früherkennung erreichen die Vorgabe nicht. Es gibt zwar im Versuchsstadium Möglichkeiten zur Geschlechtsbestimmung nach 3,5 bis 5,5 Tagen mit einer Messgenauigkeit für beide Geschlechter von über 95 %, die aber noch keine Praxisreife haben.

Die sich daraus ergebenden Untersuchungsziele der Arbeit gliedern sich in vier Bereiche, die im Folgenden näher beschrieben werden. Hervorzuheben sind vor allem die Möglichkeiten der Umsetzung und die wirtschaftliche Bedeutung.

Untersuchungsziel 1: Vorgaben und Optionen zur Aufzucht männlicher Küken
Untersuchungsziel 2: Möglichkeiten der embryonalen Früherkennung
Untersuchungsziel 3: Kosten-Nutzen-Analyse
Untersuchungsziel 4: Grenzen der Umsetzung

Ausgangspunkt für Hypothesen sind die Konsequenzen für die Geflügelwirtschaft durch die neuen gesetzlichen Anforderungen. Das hat Auswirkungen auf die Produktivität und erfordert ein konsequentes Umdenken der Marktbeteiligten.

Hypothese 1: Das neue Tierschutzgesetz mit dem Verbot des Tötens männlicher Küken führt zu einem Ungleichgewicht und zu Wettbewerbsverzerrungen im Bereich der Eierproduktion, verbunden mit Betriebsaufgaben im europäischen Handel.

Hypothese 2: Der Anteil aus deutscher Erzeugung schrumpft zu Gunsten ausländischer Mitbewerber. Die Verbraucher sind nicht bereit, die höheren Kosten beim Einkauf zu tragen.

Hypothese 3: Der ökonomische Nutzen ist fraglich, dennoch bieten sich Optionen und es erfolgt eine Neuorientierung, der Verbrauch steigt und der Markt profitiert von den neuen Vorgaben.

7.2 Literaturrecherche und Datenanalyse

7.2.1 Vorgaben und Optionen zur Aufzucht männlicher Küken

Zur Beurteilung der Ist-Situation und dem Zukunfts-Szenario ist eine statistische Analyse sinnvoll. Grundlage der Statistiken sind Veröffentlichungen der EU-Kommission, der Agrarmarkt Informationsgesellschaft (AMI), der MEG-Marktbilanz Eier und Geflügel (Beck, 2021) und des deutschen statistischen Bundesamtes. Die Standards und Produktionsvorgaben basieren auf Daten und Erhebungen der CD Consulting gUG und der IG Bio-Initiative e. V. und zahlreichen wissenschaftlichen Veröffentlichungen.

Der Verein für kontrollierte Tierhaltungsformen hat Vorgaben für die konventionelle und ökologische Aufzucht einen Leitfaden „Henne/Hahn" erarbeitet, der Ende 2019 zur Anwendung kam. Einbezogen wurde die Herkunftssicherung und Rückverfolgbarkeit, basierend auf Mengenmeldungen, die in der Datenbank des Vereins für kontrollierte alternative Tierhaltungsformen e.V. (KAT, 2021) für alle am Prozess beteiligten Stufen Vorgabe sind. Die Aufzucht männlicher Küken beträgt 10 Wochen und es soll ein Lebendgewicht von 1,3 kg erreicht werden. Das betrifft auch die Biobruderhähne, wodurch allerdings eine sinnvolle Vermarktung der Tiere kaum gegeben ist. Die IG Bio-Initiative schreibt deshalb eine längere Aufzucht und mindestens 1,6 kg Lebendgewicht vor. Inwieweit die Umsetzung auch in benachbarten EU-Ländern erfolgt, wird die Praxis zeigen.

Die Fachhochschule Südwestfalen (Schütz et al., 2018) hat umfangreiche Untersuchungen zum Marktpotential für Geflügelprodukte aus Hahnenfleisch von Lege- und Zweinutzungshybriden erstellt. Ziel der Untersuchung war es zu analysieren, unter welchen Bedingungen die Mast und Verarbeitung von Lege- und Zweinutzungshühnern in Deutschland umsetzbar sein könnte, mit dem Ergebnis, dass die Aufzucht von Hähnen der Legehybriden unter Berücksichtigung der damaligen Rahmenbedingungen nicht wirtschaftlich ist. Eine Alternative stellen die Lege- und Zweinutzungshybriden zur Herstellung von qualitativ hochwertigem Fleisch dar. Zu einem ähnlichen Ergebnis kommt eine weitere Studie der FH Südwestfalen (Schröter et al., 2018) zum Bruderhahn- und Zweinutzungshuhnkonzept. Es mangelte seinerzeit allerdings bei den Befragten an der Kenntnis der Begriffe. Der Begriff *Bruderhahn* (Bundesforschungszentrum Landwirtschaft, 2020; Bundeszentrum für Ernährung BZFE, 2021) war zu der Zeit kaum bekannt, erst mit dem anstehenden Verbot des Tötens männlicher Küken gewann die Terminologie im Ökobereich an Relevanz (Schröter et al., 2018).

In jüngster Zeit hat sich die Hochschule Osnabrück (Kaufmann & Andersson, 2021) mit der Thematik intensiver auseinandergesetzt. Wichtig erscheint vor allem die Erkenntnis, dass der Bruderhahn kein Masthähnchen im eigentlichen Sinne ist. Es handelt sich um eine Aufzucht und nicht um Mast. Das beschreibt auch die Tierschutz-Nutztierhaltungsverordnung § 2 Abs. 9 (2021), dass ein Masthuhn ein zum Zweck der Fleischerzeugung gehaltenes Tier der Art Gallus gallus darstellt.

Der Europäische Parlamentarische Forschungsdienst (2021) hat sich u. a. mit den Haltungssystemen für Geflügel befasst. Demnach liegen zwar keine systematischen Erkenntnisse über das Wohlergehen von Legehennen in Europa vor, um zu beurteilen, was sich im Laufe der Zeit verbessert hat, aber die bemerkenswerten Veränderungen bei den Haltungsbedingungen für Hennen (d. h. mit dem Verbot der Käfighaltung) führten zu einer grundlegenden Verbesserung. Das gleiche gilt für Masthähnchen mit der Einschränkung der Besatzdichte, der Optimierung der Einstreuqualität und der allgemeinen Modernisierung der Haltungseinrichtungen, was zu einer gewissen Verbesserung des Wohlergehens dieser Tiere beigetragen hat. Dennoch bleiben wichtige Tierschutzprobleme (nach wie vor zu viele Tiere pro qm Grundfläche, schlechte Luftqualität, Probleme im Zusammenhang mit schnell wachsenden Rassen) weiterhin ungelöst.

Der DLG-Ausschuss Geflügel (Grashorn, 2021) kommt zu der Aussage, dass die Hähnchenfleischerzeugung nach wie vor einen zukunftsorientierten

Betriebszweig darstellt, mit dem Gewinne erwirtschaftet werden können. Ursache hierfür ist nicht zuletzt die kontinuierlich steigende Nachfrage nach Hähnchenfleisch. Allerdings sind die Anforderungen an das Haltungsmanagement nicht zu unterschätzen. Hier gilt es, die Haltungsbedingungen so zu optimieren, dass ein möglichst hohes Tierwohlniveau gehalten wird.

Letztendlich muss der Betriebsleiter und Tierhalter entscheiden, ob er in die Massenproduktion (große Ställe; Kurz-, Normal- oder Schnellmast und deren Kombinationen) einsteigt, oder ob er sich im gehobenen Produktionssegment (Premium) besser aufgehoben fühlt. Die Initiative Tierwohl (ITW, 2021; Tiemann, 2021) sieht sich als größte Plattform für mehr Tierwohl entlang der Wertschöpfungskette. Ob und inwieweit das auch für die sog. Bruderhahnaufzucht gilt, lässt sich nach den gegenwärtigen Aussagen nicht ableiten.

Die Brudertier-Initiative (B.I.D., 2021) setzt sich für eine ethische, zukunftsfähige Nutztierhaltung in der ökologischen Landwirtschaft ein. Bio-Betriebe und verschiedene Handelsketten haben sich zur Umsetzung für das System der Querfinanzierung entschieden. Die Eier der Legehennen werden um bis zu vier Cent teurer verkauft und mit dem Erlös männliche Küken aufgezogen. Das Prinzip wird aber bisher nur bei weniger als fünf Prozent der aussortierten Legehähnchen pro Jahr angewendet.

Das Bundesministerin für Ernährung und Landwirtschaft, Ministerin Klöckner (2021), unterstützt das Forschungsprojekt „SocialLab – Nutztierhaltung im Spiegel der Gesellschaft". Unter der Koordination des Thünen-Instituts (vgl. Schulz, 2021) soll herausgefunden werden, wie Verbraucher und Landwirte die Tierhaltung und der Handel die Vermarktungssituation wahrnehmen. Eine große Diskrepanz besteht nach wie vor zwischen den tief verankerten Bildern von „Massentierhaltung" und „Museumslandwirtschaft" – verbunden mit der Erkenntnis, dass der Weg zu einem neuen „Gesellschaftsvertrag für eine landwirtschaftliche Tierhaltung der Zukunft" noch weit ist und es innovativer Kommunikations- und Diskursformate bedarf.

Der Deutsche Ethikrat (2020) hat sich in seiner Stellungnahme über die Tierwohlachtung zum verantwortlichen Umgang mit Nutztieren ebenfalls mit der Thematik befasst und den achtsamen Umgang mit tierischem Leben aus dem Respekt vor dem Leben von Tieren und zumindest eine achtsame und möglichst umfassende Verwertung getöteter Tiere gefordert. Die Aufzucht von Bruderhähnen wird den Vorgaben gerecht.

Ethisch vertretbare Tierhaltung und die Notwendigkeit neue Wege zu gehen beschreiben eine Studie, die in der Zeitschrift für Ganzheitliche Tiermedizin erschienen ist (Brendieck-Worm et al., 2021). Grundlage ist die Erkenntnis, dass Eier- und Geflügelfleisch weltweit mit genetisch stark eingeschränkten, hochspezialisierten Hybridzuchtlinien produziert wird, was zur fast vollständigen Konzernabhängigkeit sowohl der konventionellen als auch vieler Bio-Betriebe geführt hat. Ein Lösungsansatz wird durch den Einsatz moderner Zweinutzungshühner, bei denen Legeleistung und Fleischansatz ohne Hochleistung harmonisch kombiniert sind, gesehen. Dieses Ziel ist jedoch nur durch grundlegende Änderungen bei der Zucht und Haltung von Hühnern zu erreichen.

Die Hochschule für nachhaltige Entwicklung, Eberswalde (Hörning, 2021) beschreibt mit dem Beitrag „Zweinutzungshühner und Bruderhähne" neue Entwicklungen mit der Erkenntnis, dass das Verbot des Kükentötens insbesondere im Ökolandbau den Trend zu mehr Tierwohl in der Landwirtschaft mit einer neuen Positionierung der Markenprogramme und Bioverbände führt.

7.2.2 Möglichkeiten der embryonalen Früherkennung

Zum gegenwärtigen Zeitpunkt gibt es weltweit eine Vielzahl von unterschiedlichen Methoden der Früherkennung. Praxisreif und zugelassen sind allerdings in Deutschland nur wenige Verfahren. Dazu zählt insbesondere das „Seleggtverfahren" ab dem 9. Tag (Breloh et al., 2021), die aber nach dem jetzigen Stand ab 2024 nicht mehr zugelassen ist. Deshalb wird intensiv an der Geschlechtsbestimmung ab dem 6. Bruttag geforscht (Universität Leipzig, Einspanier, 2021). Die optische-spektroskopische in-ovo Geschlechtsbestimmung soll bereits am Tag 3,5 – 5,5 und eine Genauigkeit von über 95 % erreichen (Technische Universität Dresden, Steiner et al., 2021; Hurlin, 2021). Das Verfahren hat allerdings noch keine Praxisreife. Agri Advanced Technologies (AAT, EW-Group) arbeitet ebenfalls an einer technischen Lösung zur Geschlechtsbestimmung im Ei. Die Hyperspektral-Messung, ermöglicht das ab dem 13. Tag (Steiner et al., 2021). Dieses Verfahren ist mit einer Genauigkeit von über 95 % praxistauglich, allerdings nur bei sog. Braunlegern (Hühner, die braune Eier legen). Das Entwicklungsstadium des Embryos ist am 13. Tag allerdings weit fortgeschritten. Der Tierschutz aber auch Marktbeteiligte und Verbraucher lehnen deshalb das Verfahren aufgrund des Schmerzempfindens der fortgeschrittenen Entwicklung des Embryos ab. Dem hat auch der Gesetzgeber mit den Vorgaben im Tierschutzgesetz Rechnung getragen.

GMO-basierte Techniken bieten unterdessen eine 100%ige Genauigkeit, diese sind jedoch in der EU nicht zugelassen. Plantegg (Kleine, 2021) hat ein Verfahren entwickelt, das auf einer DNA-Analyse basiert und noch 2021 für den Discountbereich Anwendung finden soll.

Das Problem der derzeit relevanten Methoden ist die Fehlerquote nicht erkannter Geschlechtsbestimmung von 5 %, zum Teil auch deutlich darüber. Die damit nicht selektierten männlichen Küken müssen aufgezogen werden, was sich oftmals mangels Stallkapazitäten als kostenintensiv und problematisch erweist. 5 % Fehlerquote bedeutet auch, dass 5 % weibliche Tiere nicht erkannt werden, was wiederum zusätzliche wirtschaftliche Einbußen zur Folge hat.

7.2.3 Statistische Analyse

Statistisches Datenmaterial ist Grundlage für die weitere Recherche. Aus diesem Grund wurden Informationen vom statistischen Bundesamt, der MEG, AMI, aus eigenen Erhebungen im Rahmen der Interessengemeinschaft Bio Initiative und der CD Consulting gUG herangezogen. Die Bruderhahnaufzucht für mehr Tierwohl erfordert zudem eine detaillierte Analyse der Produktionsdaten, aber auch die Verbrauchsentwicklung und die damit verbundene Kostensituation. Letztendlich müssen höhere Produktionskosten, bedingt durch strenge Vorgaben für mehr Tierschutz und Haltungskriterien, von den Konsumenten getragen werden. Dazu gibt es bereits eine Reihe von wissenschaftlichen Analysen, aber auch Daten, die auf empirischen Erhebungen basieren.

Grundlage für diesen Beitrag sind insbesondere Erhebungen der Marktinfo Eier & Geflügel (Beck, 2021), Agrarmarkt Informationsgesellschaft (AMI, 2021) und eigene Recherchen. Sie vermitteln einen globalen Überblick der Marktentwicklung.

Zur Beurteilung der Situation im Bereich der Selektion von männlichen und weiblichen Küken ist ein Blick auf die Entwicklung der Eier- und Geflügelproduktion von Bedeutung. In Deutschland beträgt der

Tab. 1: Versorgungsbilanz Eier und Geflügel, Deutschland

Deutschland	**2018**	**2019**	**2020**
Legehennenbestand, Mio. Stück	46,8	48,0	49,2
Legeleistung pro Huhn, Stück	291	290	293
Eierproduktion, Mio. Stück	13.614	13.339	14.421
davon Bioeier	1.556	1.636	1.800
Einfuhr Schaleneier, Mio. Stück	6.640	6.460	6.100
Verbrauch			
Stück pro Kopf	234	235	239
davon Bioeier	26	27	30
davon Tierschutz	< 2	< 3	< 4
Mastbereich			
Jungmasthühner, 1.000 t	1.025	1.041	1.071
kg pro Kopf	14,3	14,4	14,8
davon Bio	0,5	0,8	1,0
davon Tierschutz, duale Linien	< 0,5	< 0,5	< 0,5
Preisgestaltung			
Euro	**2018**	**2019**	**2020**
Verbraucherpreise			
Hähnchen, frisch, pro kg			
konventionell	3,96	4,01	4,17
Bio	7,80	7,18	8,19
Eier, pro 10 Stück			
Bodenhaltung	1,37	1,27	1,36
Freiland	2,01	1,95	2,02
Bio	3,31	3,34	3,34
Futter, pro 100 kg			
Legehennen	26,76	26,64	27,56
Hähnchen	32,34	32,10	32,37
Biofutter (eigene Erhebung)	50,00	50,00	50,00

Quelle: MEG, AMI, eigene Erhebung, 2021

Legehennen-Bestand knapp 50 Millionen Tiere (vgl. Tabelle 1), das bedeutet, dass etwa die doppelte Anzahl von Bruteiern benötigt wird. Interessant sind vor allem die Daten im ökologischen Bereich. Die Produktion von Bioeiern beträgt mittlerweile ca. 15 % mit Tendenz in Richtung 20 % steigend. Das zeigt sich auch beim Verbrauch. Der Anteil ökologischer Eier nimmt seit Jahren zu. Dagegen gibt es im Bereich Tierschutz nur einen Anteil von deutlich weniger als 2 %.

Die Erzeugung von Hähnchen ist seit Jahren konstant. Das gilt auch für den Verbrauch, der bei knapp 15 kg pro Kopf liegt. Interessanterweise ist der Anteil aus ökologischer Erzeugung noch sehr gering. Das betrifft auch den Bereich Tierschutz, der durch die Priorisierung von dualen Linien preisbedingt bisher keine Marktbedeutung erlangt.

Seit dem anstehenden Verbot des Kükentötens hat die Aufzucht von Bruderhähnen stark zugenommen und wird künftig das Bild am Markt verändern. Marktexperten gehen davon aus, dass die Selektion in Deutschland nur einen geringen Anteil haben wird, während die Aufzucht von Bruderhähnen in Richtung 80 % geht. Wenn man unterstellt, dass das Schlachtgewicht eines männlichen Tieres 1 kg beträgt, dürfte das einem theoretischen Produktionsvolumen von über 40.000 t entsprechen, was zu Lasten des Verbrauchs von konventionellem Hähnchenfleisch geht.

Ein Blick auf die Preisgestaltung zeigt, dass für ökologisch erzeugte Ware deutlich größere Umsätze erzielt werden. Dies ist zum einen den erheblich höheren Produktionskosten geschuldet, zum anderen aber auch dem Anspruch auf mehr Qualität und die Bereitschaft der Abnehmer, mehr Geld in Richtung Tierwohl zu investieren. Das wird auch dem Bereich Tierschutz zugesprochen.

Die vorstehende Tabelle 2 gibt einen Überblick über das Wachstum bzw. die Gewichtszunahme von Legehennen und Bruderhähnen im Vergleich zu konventionellen Masthühnern (schnellwachsenden Rassen). Auffallend ist vor allem das starke Wachstum. Die Tiere erreichen bereits nach 6 Wochen

Tab. 2: Aufzucht Legeküken, Bruderhähne, Masthybriden

	Junghennen	**Bruderhahn**	**Masthühner** [1)]
Alter in Tagen	Gewicht in g	Gewicht in g	Gewicht in g
1	35	35	46
14	115	115	290
35	335	291	1.100
50	530	534	1.800
70	848	974	3.000
90	1.105	1.308	ausgestallt
110	1.317	1.650	ausgestallt
Futterverbrauch, g pro Tag			
1	0	0	0
14	14	17	38
35	32	31	115
50	44	50	150
70	59	64	185
90	67	75	ausgestallt
110	73	95	ausgestallt

Quelle: EZ Fürstenhof, eigene Erhebung, 2021

Anmerkung: 1) schnellwachsende Rassen

das Schlachtgewicht, während die Hybridlinien aufgrund der sehr schlechten Futterverwertung nur geringe Gewichtszunahmen aufweisen. Das Ziel der Legehybriden ist allerdings nicht der Fleischansatz, sondern eine hohe Legeleistung. Deshalb erreichen Bruderhähne erst nach 120 Tagen ein Gewicht von 1,6 kg. In diesem Zeitraum sind Masthühner längst ausgestallt. Bei einer theoretischen Mastdauer von 70 Tagen erreichen die Tiere ein Gewicht von 3 kg und sind damit als ganzes Tier nicht mehr vermarktungsfähig. Wachstum und Verbrauch bei den Legehybriden sind bei den männlichen Küken dieser Linien weitgehend identisch.

Im ökologischen Bereich, bestimmter Labelprogramme, wie zum Beispiel Label Rouge (2018) und bestimmter Tierwohlprogramme, wie zum Beispiel Deutscher Tierschutzbund, werden allerdings nur langsam wachsende Rassen verwendet, die das ideale Schlachtgewicht erst nach 50 Tagen und mehr erreichen.

Die Daten der Tabelle 3 stammen aus eigenen Erhebungen der Interessengemeinschaft Bio-Initiative bzw. des Autors. Es handelt sich um eine beispielhafte Darstellung, die einen groben Überblick vermitteln soll.

Tab. 3: Haltungsvorgaben

Bruderhahnaufzucht	**ökologisch**	**konventionell**
Besatzdichte, Anzahl Tiere pro Gruppe	10.000	derzeit keine Vorgaben
gemeinsame Aufzucht	nicht vorgegeben	nicht vorgegeben
Auslauf	ab 10. Woche	-
Auslauffläche	1 qm/Tier	-
nutzbare Fläche pro Tier, qm	max. 21 kg/LG	max. 39 kg/LG
Schlachtalter	bis 110 Tage bzw. 1,6 kg	bis 70 Tage
Umlauf pro Jahr, max., je nach Schlachtalter	2,5 (4,5-5)	4,5-5
künftiger Bestand an männlichen Küken, Mio. Stück	> 5	> 30

Quelle: IG Bio-Initiative, eigene Erhebungen, 2021

Die meisten Bio-Verbände geben inzwischen die Aufzucht von Bruderhähnen vor. Eine embryonale Selektion kommt nicht in Betracht. Allerdings beträgt die Dauer der Aufzucht wie im konventionellen Bereich meist nur 10 Wochen. Damit wird vermieden, dass den Tieren Auslauf gewährt werden muss, der gem. Bioverordnung vorgeschrieben ist. Regionale Bruderhahn-Initiativen schreiben dagegen anlog der Bio-Initiative eine Aufzucht von bis zu 120 Tagen vor.

Die Kostenanalyse von Zweinutzungslinien, Legehybriden und konventionellen Masthähnchen (vgl. Tabelle 4 und 5) basiert auf Erhebungen eines Forschungsberichts der FH Südwestfalen (Schütz et al., 2018). Eine ökonomisch sinnvolle Verwertung bei den Zweinutzungslinien ergeben theoretische Erlöse

Tab. 4: Kostenanalyse Zweinutzungslinien, Legehybriden und Masthybriden

	Zweinutzungslinien	**Legehybriden (männliche Küken)**	**Masthühner [1] (konventionell)**
Alter	10 Wochen	10 Wochen	6 Wochen
Kükenpreis	0,37	0,25	0,35
Futterverwertung	2,00	2,40	1,60
Lebendgewicht	2,40	1,53	2,59
Schlachtgewicht	1,52	0,82	1,86
Gewicht Brust	0,29	0,11	0,56
theoretischer Erlös, € pro kg	0,23	-1,89	1,96
Legeleistung (Schwester)	250	320	-

Anmerkung: 1) schnellwachsende Rassen
Quelle: FH Südwestfalen (Schütz et al., 2018)

pro Kilogramm von lediglich 0,23 € und die Legeleistung erreicht 250 Eier. Im Vergleich zur konventionellen Haltung werden 320 Eier erzielt. Der theoretische Erlös wurde mit einem Minus von 1,89 € ermittelt. Mit Kosten für Logistik, Stall, Löhne und Schlachtung/Zerlegung ist das Minus deutlich höher. Die Mast von konventionellen Tieren bewegt sich dagegen mit knapp 2 € deutlich im positiven Bereich.

Die schlechte Futterwertung von Zweinutzungslinien und Bruderhähnen, insbesondere im Bereich der biologischen Erzeugung bedingt durch die längere Aufzucht, bedeutet in beiden Fällen ein Minus bzw. Verluste in Höhe von knapp 2 Euro bzw. bis zu 5 Euro pro Kilogramm. Deshalb erscheint eine Aufzucht der männlichen Küken aus ökonomischer Sicht nicht sinnvoll. Dennoch können

Tab. 5: Kostenanalyse Zweinutzungslinien, Legehybriden und herkömmliche Masthybriden

	Zweinutzungslinien	**Bruderhähne (konventionell)**	**Bruderhähne, Bio**
Alter	10 Wochen	10 Wochen	15 Wochen
Kükenpreis	0,37	0,25	0,35
Futterverwertung	2,00	2,40	1,60
Lebendgewicht	2,40	1,00	1,60
Schlachtgewicht	1,52	0,60	1,10
Gewicht Brust	0,29	0,11	0,40
theoretischer Erlös, € pro kg	0,23	-1,89	-5,00
Legeleistung (Schwester)	250	-	-
erforderlicher Mehrpreis pro Ei, Cent	3,0 konventionell 6,0 ökologisch	1,5	3,5

Gewinne erzielt werden, und zwar über den deutlich höheren Eierpreis, der sich auch am Markt durchsetzen lässt. Damit ergibt sich hinsichtlich der betriebswirtschaftlichen Vorgabe ein anderes Bild, das erklärt auch, dass im konventionellen Bereich eine hohe Bereitschaft besteht, die männlichen Tiere zu verwerten. Die Verluste in der Aufzucht werden über den Verkauf der Eier mehr als ausgeglichen.

Die theoretische Kalkulation der Bruderhahnaufzucht (Tabelle 6), wurde von der Bio-Initiative (von der Crone, 2020) erstellt. In der Übersicht wird neben den Aufzuchtkosten auch der Anteil der Lohnhaltung, Gebäude, Energie, Personal, Schlachtung, Zerlegung und Vermarktung einbezogen. Daraus ergeben sich Ausgaben von über 16 € pro Tier, während die Einnahmen kaum über

Tab. 6: Theoretische Kalkulation Bruderhahnkonzept

Preise €/kg			
Aufzuchtkosten			5,25 €
Lohnhaltung, kalkulatorisch, Gebäudekosten, Energie, Personalkosten			3,80 €
Ein- und Ausstallung etc.			3,80 €
Schlachtung, Gefrierhaus etc.			3,70 €
Ausgaben gesamt			**16,55 €**
Kalkulierte Einnahmen:			
Basis Lebendgewicht, Durchschnitt 1,6 kg/Tier			
	kg	Preis	gesamt
Schenkel	0,5	5,00 €	2,50 €
Brustfilet	0,2	14,00 €	2,80 €
Flügel	0,15	2,00 €	0,30 €
Reste (keine Verwertung von 100 %)			0,50 €
Einnahmen gesamt			**6,10 €**

Quelle: IG Bio-Initiative (2021) sowie eigene Erhebungen

6 € pro Kilogramm hinausgehen. Das Beispiel bezieht sich auf den ökologischen Bereich, denn konventionell aufgezogene Tiere verursachen zwar weniger Kosten, bedingt durch die nur sehr geringe Verwertungsmöglichkeit des Fleischanteils ist die Erlössituation allerdings ähnlich schlecht.

7.3 Erreichung der Untersuchungsziele, Prüfung der Hypothesen, Schlussfolgerungen

Die Analyse der Bruderhahnaufzucht für mehr Tierwohl beinhaltet, wie oben beschrieben, zwei Optionen: die Aufzucht und die embryonale Früherkennung. In Deutschland sind die Vorgaben durch das Tierschutzgesetz spätestens ab 1. Januar 2022 umzusetzen, es bleibt also für die Wirtschaftsbeteiligten wenig Zeit, darauf zu reagieren.

7.3.1 Erreichung der Untersuchungsziele

Untersuchungsziel 1: Vorgaben und Optionen zur Aufzucht männlicher Küken

Die Vorgaben und Optionen für die Aufzucht männlicher Küken sind vom Gesetzgeber auf der einen und von den Wirtschaftsbeteiligten auf der anderen Seite definiert. Die embryonale Früherkennung beinhaltet zahlreiche Möglichkeiten, die von der Erkennung vom dritten bis hin zum 13. Tag nach der Befruchtung möglich sind. Hier zeigt sich bereits erheblicher Widerstand der Tierschutzorganisationen, die eine Erkennung über den 6. Tag hinaus vehement ablehnen, da ein Schmerzempfinden der Tiere unterstellt wird. Nach dem gegenwärtigen Stand gibt es allerdings noch keine vom Gesetzgeber geforderte Methode der Selektion. Damit bleibt bis auf weiteres die Aufzucht der männlichen Tiere.

Untersuchungsziel 2: Möglichkeiten der embryonalen Früherkennung

Die Möglichkeiten der Früherkennung sind damit skizziert. Die embryonale Selektion dürfte in Deutschland nicht die Bedeutung erlangen wie das zum Beispiel in anderen EU-Ländern der Fall ist. Tierschutz hat in Deutschland einen außergewöhnlich hohen Stellenwert, das gilt auch für Österreich und die Schweiz. In den Niederlanden orientiert man sich an Marktgegebenheit und gesetzliche Vorgaben in Deutschland, da etwa 50 % der Eier aus den Niederlanden stammen.

Untersuchungsziel 3: Kosten-Nutzen-Analyse

Als Option bleibt nach dem gegenwärtigen Stand die Aufzucht der männlichen Küken. Aus ökonomischer Sicht ist das zwar wenig sinnvoll, denn die männlichen Legehybriden sind auf Eierproduktion ausgerichtet und nicht auf Fleischansatz. Die Futterverwertung ist schlecht und die Aufzucht deshalb mit sehr hohen Kosten verbunden, die über den Verkaufspreis für Eier ausgeglichen werden können. Deshalb geht die Tendenz zur Aufzucht männlicher Küken in Richtung 80 %.

Untersuchungsziel 4: Grenzen der Umsetzung

Die entscheidende Frage bleibt, inwieweit der Markt die höheren Kosten für die Aufzucht von männlichen Küken trägt. Die Fleischverwertung ist im konventionellen Bereich kaum gegeben und deshalb nicht rentabel. Das gilt auch für die ökologische Produktion mit höherem Schlachtgewicht, doch gibt es damit bessere Absatz- und Verwertungsmöglichkeiten für das Fleisch. Während für konventionelle Ware die Aufzucht nicht über 70 Tage hinausgeht, sind es im Biobereich bis zu 120 Tage. In beiden Fällen können die Zusatzkosten nur über höhere Eierpreise kompensiert werden. Damit sind Grenzen der Umsetzung vorgegeben. Inwieweit die Bereitschaft der Konsumenten gegeben ist, für herkömmliche Eier die Bruderhahnaufzucht auf Dauer zu unterstützen, bleibt unsicher. Deshalb besteht mittelfristig betrachtet die embryonale Selektion als Option. Im ökologischen Bereich dürfte die Bruderhahnaufzucht dagegen erfolgreich bleiben. Aber auch hier wird es Vorbehalte geben, denn der Vorwurf von Ressourcenverschwendung steht aufgrund des hohen Futterverbrauchs schon jetzt im Raum.

7.3.2 Prüfung der Hypothesen

Hypothese 1: Das neue Tierschutzgesetz mit dem Verbot des Tötens männlicher Küken führt zu einem Ungleichgewicht und Wettbewerbsverzerrungen im Bereich der Eierproduktion, verbunden mit Betriebsaufgaben.

Die Eierwirtschaft muss sich neu strukturieren. Das Verbot des Kükentötens wird nicht dazu führen, dass es zu Betriebsaufgaben oder zu gravierenden Änderungen am Markt kommt. Im Gegenteil, es ist zu erwarten, dass bedingt durch verbesserte Tierschutzanforderungen der Verbrauch weiter steigt und das Vertrauen in das Produkt Ei noch mehr in den Vordergrund rückt. Eine ähnliche Situation gab es bereits vor einigen Jahren mit dem Verbot der Käfighaltung oder dem Verbot des Kupierens der Schnäbel. Die Lobbyverbände haben zwar das Aus der deutschen Geflügelhaltung prognostiziert, doch das Gegenteil ist eingetreten. Der Selbstversorgungsgrad und der Verbrauch sind seither gestiegen. **Aufgrund der vorliegenden Daten ist Hypothese 1 nicht haltbar.**

Hypothese 2: Der Anteil aus deutscher Erzeugung schrumpft zu Gunsten ausländischer Mitbewerber. Die Verbraucher sind nicht bereit, die höheren Kosten beim Einkauf zu tragen.

Die Verbraucherpreise für Eier mit der Auslobung „ohne Kükentöten" sind deutlich gestiegen. Die höheren Preise werden akzeptiert, wenn eine entsprechende Auslobung erfolgt. Vor allem der Biomarkt profitiert hiervon. Ausländische Mitbewerber werden sich den Rahmenbedingungen anpassen und ebenfalls mit der Auslobung „ohne Kükentöten" ihre Ware am Markt anbieten. Deshalb wird es keine Einschränkungen geben. **Aufgrund der vorliegenden Daten ist Hypothese 2 nicht haltbar.**

Hypothese 3: Der ökonomische Nutzen ist fraglich, dennoch bieten sich Optionen und es erfolgt eine Neuorientierung, der Verbrauch steigt und der Markt profitiert von den neuen Vorgaben.

Der ökonomische Nutzen ist tatsächlich fragwürdig. Die embryonale Früherkennung ist zwar ebenfalls mit Kosten verbunden, diese sind aber deutlich geringer als die Bruderhahnaufzucht oder die Verwendung von

Zweinutzungslinien. Dennoch lassen sich Gewinne erzielen. Pro Ei werden um bis zu 4 Cent höhere Preise erzielt und damit die Zusatzkosten mehr als kompensiert. **Aufgrund der vorliegenden Daten kann Hypothese 3 aufrechterhalten werden.**

7.3.3 Schlussfolgerungen

Die Aufzucht von männlichen Küken, wie auch die embryonale Früherkennung stehen klar im Interesse des Tierwohls. Viele Tierschutzorganisationen betrachten das zwar aus einem anderen Blickwinkel und befürworten die Zweinutzungslinien, die jedoch gegenwärtig am Markt kaum verfügbar sind. Hinzu kommt eine geringere Legeleistung und schlechte Futterwertung, die Zusatzkosten verursachen und vom Markt bisher nicht gedeckt werden können. Aus diesem Grund gibt es neben der embryonalen Früherkennung und zur Umsetzung der gesetzlichen Vorgaben mit dem Verbot des Kükentötens ausschließlich die Option der Aufzucht männlicher Tiere. Aus ökonomischer Sicht ist dies allerdings alles andere als sinnvoll, sehr hoher Futterverbrauch und die vergleichsweise lange Aufzucht von bis zu 120 Tagen bedeuten hohe Kosten. Viele Marktteilnehmer betrachten deshalb die Aufzucht als Ressourcenverschwendung. Der Tierschutz will unterdessen keine embryonale Früherkennung über den 6. Tag hinaus, da ein Schmerzempfinden bei der Selektion unterstellt wird. Wissenschaftlich erwiesen ist das allerdings nicht. Die Erkennung bis zum sechsten Tag, wie vom Gesetzgeber vorgegeben, ist derzeit noch nicht marktreif. Es ist deshalb zu bezweifeln, dass mit Inkrafttreten der neuen Bestimmung tatsächlich in ausreichendem Umfang ein solches Verfahren zur Verfügung steht. In anderen Ländern, zum Beispiel in Frankreich, erfolgt die Selektion ab dem 13. Tag oder noch später. Das ist ebenfalls nicht zu akzeptieren.

Trotz schlechter Rahmenbedingungen der Aufzucht von Bruderhähnen, ergeben sich für die Legehennenhalter und -vermarkter durchaus Vorteile. Verbraucher und auch der Lebensmittelhandel sind bereit, für Eier von den sogenannten Schwestern einen deutlich höheren Preis zu akzeptieren. Es werden bis zu vier Cent mehr verbucht. Unterstellt man einen Verbrauch in Deutschland von 18 Milliarden Eiern, ergibt sich daraus eine sehr hohe Summe. Damit können die Zusatzkosten für die ineffiziente Bruderhahnaufzucht mehr als kompensiert werden. Ein entscheidender Mangel besteht allerdings darin, dass es derzeit keine Vorgaben für die Aufzucht gibt und letztendlich auch keine Kontrolle.

Prognosen entsprechend werden bis zu 80 % der geschlüpften Küken in Deutschland der Bruderhahnaufzucht zugeführt, in der Regel mit einer Aufzuchtdauer von allenfalls 70 Tagen. Eine Verwertung des Fleisches ist kaum vorstellbar. Die Schlachtgewichte liegen zum Teil weit unter 1 kg Lebendgewicht und damit stehen bei einer Ausbeute von 50–60 % verwertbarer Teile (Brust und Schenkel) allenfalls 300 g vermarktungsfähige Ware zur Verfügung. Deshalb hat dieses keine Marktbedeutung und es ist die Aufzucht mit diesen Vorgaben als nicht sinnvoll zu betrachten. Im ökologischen Bereich, mit der Vorgabe einer Aufzucht von bis zu 120 Tagen und einem Lebendgewicht von 1,6 kg gibt es dagegen andere Ergebnisse. Eine Verwertung ist gegeben, zumal Ökoprodukte in der Gunst der Verbraucher einen höheren Stellenwert haben.

Mittelfristig gesehen ist die Bruderaufzucht allerdings kein Zukunftsmodell. Zweinutzungslinien sind deshalb eine bessere Alternative. Die Legeleistung ist zwar um 20 % geringer und die Aufzucht der männlichen Tiere aufgrund der schlechteren Futterverwertung mit höheren Kosten verbunden, doch hat die Aufzucht dieser dualen Linien Zukunft, insbesondere im ökologischen Bereich. Defizite im Bereich der Produktionskosten können durch höhere Verkaufspreise für Eier und Fleisch kompensiert werden, wodurch sich durchaus Perspektiven bieten. Außerdem besteht Optimierungspotential im Bereich der Genetik und Züchtung.

Deshalb wird sich mittel- bis langfristig im konventionellen Bereich die embryonale Selektion durchsetzen. Derzeit ist das Ziel einer Erkennung unter sechs Tagen zwar noch nicht erreicht; es ist allerdings abzusehen, dass die Wissenschaft bald marktreife Selektionsmethoden vorgibt. In anderen Ländern außerhalb der EU ist das bereits der Fall, zum Beispiel durch gentechnische Verfahren, die schon am ersten Tag eine Selektion mit einer Genauigkeit von 100 % ermöglichen. Das Verfahren ist jedoch bisher in der EU verboten.

Die gegenwärtigen Untersuchungen beziehen sich primär auf den deutschen Markt. Die Eigenversorgung beträgt in Deutschland 70 %. Damit muss ein großer Anteil aus benachbarten Ländern importiert werden. Das Gros stammt aus den Niederlanden. Um den Markt auch künftig bedienen zu können, werden die dortigen Produzenten die deutschen Vorgaben ebenfalls umsetzen, entweder durch die Früherkennung oder über die Aufzucht von männlichen Küken.

Literaturverzeichnis

AMI (2021). *AMI Markt Bilanz Öko-Landbau 2021*. https://www.AMI-informiert.de

Beck, M. (2021). *MEG-Marktbilanz Eier und Geflügel 2021*, https://www.marktinfo-eier-gefluegel.de

B.I.D. Brudertier-Initiative Deutschland (2021). https://brudertier.bio

Bio-Initiative e. V. (2021). *Systemvorgaben für die ökologische Erzeugung.* www.ig-bio.de

Breloh, L., Meter, T. & Einspanier, A. (2021). Universität Leipzig, https://www.seleggt.com/de/

Brendieck-Worm, C. & Spielberger, U. (2021). Ethisch vertretbare Tierhaltung. *Zeitschrift für Ganzheitliche Tiermedizin,* 35, S. 17–22.

Bundesforschungszentrum Landwirtschaft (2020). *Was ist ein Bruderhahn*? https://www.landwirtschaft.de/landwirtschaft-verstehen/haetten-sies-gewusst/tierhaltung/was-ist-ein-bruderhahn

Bundesgesetzblatt (2021), https://www.bgbl.de/xaver/bgbl/start.xav?startbk=Bundesanzeiger_BGBl&start=//*[@attr_id=%27bgbl121s1828.pdf%27]#__bgbl__%2F%2F*%5B%40attr_id%3D%27bgbl121s1828.pdf%27%5D__1630825213035, S. 1828-183

Bundesministerium für Ernährung und Landwirtschaft BMEL (2021). *Tierwohlkennzeichen.* https://www.bmel.de/DE/themen/tiere/tierschutz/tierwohl-kennzeichen/tierwohl-kennzeichen_node.html

Bundeszentrum für Ernährung BZFE (2021). *Bruderhahn-Eier und Hähnchen,* www.bzfe.de/nachhaltiger-konsum/orientierung-beim-einkauf/bruderhahn-eier-und-haehnchen/

Deutscher Ethikrat (2020), *Tierwohlachtung – Zum verantwortungsvollen Umgang mit Nutztieren,* www.ethikrat.org

Einspanier, A. (2021). *Früherkennung ab 6. Tag.* Universität Leipzig.

Europäischer Parlamentarischer Forschungsdienst (2021). https://www.europarl.europa.eu/at-your-service/de/stay-informed/research-and-analysis

EZ Fürstenhof (2021). *Analyse Aufzucht Legeküken, Bruderhähne, Masthybriden,* https://www.ez-fuerstenhof.de

Grashorn, M. (2021). *Haltung von Masthühnern.* DLG-Ausschuss Geflügel.

Hurlin, J. (2021). *In ovo Geschlechtsbestimmung.* https://www.agri-at.com

Hörning, B. (2021). *Zweinutzungshühner und Bruderhähne.* https://www.hnee.de/de/Startseite/HNEEberswalde-Startseite-E9875.htm

ITW – Initiative Tierwohl (2021). *Mehr Tierwohl in der Nutztierhaltung.* https://initiative-tierwohl.de

Kaufmann, F. & Andersson, R. (2021). *Bruderhähne – Chancen und Grenzen.* WPSA Frühjahrstagung. Hochschule Osnabrück.

KAT e. V., Verein für kontrollierte alternative Tierhaltungsformen (2021). *Vorgaben für Legehennenhaltung und umfassende Herkunftssicherung.* https://www.was-steht-auf-dem-ei.de/de/

Klöckner, J. (2021). *Social LAB – Nutztierhaltung im Spiegel der Gesellschaft.* BMEL.

Kleine, M. (2021). *In-Ovo Geschlechtsbestimmung*. PLANTegg. www.plantegg.de

Label Rouge (2018). http://www.volaillelabelrouge.com/huhner

Schröter, I., Schütz, K., Braunisch, M., Wittmann, M. & Mergenthaler, M. (2018). *Bruderhahn- und Zweinutzungshuhnkonzept: Kenntnisse und Begriffsverständnisse der Kundschaft einer Bio-Fleischerei am Point of Sale.* Notizen aus der Forschung. Soest: Fachhochschule Südwestfalen.

Schütz, K., Mergenthaler, M. & Wittmann, M. (2018). *Marktpotential für Geflügelprodukte aus Hahnenfleisch von Lege- und Zweinutzungshybriden.* Soest: Fachhochschule Südwestfalen.

Schulz, I. (2021). *Nutztierhaltung im Spiegel der Gesellschaft*, SocialLab-Konsortium, Thünen-Institut für Marktanalyse, Braunschweig

Steiner, G., Otte-Kinast, B. & Hurlin, J. (2021). *Optisch-spektroskopische in-ovo Geschlechtsbestimmung des Hühnereies für den praktischen Einsatz in der Brüterei.* Technische Universität Dresden.

Tiemann, I. (2021). *Diskussionstand AG Geflügel des Kompetenznetzwerks Nutztierhaltung.* BMEL, ITW, Institut für Tierzuchtwissenschaft, Rheinische Friedrich-Wilhelms-Universität Bonn, https://www.itw.uni-bonn.de/institut/tierzucht/

von der Crone, C., Mau, M., Gauly, M. & Lang, H. (2018). Ausstieg aus dem Verfahren des Tötens männlicher Küken. *Journal of Economy & Society, 2018*(3–4), University of Sopron.

von der Crone, C. (2020). *Housing Condition Score (HCS) Masthühner.* CD Consulting gUG, http://www.cvdc.de

Innovatives Wissensmanagement

Innovative Knowledge Management

Herausgegeben von Prof. Dr. Dr. Dr. habil. Bernhard F. Seyr

Band	1	Bernhard F. Seyr (Hrsg.): Innovations- und Wissensmanagement in der Praxis: Konzepte, Forschungsergebnisse und Fallstudien. Innovation and Knowledge Management in Practice: Concepts, Research and Case Studies. 2020.
Band	2	Bernhard F. Seyr (Hrsg.): Multidisziplinäre Perspektiven im Innovations- und Wissensmanagement. Multidisciplinary Perspectives in Innovation and Knowledge Management. 2021.
Band	3	Bernhard F. Seyr (ed.): Applied Innovation and Knowledge Management in Organizations. Angewandtes Innovations- und Wissensmanagement in Organisationen. 2022.

www.peterlang.com

www.ingramcontent.com/pod-product-compliance
Ingram Content Group UK Ltd.
Pitfield, Milton Keynes, MK11 3LW, UK
UKHW041826031026
15587UKWH00002B/589

9 783631 874141